Advance praise for

THE LIFE & LEGACY OF

Baroness Betty DE *Rothschild*

"In this fascinating and far-reaching biography of Baroness Betty de Rothschild, Laura S. Schor went beyond the bejeweled image of a wealthy aristocrat celebrated by Ingres and discovered a political woman bent on reconciling Jewish life with the modern world, and a philanthropist determined to educate both boys and girls for a fulfilling existence in contemporary France."

Anka Muhlstein, Author of Baron James: The Rise of the French Rothschilds
and Prix Goncourt Recipient for her 1996 Biography A Taste for Freedom:
The Life of Astophe de Custine

THE LIFE & LEGACY OF

Baroness Betty

DE *Rothschild*

PETER LANG
New York • Washington, D.C./Baltimore • Bern
Frankfurt am Main • Berlin • Brussels • Vienna • Oxford

LAURA S. SCHOR

THE LIFE & LEGACY OF
Baroness Betty
DE *Rothschild*

PETER LANG
New York • Washington, D.C./Baltimore • Bern
Frankfurt am Main • Berlin • Brussels • Vienna • Oxford

Library of Congress Cataloging-in-Publication Data

Strumingher, Laura S.
The life and legacy of Baroness Betty de Rothschild / Laura S. Schor.
p. cm.
Includes bibliographical references and index.
1. Rothschild, Betty Salomon de, baroness, 1805–1886.
2. Rothschild family. 3. Jews, German—France—Social conditions—19th century.
4. Women in public life—France—Biography.
5. Jewish women—France—Biography. 6. Jewish bankers—France—Family
relationships—History—19th century. 7. Upper class—France—
Paris—Biography. I. Title.
DS135.F9R6667   332.1′092—dc22   2005010682
ISBN 0-8204-7885-7

Bibliographic information published by **Die Deutsche Bibliothek**.
Die Deutsche Bibliothek lists this publication in the "Deutsche
Nationalbibliografie"; detailed bibliographic data is available
on the Internet at http://dnb.ddb.de/.

Cover art: J.Ingres, *Baroness Betty de Rothschild,* 1848. Private collection.
Cover design by Sophie Boorsch Appel

The paper in this book meets the guidelines for permanence and durability
of the Committee on Production Guidelines for Book Longevity
of the Council of Library Resources.

© 2006 Peter Lang Publishing, Inc., New York
29 Broadway, New York, NY 10006
www.peterlangusa.com

Printed in Germany

In memory of my father, David C. Gross,
and in honor of my mother, Esther R. Gross,
and my husband Joseph M. Schor

Contents

Illustrations

Preface

A few years ago, the Baron Elie de Rothschild and his late wife, the Baroness Lilliane, graciously welcomed me into their elegant Parisian home. I had written to ask for an opportunity to speak with them about Betty de Rothschild, the matriarch of the French Rothschild family. Lilliane, the vivacious family historian, was eager to share sources and anecdotes. Elie, a charming octogenarian, asked me several questions: "Why write a biography of my great-grandmother?" He wanted to know: Why would anyone want to read about Betty? What did she accomplish that might be meaningful for today's readers?

Born in the narrow streets of the *Judengasse*, the storied Frankfurt ghetto, Betty de Rothschild grew to young womanhood in the relatively secure world of affluent Jewish families. In 1819, Betty's childhood ended abruptly with anti-Semitic riots in Frankfurt and neighboring towns. Following weeks of mob violence, Betty's life returned to its normal rhythm of music and dancing lessons, drawing classes, and trips to Alpine spas. At nineteen, Betty married her young uncle, James, founder of the French Rothschild Bank, and moved to his opulent new home in the heart of romantic Paris. Here she developed a famous salon, hosting Balzac, Heine, Meyerbeer, Scheffer, Rachel and Chopin, along with the diplomatic corps. The celebrated portrait painter, Ingres, captured Betty's graciousness as a salon hostess as the July Monarchy came to an end.

Betty and James had five children: Charlotte, Alphonse, Gustave, Salomon, and Edmond. Betty was a devoted mother, regularly spending hours with her children and their tutors studying a wide variety of subjects that bridged a classical curriculum with modern interests and Jewish tradition.

These studies were a unique form of continuing education for Betty whose intelligence and energy were frequently noted by family members.

Keenly aware of the importance of education to enable poor girls and boys to earn a respectable income, Betty devoted time and money to providing continuing vocational education and moral instruction to girls. Her efforts resulted in significant benefits to thousands of young women as well as to the creation of the first modern Jewish women's organization in France. Betty continued to develop the role of modern Jewish woman philanthropist throughout her life. Her philanthropy knew no geographic or religious bounds; her committment to girls and women remained constant.

Betty's patriotism surfaced during the Franco-Prussian War and the Commune of 1871. In hastily constructed "ambulances" in the courtyard of her homes as well as in the Rothschild Hospital she provided medical care for wounded soldiers and for the malnourished and sick. She remained in the besieged Paris for months assisting those in need.

Betty de Rothschild died in 1886. She was eulogized for her philanthropy in the French press for many weeks. However, in the years since her demise there have been no biographies and no collections of her letters. The village named for her in Israel, Mazkeret Batya, has scant information about Betty in their library. The famous portrait by Ingres is held in private hands and is rarely loaned to major museums.

Fortunately, the Rothschild Archive in London (RAL) possesses thousands of letters, some from Betty, others to her, and many more in which she is mentioned. The archive also holds numerous legal and financial documents including: Betty's marriage license, her husband's will, pages from Betty's account books, her last letter to her children, and her will. These documents were captured by the Germans during the Second World War, moved to Frankfurt, recaptured by Russian forces, and ultimately brought to Moscow where they languished until 1994. The RAL negotiated with Russian archivists and acquired this treasure of documents over a ten-year period.

I am indebted to Melanie Aspey, Director of the RAL, whose knowledge of the Rothschild holdings was critical throughout the research for this biography. Her kindness during each of my visits to the Archives was unfailing. I would also like to single out two colleagues, Karen Offen and Robert Seltzer, both early readers of the manuscript, whose thoughtful suggestions resulted in further research and analysis and to Ellen Marson who read the penultimate draft with care and attention to detail. In Paris, Pauline Prevost-Marcilhacy and Evelyn Lejeune-Resnick shared my enthusiasm for this project and offered help in finding obscure references in French archives. Jean-Claude Kuperminc and Philippe Landau welcomed me to the Archives of the Alliance Israélite Universelle and to the Consistoire de Paris. Evelyne Chemouny and Rosa Attali provided French translations, while Heidi Burns and Ingebord Lasting translated from German, and Robert Binder located and translated Hebrew sources. Donald Held was responsible for redacting numerous drafts; Ruiyan Xu and Indra Rios-Moore prepared the text for publication.

Finally, I want to thank Baron Elie de Rothschild for his questions. The following chapters are my attempt at an answer.

CHAPTER ONE

A Frankfurt Girlhood

It does not look rosy for us as regards our citizenship . . . As far as I can see from a distance, we still have a long struggle before us. This matter interests me so much that if I catch a simple word about it, I listen eagerly to what is said . . . I am very curious to know what the result will be.
    Caroline Rothschild, Frankfurt, to her husband Salomon, London, July 21, 1814

I cannot tell you how much pleasure I experienced when I read the kind words of your sweet epistle. I assure you it caused tears of love to come to my eyes. There was so much sensitivity and sincerity in the wish it carried, and the letter revealed so much innocence.
    Betty de Rothschild, Frankfurt, to her cousin Charlotte Rothschild, London,
                                                                November 19, 1822

In the summer of 1819 Betty de Rothschild was fourteen-years-old. As a result of her family's wealth, she grew up in relative comfort in her natal city, Frankfurt, despite the continued restriction on civil rights for Jews. During the Napoleonic conquest of Frankfurt, Betty and the rest of the Jewish community experienced new freedom, but the restrictions and traditional anti-Semitism returned with his defeat. In 1816, Professor Friedrich Fries of Heidelberg University published *Threat to the Welfare and Character of the Germans by the Jews,* calling for the extermination of the Jews. A group calling themselves Teutomaniacs declared: "Christian hate will call down the Day of Judgement on the Jews, the accomplices of profiteering." Among the literate, the romantic glorification of the mystical unity of the *Naturvolk,* a precursor to the Aryan mythology of the twentieth century, was popular fare.[1]

On August 5, 1819, news of anti-Jewish riots led by university students in neighboring Wurzburg reached Frankfurt. Jew baiting spread to Bamberg, Hamburg, and Karlsruhe. That summer, as in ancient times, Jews huddled in fields surrounded by the belongings they managed to rescue from their attackers. In Frankfurt, poor harvests led to empty stomachs and fear of famine. Long-smoldering anti-Semitic sentiments burst into the open. Cries of Hep-Hep, an abbreviation of *Hierosolyma est perdita* (Jerusalem is lost), and *Jude verreck* (death to the Jews) echoed ominously in Frankfurt's cobblestone streets. Menacing crowds of the unemployed loitered in the Jewish quarter, the Judengasse. A rumor spread that Jews had beaten a Christian. At nightfall, bands of clerks, craftsmen, and the unemployed, armed with clubs, knives, and stones, forced their way into the Judengasse where members of Betty's family lived. The mob, unimpeded by the police, broke plate-glass windows and vandalized shops and homes. The dwellings of wealthy Jews were special objects of the attackers, and among the houses attacked was Grunen Schild, the House of the Green Shield, belonging to Betty's grandmother, Gutle Rothschild, widow of Mayer Amschel, founder of the Rothschild banking business.[2]

The Rothschilds had deep roots in the Judengasse. Mayer Amschel, Betty's grandfather, was born there on February 23, 1744, and remained until his death in 1812. The narrow streets of the Jewish ghetto, with its fetid atmosphere caused by crowding and lack of adequate sanitation, were his playground. As a child, he attended *heder*, a Jewish school where he studied the Bible and Talmud. At the age of eleven, he was sent to the Jewish seminary in Furth, where he was a promising pupil. But Mayer Amschel was orphaned before his twelfth birthday, and forced to cut short his studies. At thirteen, he started as an apprentice of the Oppenheim Bank in Hanover where he learned to evaluate and trade rare coins. Six years later his apprenticeship ended; Mayer Amschel returned to the Judengasse where he slowly developed a business trading coins. There, he achieved success by financing the Landgrave of Hesse, who provided soldiers for England's army. In 1770, at the age of twenty-six, he married nineteen-year-old Gutle Schnapper, daughter of a prosperous moneychanger, Wolf Salomon Schnapper. Gutle and Mayer Amschel formed a remarkably productive and reproductive family. Gutle gave birth to nineteen children and raised ten of them to adulthood. During these years, Mayer was appointed Court Agent to Hesse-Hanau in 1783, Court and Chamber Agent to Hesse-Kessel in 1803, and Councillor of Frankfurt in 1810. He left a thriving family business in the hands of his five sons, admonishing them to remain united. In his will he avoided disclosing the value of his assets by selling all his shares in the business and all his other possessions to his five sons for a nominal sum of 190,000 gulden, which were to be distributed for the benefit of his wife and five daughters.[3]

Mayer and Gutle's children were all raised in the Judengasse, and most of them followed their parents' example, marrying into successful families who lived within the same narrow streets. Jeannette, the eldest child, was born in 1771; in 1795 she married a merchant, Benedikt Moses Worms. Amschel Mayer, the oldest son, was born in 1773; in 1796 he married Eva Hanau, daughter of businessman Lehmann Isaac Hanau. Salomon Mayer was born in 1774; in 1800 he married Caroline Stern, daughter of Samuel Hayum Stern, a wine merchant. Nathan Mayer was born in 1777; he moved to London where in 1806 he married Hannah Cohen, daughter of a wealthy banking family. Isabella was born in 1781; in 1802 she married Bernhard Juda Sichel, a local businessman. Babette was born in 1784; in 1808 she married Siegmund Leopold Beyfus, a neighboring banker. Carl Mayer was born in 1788; in 1808 he married Adelheid Herz, daughter of a wealthy Hamburg family. Julie was born in 1790; in 1811 she married Mayer Levin Beyfus, a local banker. Henriette was born in 1791; she married Abraham Montefiore in London in 1815. James Rothschild was born in 1792; in 1824 he broke with family tradition, marrying his niece Betty.

The children and grandchildren of Mayer de Rothschild remained close to Gutle throughout her long widowhood. During the riots of August 1819, it is possible that fourteen-year-old Betty hid with her family in a back room of the Rothschild family home waiting for the rampage to cease. Grandmother Gutle, Uncle Amschel and his wife Eva, Uncle Carl and his wife Adelheid, and Betty's parents Salomon and Caroline probably gathered there in the face of danger. Betty's cousins, the children of the Worms, Hanau, Stern, Sichel, and Beyfus families also lived in the small streets in or near the Judengasse. They, like Betty, would have awakened on August 6th to find the hateful words Hep-Hep inscribed in large letters on the quaintly named streets of the old city: Pewterer's Lane, Cloister Lane, Fisherman's Lane, At the Smithy, The Roll Market, Rose Corner, Swordsmith's Lane, and Behind the Little Lamb. As the disturbances increased, city authorities began to fear a general rising. Finally, anticipating possible anarchy, the authorities called in troops to hold the populace in check.[4]

Growing up in Frankfurt, Betty had witnessed some manifestations of anti-Semitism, including the notorious Judensau (Jew's sow), a painted relief prominently displayed on the main city gate showing Jews suckling from a sow. Nevertheless, the experience of being the object of direct attack was new to her in 1819. Regrettably, this was not to be her last experience with violence and the unexpected hostility of Christian neighbors. Betty lived through the tumultuous years of 1830, 1848, and 1870–71 in Paris. Each political upheaval was accompanied by anti-Semitic rhetoric and sometimes by mob activity. Every new threat stirred memories of previous attacks and destruction of property.

The riot of 1819 was part of a pattern of behavior familiar to the older residents of the Jewish quarter. In the two decades since the removal of the locks on the gates of the walled ghetto, the Jews of Frankfurt had experienced frequent changes in their legal status as well as changes in the mood of the Christian citizens of Frankfurt. The dispersal of the rioters in 1819 did not mean an end to the attacks on Jews. Indeed, in the weeks that followed, Betty's uncle, Amschel, received several anonymous threats. One letter informed him of the day on which he was to be murdered by a secret society dedicated to ridding Frankfurt of all its Jews.[5] News of the desecration of synagogues, destruction of Torah scrolls and prayer books in nearby Sommersack and Rimpar reached Frankfurt.[6] Uncle James, writing from Paris, urged his brothers to leave Frankfurt for good, fearful that the massacre of Jews there had only been postponed.[7]

Because of complex laws and customs limiting Jewish mobility, it was diffi-cult for German Jews to move away from the violence and threats. The right to rent or buy housing, the right to set up shops, and access to employment were limited in Frankfurt and the adjacent towns. In addition, some Jews were reluc-tant to leave for other reasons. Exposed to Enlightenment ideas calling for equal civil rights, the first stirrings of patriotism and nationalism began to affect their outlook on the world.[8] The Jews of Frankfurt had demanded and finally obtained citizenship for three years during the French occupation of the city. The more educated were gradually forming identities as Frankfurters and Ger-man Jews. Some, like Heinrich Heine, converted in an opportunistic effort to win the approval of their Christian neighbors who expected enlightened Jews to become Christians. Most, like the Rothschilds, the Sichels, the Wormses, the Beyfuses, and the Hanaus, remained Jews.

These families stayed in Frankfurt where they experienced a strong Jewish communal life; they assumed that conditions for Jews would improve slowly. During the previous century, to make room for the growing population, most of the old wooden houses were subdivided. Two or three story additions were placed on top of the original structures and a row of houses was built behind the original dwellings in the narrow backyards. Very little light penetrated the homes, the four synagogues, the public bathhouse, and the communal bakery where bread was baked on weekdays and *cholent* (cassoulet of meat and beans) was prepared for the Sabbath. Unwilling to allow Jews to live among Christians or to expand the Judengasse, the authorities tried instead to limit the growth of the Jewish population. Laws limited the number of marriages to twelve per year and required the bridegroom to be at least twenty-five-years-old.

For a century Jews were permitted to enter the rest of the city only on business and never more than two abreast. When Betty's parents were chil-dren, the gates of the Judengasse were guarded by soldiers and were locked at night, all day on Sundays, and on Christian holidays. Jews were forbidden to linger in a public square, visit an inn or a coffee house, enter a park, or walk in one of the new promenades. They were banned at all times from the vicinity of Frankfurt's main cathedral and could enter the town hall only through the back entrance. They were not permitted to farm, nor could they trade in weapons, spices, or other commodities. A few Jews had shops dealing in luxury goods: silk, lace and jewelry. Most were pawnbrokers, moneychangers, and dealers in second hand clothes. Some were registered as butchers and bakers;

some were religious officials; some were doctors and lawyers. Inside the ghetto, Jews enforced their own customs, which required modest clothing; no berets for men, silk and jewelry for women only on the Sabbath.[9]

Closed off from the rest of society, the Judengasse developed a reputation for Jewish scholarship. In Mayer Amschel's youth the community boasted eight rabbis, twelve teachers, five cantors, one notary, and two doctors. Though Jews lived in a confined space with many restrictions on their freedom and on their ability to earn a living, the community educated its children. Literacy was much higher in the Judengasse than in the rest of the city.[10]

Commencing with the turn of the nineteenth century, the struggle for the abolition of the ghetto proceeded in fits and starts; yet, the Jewish community gradually began to integrate into the larger Christian community that surrounded them. Formerly their contact was restricted to business dealings and tax payments, but French revolutionary influence and German Enlightenment ideas began to make inroads even in Frankfurt, which the French occupied from 1806 to 1814. Napoleon appointed Archbishop Carl von Dalberg the Grand Duke of Frankfurt; Dalberg opened public parks to the ghetto-bound Jews as soon as he arrived in the city. But when Jewish communal leaders requested civil rights, freedom to acquire land, and the right to pursue various business interests, Dalberg, knowing the staunch opposition of Frankfurt's citizens, hesitated. Goethe, Frankfurt's celebrated author, probably expressed the ambivalence of many in his diary entry which recorded a trip to the ghetto:

> The confinement, the dirt, the swarm of people, the accents of an unpleasant tongue, all made a disagreeable impression, even when one only looked in when passing outside the gate. It took a long time before I ventured in alone; and I did not return easily after once escaping the obtrusiveness of so many people untiringly intent on haggling, either demanding or offering . . . *And yet, they were also human beings, energetic, agreeable, and even their obstinacy in sticking to their own customs, one could not deny respect.*[11] [my emphasis]

Though new ideas on the proper position of Jews in society had been circulating in German lands since the early 1780s when Christian Dohm's *On the Civil Improvement of the Jews* appeared, Frankfurt remained largely resistant to changes that were promulgated elsewhere. In the first decades of the century, Berlin was the center of advanced ideas about Jewish civil rights. There, Jewish salon hostesses Dorothea Mendelssohn, Henriette Herz, and Rachel Varnhagen entertained the leading philosophers of the day. Wilhelm Humboldt, the humanist and statesman, and his brother Alexander, the scientist and philosopher, along with Friedrich Schleiermacher, the theologian, were guests in the salons of these Jewish women.[12] Soon thereafter, in Paris, Napoleon convened a Sanhedrin, a Jewish Court of Justice, composed of seventy-one learned men, mostly rabbis, who were asked to reflect on the civic responsibilities of

Jews. But the Jews of Frankfurt, most of whom could not speak proper German, remained a traditional community long after Berlin and Paris had entered the modern world.

One of the Jewish couples permitted to marry in the Judengasse on December 26, 1800 was Caroline Stern, the eighteen-year-old daughter of Samuel Hayim and Sarah Kulp, and Salomon Rothschild, the twenty-six-year-old son of Mayer Amschel Rothschild and Gutle Schnapper. The traditional Jewish wedding united two successful families. The marriage contract stipulated that Mayer Rothschild would give his son 5,000 thalers and half of his house, furnished and with full property rights, in accord with local custom, as well as one-fourth share in his business and appropriate trousseau and gifts. Caroline received 10,000 thalers from her father, the promise of an additional 500 florins on the birth of her first child and 500 florins for the birth of the second child, a trousseau, and gifts. She was promised an inheritance equal to half that of her brother. [13]

Caroline Stern, Betty's mother, had an unusually broad education for a woman raised in the Judengasse. She wrote German and French as well as Judendeutsch, the lingua franca that Goethe found so loathsome. She also read Hebrew, the language of the synagogue, where she had a permanent place in the women's section purchased by her father at the time of her marriage. Salomon, Betty's father, had a traditional education based on the Bible and Talmud, but he was continually learning new skills as an adult. The wealth of both families and the education and health of Caroline and Salomon were weighed carefully before all parties agreed to the match. [14]

Following local tradition, the new couple lived for several years with the Sterns in Kaltes Bad, and for a few additional years with the Rothschilds in Grunen Schild. In 1807, Salomon, the father of two children, Anselm born in 1803 and Betty in 1805, received the coveted permission from city authorities to move out of the Judengasse to a house on Schafergasse. [15] Though his younger brother Nathan was already living in London, Salomon was the first of the Rothschild brothers who remained in Frankfurt to move out of the ghetto. It was in this new home that Betty and her brother spent most of their youth; yet the Judengasse was close by, and connections with grandparents, aunts and uncles, and cousins were strong.

Very little is known about Betty's early childhood. From the windows of her new home, she could see life in the city outside the Judengasse and she could look out onto the market where farmers gathered each day to sell their fruits and vegetables as well as live hens, ducks, and piglets. In winter, she and Anselm might enjoy a sleigh ride, a popular amusement for the city's affluent children. Among her cousins, there was one girl close in age; Henriette, the daughter of Salomon's sister, Jeannette, was two years older than Betty. [16] It is possible that they played together at Grandma Gutle's house, which seemed spacious since the Rothschild business, formerly located in the family home, had moved into a larger building on the outskirts of the ghetto. At a time of scant scientific knowledge about childcare, the experiential knowledge of Gutle, who had raised ten children to adulthood, was of inestimable value in tending to common childhood illnesses. In addition to her contributions to the family's health, Gutle remained the spiritual center of her family throughout Betty's childhood.

For the Rothschilds in Frankfurt, family life reflected Jewish law: the Sabbath was honored with the cessation of business, the family ate only kosher food, and life was marked by the annual celebrations of Jewish holidays. The Jewish New Year and Day of Atonement were occasions in September or October for synagogue attendance and large family meals. Sukkot was celebrated *en famille* in open-air booths on the roof of a shed behind the Grunen Schild. Later, when Uncle Amschel bought a garden, the family celebrated Sukkot in the midst of its splendor.[17] Chanukah was celebrated each December by lighting an eight-branched menorah and playing games of chance with a dreidel. Heinrich Heine, having abandoned the faith of his fathers, nostalgically noted the continuing tradition of Gutle Rothschild:

> How gaily the candles sparkle–those candles which she has lit with her own hands in order to celebrate the day of victory on which Judas Maccabeus and his brothers liberated their fatherland as heroically as did in our day King Frederick William, Emperor Alexander and the Emperor Francis II! When the good lady looks at these little lights, her eyes fill with tears, and she remembers with melancholy joy her younger days when Mayer Amschel Rothschild, of blessed memory, still celebrated the Feast of Lights with her, and when her sons were still little boys who placed candles on the floor and leapt over them with childlike pleasure, as is the custom in Israel.[18]

Purim, a spring holiday of merry-making, was celebrated in the ghetto with costumes and joyous eating and drinking. Passover, commemorating the exodus of the Hebrews from Egypt, was celebrated with the eating of unleavened bread, matzo, and a ritually prescribed family meal, the Seder. Seven weeks later, the holiday of Shavuot completed the celebrations of the year. Betty participated in the holiday preparations and celebrations. She was also present at traditional family weddings. She was probably there when Aunt Julie married Meyer Beyfus in 1811 and when Uncle Carl married Adelheid Herz from Hamburg in 1818.[19] She also attended several Bar Mitzvah ceremonies. By the time she was an adult, Betty knew enough about each of these customs and rituals to take them with her when she left the traditional Jewish community of Frankfurt to set up house in Paris.

Like most children whose parents could afford to hire tutors, Anselm and Betty were taught primarily at home in their early years. Betty refers fondly to one of her tutors, Mlle Josephine, who is mentioned in all of her letters to Cousin

Charlotte. Anselm and Betty studied French, German, English and Hebrew; with their family they spoke Judendeutsch. Anselm studied finance with his father and uncles, while Betty studied piano and voice as well as painting. Anselm was the first Rothschild to go to college, studying science first in Berlin and later at Cambridge; but it is unlikely that Betty attended school. Her age-mates, Marie Flavigny (later Marie d'Agoult) and Catherine Boode, the niece and sister-in-law of Moritz Bethmann, one of the leading bankers and enlightened men of Frankfurt, attended Herr Engelmann's finishing school.[20] Despite the fact that Salomon Rothschild and Moritz Bethmann had business and limited social relations, Betty would not have been sent to Herr Engelmann's with its Christian values and non-kosher food.

The Bethmann and Rothschild banks had frequent business dealings throughout Betty's childhood. Moritz Bethmann took pleasure in giving dinner parties and receptions. Though the Rothschilds would not eat the pheasant from the Bethmann estate in Bohemia nor drink the fine Rhineland wines he offered his other guests, they shared his enthusiasm for the arts. No talented writer, musician, or artist visited Frankfurt without being invited to the Bethmann's. As many of these artists also performed in London and Paris, it was likely that by the time they arrived in Frankfurt they would have already met at least one of the Rothschilds, perhaps coming to Frankfurt with letters of introduction from Nathan or James. The liberal-minded Bethmann would invite his neighbors, the Rothschilds, to enjoy a musical performance at his home. These visits were reciprocated. When Moritz Bethmann attended a dinner party in May 1816 at the home of Salomon and Caroline Rothschild, he commented on the excellence of the fare and on the well-behaved children. Bethmann made specific mention of the high level of education achieved by Betty.[21]

Affluent families like the Rothschilds wanted to extend the rudiments of German culture, reading, writing, arithmetic, and French to all Jewish children in Frankfurt. They tried to establish a Jewish school for the secular instruction of poor children who were still attending traditional schools, like the one in which Mayer Amschel had studied fifty years earlier. Traditional schools taught only the Bible and Talmud and used Judendeutsch as the language of instruction. The school, proposed in 1794 and again in 1801, combined traditional subjects with modern ones. The plan failed because of stiff opposition from the rabbinate and the traditional communal leadership. But parents who valued a more secular education sent their children to local non-Jewish schools. Between 1800 and 1803, twenty-nine Jewish boys attended the Frankfurt gymnasium, whereas only six had attended in the previous decade. In 1803, when the city opened a model school offering poor boys a chance to learn, twenty-two pupils, one-fourth of the students registered, were Jewish. Other parents sent their sons out of the city to Jewish secular schools. Thirteen boys from Frankfurt were sent to Westphalia to study with the enlightened Israel Jacobson. Girls were also sent to non-Jewish schools in this period. Of the thirty girls attending the model school between 1803 and 1804, one-quarter were Jewish.[22]

In 1803, Mayer Amschel Rothschild, having become a successful banker and community leader, funded the establishment of a new school for poor Jewish children in Frankfurt; permission to lease a school building outside the Judengasse for this purpose was obtained from the authorities. In 1806, Michael Hess, who had been hired by Rothschild as a tutor for his youngest son, James, was appointed head teacher of the new school, Philanthropin. The school aimed to prepare boys for practical life, especially for commercial careers, but great attention was also given to religious instruction. Many hours each week were devoted to teaching Hebrew so that pupils would understand the Bible in the original text. In addition to traditional sacred studies, German, French, geography, natural history, and modern philosophy made up the curriculum. In January 1810, a department for girls was opened. In addition to the boys' curriculum, girls were trained for their future duties as wives and mothers. All students were taught how to negotiate the changing world; they were taught to be a Jew at home and an honorable person in the world.[23] These values also permeated the private instruction Betty received at home.

Concern about occupational training for Jews was widespread at this time. Enlightened Christians and Jews saw vocational education as a way to raise Jews out of poverty. Jews in Berlin, Breslau, Seesen, and Dessau had already founded schools to provide training, especially for poor children; yet artisans frequently refused to take on Jewish apprentices, and the centuries-old guild system precluded Jewish membership. Thus, despite its philanthropic origins, the Philanthropin gradually evolved into a middle-class institution. From its inception, the school accepted tuition-paying students to help balance the budget, and after the first two years, tuition-paying students predominated. In 1822, the Philanthropin, renamed Burger und Realschule, became the official school of the Jewish community of Frankfurt. By that time, its emphasis had changed from training in manual skills to commercial education.[24]

Archbishop von Dalberg was favorably impressed by the efforts of the Jews to move toward a more practical education for their children. In 1807 he issued a new ordinance emphasizing religious and educational reform and provided annual funds for the Philanthropin from his own pocket;[25] but little progress was made on other issues. Trade restrictions continued to exist, hampering the efforts of the Rothschild brothers, and the ghetto was maintained, albeit in a modified form, without walls and gates.

When Amschel Rothschild decided to follow his brother Salomon to live outside of the ghetto, he had to apply for a special permit for the house and a year later for another special permit for the right to own a garden. The permits allowed him to fulfill his strong desire to buy land outside the ghetto. Amschel, a traditional Jew and hard-working Rothschild, was at heart a keen horticulturalist. As he did not travel much, he asked his more peripatetic brothers to send him exotic plants that he tended with care, offering cuttings of rare species to special guests. The description of his garden in a local guide-book of the 1830s illustrates the continuing ambivalence of the Christian community to the Jews living in their midst:

> The flowers are glittering in gold and the beds are fertilized with crown thalers, the summer houses are well papered with Rothschild bonds . . . A magnificent wealth of foreign flora spreads across the garden . . . To my mind, in his garden Amschel von Rothschild resembles a lord in his seraglio.[26]

In 1811, having received numerous petitions and requests, Dalberg was prepared to grant the Jews of Frankfurt citizenship in return for a large pay-ment in lieu of the annual 25,000 gulden tax which the Jewish community had been required to pay to live in the ghetto. Mayer Amschel Rothschild, a notable of the community, proposed a lump sum payment of 440,000 gulden, of which he promised to pay 100,000. By the end of the year, the Official Gazette proclaimed:

> Henceforth the *Israelitish* dwellers in the city of Frankfurt are to enjoy the same rights and powers as the Christian citizens . . . the *Israelitish* citizens are to have the right to the same treatment by all court and administrative offi-cers as the rest of the citizens.[27]

The Jews took the oath of citizenship before Mayor Guiollette, fulfilling the dreams of progressive Jews in Frankfurt.

Seven months later Mayer Amschel Rothschild, having been one of the first nineteen family heads to sign the oath of citizenship, was dead. Mayer Amschel's widow and children did not remain Frankfurt citizens for long. In 1814, with the defeat of Napoleon, the French left Frankfurt and the Austrian government revoked the recently granted citizenship and revived all the old laws concerning Jews. Amschel, now the head of the Frankfurt bank, and his four brothers, Nathan in London, James in Paris, and Salomon and Carl travel-ing extensively to support the family enterprise, were all concerned about the deteriorating conditions for Jews in Frankfurt and elsewhere in the former French-occupied lands. But it was Salomon's wife, Caroline, who remained in Frankfurt, who voiced her devotion to Jewish rights.

Writing in July 1814 Caroline asked Salomon and his brothers to remem-ber the Jews of Frankfurt:

> It does not look rosy for us as regards our citizenship . . . As far as I can see from a distance, we still have a long struggle before us. This matter interests me so much, that if I catch a simple word about it, I listen eagerly to what is

said . . . I am very curious to know what the result is going to be. Can't you, my dearest Salomon, contribute to this through your acquaintances over there? This would be a heavenly good deed, which cannot be bought even with very much money. Perhaps a minister there would give you an intro-duction to Austria, Russia or whomsoever has a say in this matter. *You may ask what has a woman to do with public affairs? Better she should write about soap and needles. However, I see what I am doing as necessary. Nobody is doing anything about the matter. Time is passing slowly and we will reproach ourselves for not having done more . . . This matter is now most pressing; and here in Frankfurt nobody is doing anything.*[28] [my emphasis]

Caroline's comments offer rare insight into the thoughts of a Rothschild woman early in the nineteenth century. The mother of two children—Anselm was eleven and Betty was nine—Caroline Stern had participated in Rothschild family discussions since her marriage to Salomon in 1800. She was surely involved in the conversations about the creation of the Jewish school funded by her father-in-law and likely consulted with its director, Michael Hess, in hiring tutors for her children. As an educated Jewish woman, Caroline probably sub-scribed to *Sulamith*, a German-language periodical published in Dessau since 1806, whose authors focused on the moral improvement of German Jewry. Atypically for the day, this monthly review specifically addressed Jewish women as well as men. Acting on behalf of the Jews of Frankfurt, Caroline asked her husband to spend some time to address their conditions. She couched her request in feminine rhetoric, wondering if he would think that she had entered a male sphere of activity. Caroline's consciousness of the moral impera-tive to act outweighed her fears of overstepping traditional boundaries. Betty learned from her mother's courage.

Caroline was not the only woman in Frankfurt thinking about the condi-tion of the Jews and writing her thoughts in epistolary form. Rahel Levin Varn-hagen, the Berlin salon hostess, lived in Frankfurt from 1815–19. Though she had already converted to Christianity, Rahel voiced her concerns about anti-Semitism in a letter to her brother Ludwig Robert in 1819:

I know my country! Unfortunately. A cursed Cassandra! For three years I have been saying the Jews will be attacked . . . This is the German courage of rebellion. And why? Because it is the most proper, good-natured, peace-loving, slavish people . . . there is also room for envy towards those Jews—whom one was, thanks to religious excesses, permitted to hate, despise, and persecute as inferior beings.[29]

Despite the persistence of anti-Semitic feelings, during the years following the Congress of Vienna of 1815, most German towns reinstated some of the privileges accorded Jews during the Napoleonic occupation. Frankfurt remained alone in its adherence to the old rules and rituals. In 1819 the Jewish leaders of the city took the initiative and wrote to the German Confederation meeting in Carlsbad:

> All states in the German Confederation have found it more or less appropri-ate to the spirit of the times to elevate their protected Jews to citizens of the state. Why only in Frankfurt should the Jewish citizens be degraded once again to the status of protected Jews? Have not the Jews of the city fought along with the other citizens for the liberation of Germany? Have they not borne collective war-taxes and contributions for the freedom of their native city? Were they to accept their disparagement before the eyes of the world willingly, so would they openly become unworthy of the title of citizen.[30]

But the Confederation was preoccupied with other matters. Instead of acceding to the requests of the Jews, the authorities were obliged to quiet the *Hep-Hep* uprising that was, in part, a response to Jewish agitation for reform. The Jews of Frankfurt continued to live and work without civil rights until 1824.

Betty's identity was formed during the struggle for Jewish civil rights as it was discussed by the Rothschild family and the broader Jewish community of Frankfurt. Throughout her long life, she was influenced by a strong sense of re-sponsibility for the Jewish people that she learned first from her mother and later from other members of her family. Another major preoccupation of her youth was the physical health of her family. A preoccupation with well-being was com-mon to all the Rothschilds, whose wealth could not immunize them against everyday illnesses. The Rothschilds constantly sought advanced medical atten-tion, consulting physicians and attending spas in an effort to ward off illness and the effects of aging. The earliest known letter from Caroline to her husband, dated approximately 1813, called on Salomon to take care of his health:

> My dearest beloved,
>
> I was very surprised at your much appreciated letter of the 12th of this month, and have learned from it with the greatest vexation that unfortu-nately you are not yet well. Much as I long for your earliest return, do not quicken your departure, my beloved, if a longer sojourn would improve your health. I could never endure that by a too early departure you might fail to recover your health that being your foremost duty. Therefore, my dearest, may I beg you not to become impatient because you must know that with God's help all will be well again. At any rate, you must be com-pletely recovered for the journey . . . If only you would be in good health as I wish for you; have you already had Turkish baths? . . .
>
> Your ever loving . . . [31]

This charming, wifely letter followed the style recommended to Jewish wives in the popular *Brandshpigl*. Women were instructed to pray for their husbands' safety, asking God to protect them from officials, evil spirits, wild animals and vicious persons.[32] Salomon had apparently taken a few days or weeks at a health spa hoping to be cured of some unspecified illness. The Rothschilds paid considerable attention to their health and spas were a preferred treatment for all ailments in the first half of the century. Caroline remained at home with Anselm and Betty. Though there are many letters attesting to Caroline's unhappiness about the length of time spent by her husband traveling for the family business, she was pleased when he spent time on his health.

Salomon also resented the long absences from his wife and children. Letters from Salomon to his brother Nathan, who acted as head of the family following the death of Mayer Amschel, insisted that he had to spend more time with his wife and children. In 1814 he wrote to Nathan: "If you had been away from your wife and children for a year and a half you would begin to feel anxious too." In 1815 he was even more emphatic: "I shall first go home and fetch my wife because I am sick and tired of the life of a recluse. I shall not travel anymore without my wife, dear brother." And in December 1815 he wrote from Paris:

> I shall leave here on the 26th of this month . . . because you will see from the enclosed letters that my only son is to be Bar Mitzvah in three or four weeks time. My child will lose his filial love for his parents if I do not attend this one festival which as Jews we hold most sacred; particularly since I have hardly spent three weeks at home in the last three years.[33]

Eighteen months later Salomon chided Nathan about "trying to build Rome in one day" and not allowing members of the family enough time to be together. He expressed the need to stay in Paris to conclude business discussions with James and to await the arrival of Carl who also had business dealings to review. The fact that Caroline and Hannah were also in Paris was added incentive for him to stay. Nevertheless, the bond of brotherhood, formed during childhood and fostered by their father in his lifetime as well as in his will,[34] clearly was deeper than any passing quarrel.

This bond extended to the spouses. James and Salomon were both fond of Nathan's wife Hannah, who filled a central role in the Rothschild family from her home in London. Hannah provided family dinners for the traveling brothers. Surrounded by her children: Charlotte, Lionel, Anthony, Nathaniel, Hannah Mayer, Mayer, and Louise, Hannah became the second Rothschild matriarch, following the tradition started by Gutle. She took a lively interest in the family business and maintained a deep concern for the

Jews of London as well as elsewhere. Hannah visited the family in Paris and Frankfurt regularly, forming a close relationship with Caroline and Salomon as well as with James.

The closeness of the family can be glimpsed in letters. James wrote to Hannah in 1815 about the impending marriage of his sister, Henriette, to Abraham Montefiore. Hannah's sister Judith was married to Moses Montefiore, Abraham's brother. The growing links in the relationships among leading Jewish families continued the practice started in the Judengasse. The ties of friendship can be seen in commissions performed by James and Salomon for Hannah: for example, buying stylish silk sleeves for her dresses in Paris. Letters to Nathan, in London, from Caroline and Eva, who remained in Frankfurt, also attest to family cohesiveness.

Caroline and Hannah developed especially close ties. Caroline shared Hannah's interest in the business that occupied their husbands. Both had independent control of some of their resources and invested in their husbands' company. Caroline, like Hannah, was deeply committed to helping the Jews of her hometown and elsewhere. When her children were older, Caroline, unable to keep Salomon at home, began to travel with him. Frequently Caroline and Hannah met in Paris, the logical mid-point between Frankfurt and London. The women spent time discussing the various renovation projects for their homes, attended concerts and theater together, and met and greeted each other's friends. They also spoke about their children's development and their future. It is likely that Hannah and Caroline started talking about marriage possibilities for their daughters, Betty and Charlotte, perhaps even consulting Gutle when Caroline returned to Frankfurt.

The family letters also reflected some of their fears. Gutle and her older sons were originally opposed to the idea of Carl's marriage to Adelheid Herz. Though her family met the criterion of being financially successful, they were from the less traditional Hamburg Jewish community. The family feared that Carl, his bride, and their children would not be religiously observant. Though Carl's desire to marry Adelheid caused some concern, the bigger worry was the continuing bachelorhood of James, the youngest son, living far from family supervision in Paris.

With the family scattered in five cities, distance was a constant obstacle to family unity. Travel, even for the Rothschilds, remained hazardous. Brigands were a concern; natural disasters another. They designed special coaches with secret compartments to carry the family, often encumbered by substantial wealth, to their destinations. On Friday, July 11, 1817, Caroline and Salomon arrived in Rotterdam after a particularly harrowing journey. Caroline wrote to Nathan and Hannah in London describing their ordeal:

> We arrived here this morning after a dangerous journey. My dear Salomon being so exhausted by the many difficulties that we went through that he is

unable to write, therefore I am writing you a few lines . . . It will be a pleasure for you to hear how lucky we were to escape a great danger.

We traveled quite well until Moerstyle. A half-hour after starting to cross the river called Moerts—it was 11 PM—a terrible storm came . . . which threw us into the greatest panic and danger. A crossing which normally lasts one hour lasted three hours; twice we were thrown against the sandbanks . . . How we escaped I don't know even now . . . After landing at last we had to walk on a swampy road. Every moment we were in danger of sinking into the bog . . . All this made such a violent impression on my dear Salomon that he had an attack of pains in the joints which made the Doctor whom I summoned as soon as we arrived forbid him to proceed to the Hague, or to write. He ordered him to bed. However, I assure you that it is of no real significance and you will certainly receive from him long letters again within a few days . . . We carried so many valuables, and this was the reason that we forced the pace, traveling during the nights, without leaving the carriage since Tuesday midday when we started the voyage in Paris.

Salomon was not to be coddled. He added a humorous note to the letter:

The Doctor should hang himself! I must not write . . . He put me to bed. My worst pains are in my stomach and my joints . . . I was frightened not a little; I suffered agonies of death . . . We were 99% lost; God helped us. However, fright and terror are felt only after you get over them. Now I know what sandbanks are . . . I did not write about it to Frankfurt because the whole Judengasse would make my mother crazy . . . It was truly hard to travel three days and nights without a break and to be plagued by the fear of death.[35]

Caroline and Salomon's trips often took them away from their children who grew up surrounded by tutors and servants and the Frankfurt family. Betty's childhood was devoted to lessons, punctuated by the Jewish holidays, and by periodic trips taken with her parents. It is likely that Betty wrote journals of her thoughts and experiences; sadly none have survived. The first words spoken across the centuries by Betty are found in a letter to her English cousin Charlotte. Betty wrote from Schwalbach, on July 23, 1819, in French with a fine girlish handwriting. Betty and Anselm had accompanied Caroline to the nearby spa to help her recover from the shock resulting from the death of her father. Betty, now fourteen, wrote to the twelve-year-old Charlotte whom she had not yet met:

My very dear friend,

I am eager to reply to your kind letter which gave me the greatest pleasure and for which I am most obliged to you. I rejoiced to learn of the happy arrival of my dear Papa and my uncle at your family's home. The latter wrote

Female ties/family [handwritten margin note]

to us so many nice things about you that I can't believe that he is indulgent to you as your modesty says. It only served to arouse in me still more the real need I have to know you and to love you more. It is not from Frankfurt, my dear friend, that I have the pleasure to write to you, for at the moment we are at the waters in Schwalbach which my dear mother is taking to get her health back, for the cruel loss of our dear grandfather put her out a bit. I was careful to pass on your greetings that gave her the greatest pleasure, and she told me to pass on to you many kind words on her behalf.

We are having such a nice time here, and to give you an idea of it, I shall give you a little description. Schwalbach is beautifully situated among fine mountains and rocks, and allows us many walks that we sometimes take on the donkeys and other times by carriage, and often on foot. On all sides there are such charming and varied views that it is a real joy to behold them.

You'll think it very funny, my dear friend, if I tell you that the donkeys are the most famous walkers in Schwalbach, and maybe you will laugh if I tell you that these long-eared animals contribute greatly to our pleasure, for you cannot imagine how nice it is to ride them, how comfortable one is and how free from all anxiety that they will rush off with the bit between their teeth.

There are two springs here and the water is very good, very healthy and nice to drink, and as we are staying near one of the springs, I combine business with pleasure and drink my three glasses, afterwards going for a walk round the spa where a sparkling society gathers each morning. Delightful music charms our ears.

But I am horrified to see that my seldom-used pen has bored you too long already, my dear cousin. Will you have the patience to listen to me longer? I doubt it, so I shall quickly stop, say farewell to you, and beg you not to forget . . .

Your affectionate friend,
Betty de Rothschild

My brother is most touched by being remembered by you and by the kind lines you were good enough to add for him. He begs me to thank you for them and to send you a thousand affectionate wishes on his behalf.[36]

There is much that can be discerned from this first letter. Betty's French was already fluent; she not only communicated, she even joked in French. In addition, we can see that Betty was comfortable in the newly fashionable world of spas with their ritual drinking, eating, exercise, and musical recitals. She was also evidently eager to keep up with Uncle James. According to family lore, the six-year-old Betty asked James to write to her regularly when he left home for Paris. Every one of Betty's surviving letters to Charlotte mentioned James. Similarly, every one of them mentioned Anselm, who married Charlotte two years after Betty married James. From the first letter, there was great ease in communication, though the girls had not yet met, since the families were close and family news was shared regularly. One additional indication about Betty's personality is evident in her signature. She used the particle "de" indicating the status awarded her father and his brothers by the Austrian Empire in 1817.

In a letter of the following year, we get another picture of family closeness. Caroline, recovered from her loss and from the *Hep-Hep* riots, wrote an affectionate letter to her thirteen-year-old niece, Charlotte. Again, the language of communication was French, but Caroline wrote in a less confident hand and displayed less command of the language. She told Charlotte that though she hadn't written in a long time, she still held her very dear. She noted, "My dear little Betty wants so much to make your acquaintance." Caroline sketched Charlotte's portrait for Betty, but feared that she did not do it justice, since everyone had told her that Charlotte had changed and become even prettier. Caroline then inquired about Charlotte's new baby sister, Louise, who was born on July 6, 1820. "Do you love her a little bit yet? Is she as pretty as the little Hannah Mayer?" Caroline wondered whether the four-year-old Hannah Mayer was jealous of her "small rival" and inquired about Mayer, her two-year-old nephew: "Is he talking yet?" She was eager to see him. She also asked about Mlle Andreus, Charlotte's tutor who had been suffering from an eye ailment, and sent Mademoiselle her greetings. She wondered how Charlotte spent the summer, asking if the family took an excursion to Brighton or stayed at home in the countryside. She concluded by reiterating that she longed for family news and asked Charlotte to kiss and hug her sisters and brothers for their affectionate Aunt Caroline.

Betty added a postscript:

> I will benefit my very dear cousin from the small space left me by my good mother to remind you of my affection, and to say in a few small words how much I love you and am devoted to you.
>
> Your affectionate friend and cousin,
> Betty[37]

While Betty and Caroline focused on family matters, Salomon, like his brothers, concentrated on business. Salomon was doing more business in Vienna, where he had opened a branch of the Rothschild Bank, and as a result, spent a good deal of time there. His frequent business travel took a toll on Caroline and the children; Caroline did not want him taking extra trips to St. Petersburg or to London. After the *Hep-Hep* riots of 1819, she joined Salomon in Vienna with Anselm and Betty, where they took up residence in the Hotel of the Roman Emperors. Unable to buy a home in Vienna due to restrictions on the Jews, Salomon eventually took over the entire hotel. When Caroline learned that Salomon was planning more trips, she wrote in an uncharacteristically sharp tone: "In any event, dear Salomon, you are not going to London without my knowing the reason why. Understood, my dear husband? You are not doing it."[38] It is not clear what the outcome of this quarrel was, but by 1820 the family was living together in Vienna.

A year later, the family traveled to Paris. Another letter from Betty to Charlotte reveals a more mature Betty. This letter, from September 26, 1821, implies that by this time the girls had met, perhaps in Paris or London, and that by now Betty is familiar with Paris, or at least with Uncle James's Parisian home. It is quite possible that Hannah and Charlotte spent time with Caroline and Betty in Paris in August of 1821, and that while Hannah and her daughter had returned home for the Jewish New Year, Caroline and Betty had remained in Paris to spend the holiday with James.

Despite the affluence that permitted tutors and travel, Betty's teen years were not always rosy. Betty confided in a letter to Charlotte that her mother was ill with grief and confined to her bed. The cause of Caroline's grief is not known. It is possible that she was not happy living among strangers in Vienna, and that she continued to quarrel with Salomon about his frequent business travel. Caroline traveled back and forth between Frankfurt and Vienna, often accompanied by her daughter. Betty wrote, "You can judge for yourself, my dear friend, how much I suffered when I saw my beloved Mama in such a state."[39] Betty's strong attachment to her mother was to continue until the latter's death in 1854.

The letter from Paris includes a humorous account of a soiree held at Uncle James's on the tenth of September:

> . . . after tasting the dishes prepared by uncle's good cook, the ladies and demoiselles tried in vain to sing a little song and decided instead for a *con-tre-danse* which soon ended as the dancers had all forgotten the turns. It was very funny to see each new pair beginning and not being able to finish. And at this French soiree dancing was replaced by outbursts of laughter, and so I thought more often of you, my dear Charlotte, who, with your great talent on the harpsichord, would have given us great pleasure that evening.

Betty's wry comments about the soiree at rue Laffitte show how comfortable the sixteen-year-old girl from Frankfurt was in the elegant Paris setting. She was able to laugh at the awkwardness of the guests, perhaps because she had attended more decorous evenings in Frankfurt, which had become the capital of the Confederation of German States. Balls, concerts and banquets were the order of the day there. The Frankfurt opera offered performances by Gluck, Spontini and Mozart.[40]

Nevertheless, the awkward relations between Jews and Germans in Frankfurt remained. Amschel Mayer von Rothschild sent an obsequious letter to the

Austrian Chancellor Prince Metternich in 1821 illustrative of the remaining distance between the worlds of the Rothschilds and the Metternichs despite their many business dealings:

> Your Serene Highness, Gracious prince and Master, I hope that your Highness shall not take it amiss and consider it impertinent of me when I make so bold as to request that your Highness do me the great honor of taking soup with me this noon. This happiness would mark an epoch in my life."[41]

Metternich accepted the invitation, arriving with his mistress, the Comtesse Dorothy de Lieven, and was treated to a splendid banquet at the home of Amschel and Eva von Rothschild on Bockenheimer Landstrasse.[42] This event was noted with disapproval in Frankfurt while in Paris, where the social system of the nineteenth century was far more fluid, Metternich dined regularly at the Rothschilds along with a host of other notables.

Betty's letter to Charlotte concludes with a special wish for her cousin on the eve of the Jewish New Year, a time of pervasive sweet hopefulness. Betty, thinking about herself as well as her cousin, suggested that Charlotte enjoy the happiness of being with her parents a while longer, implying that marriage was not far off. She urged Charlotte to continue to make them happy; a role she certainly tried to fulfill for her own parents, Caroline and Salomon. Two weeks later, Betty and her mother were still in Paris. Salomon, however, was once again on his way to London. Betty dashed off a quick note to Charlotte thanking her for the letter she had received that morning and declaring her devotion and affection. Again she mentioned Uncle James. Her childish affection for her adventurous and educated uncle was developing into something more mature.[43] Charlotte's letters and periodic visits were very important to Betty, who had no sisters in whom she could confide. In May 1822 when Betty again addressed Charlotte, this time from Frankfurt, she refers to her cousin as her dear and best friend. She thanked Charlotte for her recent letter in which she assured Betty of her true friendship. Betty then chided Charlotte in a humorous tone for not keeping her promise to visit her in Vienna:

> The castles in the air that I had already built have suddenly fallen crumbled. Moreover, it is not fair to break one's word, and especially not of a nice Banker, for I remember very well that your father promised Mama he would come and see Papa, and bring you with him, and if he undertakes the dry commitment to business, why does he not fulfill the pleasant commitment of the heart?[44]

Betty then changed the tone of her letter, writing earnestly once again about Uncle James. She was delighted to hear from Charlotte that the previously ailing James was better and asked her to inquire whether James had received the two letters written to him by Betty and her family. Not having had a response, they were concerned that the letters may have been lost.

Betty's letter included more information about her growing social world. She mentioned that the Rother family, business associates of the Rothschilds, would be visiting soon and that she was eager to hear from them about Charlotte since they were arriving from London and had just spent time together. She mused, "How I envy them for having been so long in your wonderful company." She went on to respond to Charlotte's appreciation for Ignaz Moscheles, the tutor of Felix Mendelssohn, whose playing and instruction pleased Charlotte. Betty, too, had heard him perform and probably had some lessons with him when he visited Frankfurt. Charlotte also enjoyed Mlle Catalani's voice and Betty wrote, "This nightingale has already enchanted many people among whom I surely count myself." Finally, Betty reported that she spent the whole evening with an unidentified Mlle Hertz but that she no longer found her so pretty, and "I assure you, my dear, it will never be she who puts you in the shadow."

Betty signs off as follows:

Forgive this dreadful scribble, my dear, kind friend, and show your friend-
ship by not showing this to anyone.
For life and for death,
Your totally devoted and affectionate and sincere friend,
Betty
My best wishes to your dear Parents.
Mama asks me to pass on her regards.
Best wishes to Mlle Andreus.
Mlle Josephine sends a thousand wishes.[45]

Six months later, writing from her new home in Vienna, the Hotel of the Roman Emperors, Betty expressed her great pleasure in the recent letter she received from Charlotte. "I assure you it caused tears of love to come to my eyes." From the tone of the letter, Charlotte and Betty were sharing important girlish secrets. Betty tells Charlotte, "You may be sure that if the heavens refuse me all the happiness you wish for me, I would not complain since I have been granted the joy, so rare in this world, of a true friend who loves me as much as I love her, who shares my feelings and sentiments."[46]

The letter continued in a lighter tone. Charlotte had requested information about life in Vienna. Betty wrote that they do not go out into society since Salomon left for Paris. Theatre had become their only entertainment, and only one of them, which performs German tragedies, met Betty's standard. Betty pro-claimed that she had never seen such a good troupe and that her German has improved immeasurably. As far as friendships were concerned, Betty reported having made the acquaintance of the Eskeles family. Mme Eskeles, the wife of one of the leading bankers of Vienna who kept one of the largest homes in the city, frequently entertained Betty and Caroline. Nevertheless, they both felt excluded by the generally cool reception they received from Viennese Jews, who took scant notice of the Rothschilds. Life in Vienna improved during a visit by Uncle James who introduced Betty to Mlle de Stahl, the daughter of his acquaintance Ritter von Stahl. Betty learned that Mlle de Stahl enjoyed painting; soon the two young women shared an art teacher and spent time together painting.

Three months later, writing from Vienna, Betty, now seventeen, again addressed Charlotte, who was fifteen. The girlhood friends had become young ladies. Betty sent her portrait to Charlotte and was happy that her friend has received it "kindly," though she herself professed that it had no merit. Betty awaited eagerly Charlotte's promised portrait. Regrettably, these images have not survived, but subsequent portraits of the young women (figures 1 and 2) illustrated their developing sense of self.

Betty resumed her letter by announcing her relief that the Carnival season in Vienna is over. She enigmatically related:

> I'm not stepping out into society at all from now on, and then there are reasons for this that I couldn't tell you about, except face-to-face. Vienna is a very nice city, but has, at the same time, faults that are very obvious and even painful sometimes for foreigners. And this is what has made me make this decision. [47]

Betty told Charlotte that she had much to confide in her, and that when seated side-by-side, she could "pour her heart out" freely to Charlotte, whose love will ameliorate the pain. Betty may have suffered disappointment or hurt due to her unusual status as a Rothschild; she was both an aristocrat and a Jew. She was entertained by nobility and in turn entertained them by singing and playing the piano; however, despite the social interaction, Betty was not prepared to convert to Christianity as several of the celebrated Jewish Berlin salon hostesses had. She was a beautiful and talented young woman who may have received attentions from someone whose religious and social standing made a lasting relationship impossible. The secrets Betty wanted to share with Charlotte have never been revealed.

Betty's letters were not only self-referential. She also had Charlotte's future in mind when she sang the praises of her brother, Anselm. According to Betty, though gallantry is not Anselm's strong suit, Charlotte's goodness could bring about the necessary changes in him. Betty counseled, "You must be a bit indulgent with him if he is not very good at replying, for business takes up so much of his time now that he is not able to turn his thoughts to friendly letters very often. Honestly, it's an age since he wrote to me."

Betty's concern that she may have written too much for prying eyes prompted her to add a post script to this letter: "Never show this letter to anyone and please don't repeat the silly things I've scribbled in it." The letter, dated

Fig. 1. G.H. Harlow, Betty de Rothschild, n.d. The Rothschild Archive London.

February 20, 1823, with its mysterious content, is the last surviving letter from Betty before her marriage to James seventeen months later. It leaves the impression of an intelligent, cosmopolitan, lively, and loving young woman. She knew the life of the Judengasse as well as the life of the Vienna salon. She was privileged as a result of wealth and education, yet her social prospects were limited because of the anti-Semitism of polite society. Betty knew that she had a close friend and confidant in Charlotte; the cousins would remain intimate until Charlotte's death in 1859.

Fig. 2. G.H. Harlow, Charlotte de Rothschild, n.d. The Rothschild Archive London.

Betty's marriage to James was a break in the Rothschild tradition of marrying Jewish families of similar backgrounds and wealth. All of James's siblings had married by 1824, uniting some of the most influential Jewish families in Frankfurt, Hamburg, and London. The last to marry was Carl, who wed Adelheid in 1818. But James found no suitable partner in the French Jewish community. The affluent and sophisticated Parisian Sephardic families were close-knit and did not welcome James Rothschild, whom they saw as a business rival. James had little interest in Parisian Jews from Alsace, the largest community of

Jews in France, whom he saw as less sophisticated and less educated than the Jews of Frankfurt.

The solution was to marry his niece, Betty, whose education and social grace made her an ideal partner for James. Marriage between close relatives was commonplace in the ghettos of Europe. The Rothschild family was delighted with the chance to forge even closer ties among its branches. As her letters attest, Betty had been attracted to her young uncle for years. Her youthful inclinations and the family's interests coincided, making Betty a happy bride, eager to take up her new role in a new city.

Hannah Rothschild and her sons Lionel and Anthony journeyed to Frankfurt for the wedding. Charlotte had arrived earlier to spend time with her friend Betty. Hannah reported happily to her husband, Nathan, that Betty was looking exceedingly well and was as amiable as ever; Charlotte and she were inseparable. She added that Gutle was in excellent spirits, very pleased with her youngest son's marriage, and she also made reference to the tasteful gifts of jewelry and shawls brought by James for his bride. Brother Carl arrived from Naples. Congratulations poured in from friends and family all over. Hannah noted that Moritz Bethmann came to pay his respects to the family. Ever mindful of the importance of political power for business relations, James and Salomon visited Prince Metternich to invite him to the wedding; however, Hannah assumed that the Prince, who was spending time at his nearby home in Joannesburg, would not attend the wedding "on account of the family being numerous beside the necessity of making different arrangements in the kitchen for his party."[48]

Dinners and lunches for family and friends preceded and followed the wedding that took place on July 11, 1824. Betty's dowry was a munificent 1.5 million francs, much larger than any Rothschild dowry to this point, and on a par with some royal marriages of the period. In addition to the dowry, gifts from James and other members of the family included: diamond necklaces and bracelets; ostrich feathers; ermine furs; materials embroidered with gold and silver; shawls of lace and silk and cashmere. Betty was being outfitted for her new role as a Parisian society lady. Along with her trousseau, music books, and novels, Betty took a prayer book and a Bible to Paris. In addition to her paints and brushes, jewelry and shawls, she brought ceremonial items for her new home: a mezuzah to place on the door post, a brass candelabra for the Sabbath, a spice box for the ceremony at the conclusion of the Sabbath. To celebrate Jewish holidays, she brought a Passover tray for mazzot, a menorah and dreidel for Chanukah, and recipes for special holiday fare. Caroline Stern, Betty's mother, certainly provided her with a linen cloth to cover the mazzot, probably embroidered in silk and personalized for Betty.[49]

Shortly after Betty and James left the city for their new home in Paris, a law was passed in Frankfurt regulating the status of Jews in regard to political and civil rights. This law was a victory for Jews, as it abolished the tax paid by Jews to remain in the city. Once again Jews were designated *Israelitish* citizens. Nevertheless, oppressive restrictions, such as fixing the maximum number of marriages at fifteen per year and retaining some limitations on trade, remained in force. Full civil and political equality for the Jews of Frankfurt was not won until 1864.[50]

CHAPTER TWO

Madame la Baronne James de Rothschild

Laffitte gave a great ball; I was not invited. I have no house to receive people. A house without a wife is like a ship without a captain . . .
                James de Rothschild, Paris, to his brother, Amschel, Frankfurt, 1817

On Saturday we dined at a sumptuous feast at Rothschilds. He has married his niece, a pretty little Jewess, née coiffée [born lucky], a very good thing at Paris, for, just out of her nursery, she does the honors of her house as if she had never done anything else.
                Lady Granville, Paris, to her sister, Lady Georgiana Morpeth, London,
                                                    December 12, 1824

James Rothschild (originally named Jacob) was born in May 1792, the last of Mayer Amschel and Gutle's ten children. He was born in Grunen Schild, where he shared a narrow bedroom under the eaves with his four brothers. In later years, when the successful brothers lived in palatial estates in the capitals of Europe, they sometimes reminisced about the camaraderie of their tiny attic room. In addition to James's sisters, brothers and parents, the house accommodated clerks who worked for Mayer Amschel's growing business. As the older siblings married, some of the spouses lived with the Rothschild family for a few years as the young couples waited for access to the limited housing in the Judengasse. The house had three stories and a cellar. The first floor included a water pump in the entrance vestibule, a tiny kitchen with a hearth large enough to hold one pot, and the parent's small bedroom; the second floor was a family/living room with a terrace that connected it to a back room that served as the business office; the attic housed the children's bedrooms. The house also had two cellars, one hidden behind a false wall, and many secret shelves hidden in the walls.[1] By the standards of the Judengasse, this was the house of a prosperous family.

The years of revolution and counter-revolution that followed James's birth were a time of financial success for Mayer Amschel; though his fortunes continued to climb, he was not yet first among the financial leaders of the Judengasse. In 1795, the rudimentary system of accounting created by Mayer and his daughters failed to spot a thief in his employ. To avoid similar problems in the future, Mayer hired a liberally educated Jewish agent, Seligmann Geisenheimer, a native of Bingen in the Rhineland, and now a French citizen, to supervise the accounts. Geisenheimer brought more to the Rothschild household than accounting procedures. He was fluent in five languages and a proponent of secular education for Jews. Under his influence, Mayer hired Michael Hess to teach James German, arithmetic, and geography; at the same time, James also attended *heder* like his father and brothers.[2] James read Schiller and Goethe; he was the first of his family to take a keen interest in music and the visual arts, and he was also the first to lessen his religious observance. Inspired by his tutor, who in turn was enlightened by the ideas of Moses Mendelssohn, James came to believe that Jews should be able to move freely in the larger society of which they were a part.

When James was eight-years-old, his father and eldest brother were appointed Imperial Crown Agents by Emperor Francis II of Austria. The patent, dated January 29, 1800, also awarded Mayer Amschel Rothschild and his oldest son, Amschel Mayer, the right to bear arms and free passage in the Austrian Empire, exempting them from any levies, tolls, and taxes usually paid by Jews. This award, in recompense for the Rothschild's assistance in helping to finance the war against Revolutionary France, was in keeping with the imperial tradition of singling out individual Jews whose contributions to the Empire were so significant that they obviated the stigma of being Jewish. The favors granted to Court Jews did not extend to other Jews.[3] If the Rothschilds felt any ambivalence about supporting the Austrian Empire, with its discriminatory policy towards Jews, instead of France, which had given Jews citizenship, it did not stop them from doing business with the nobility of neighboring Hesse and Hanau, nor from seeking to win bigger commissions from the Imperial Government. At the turn of the nineteenth century, the Rothschilds focused on protecting their family through economic advancement. Only in later years would they take leadership positions in fighting for civil rights for Jews.

By the time James reached Bar Mitzvah, four of his older siblings were married to women from prominent Jewish families in the Judengasse. James had completed his formal education and was now ready to join his sisters and sisters-in-law in the counting house, located in the back of the house, where he would start to learn about the business being built by his father. Soon he graduated to more responsible work as a courier, moving messages and money between London, Amsterdam, Hamburg, Hanau, Prague, and Frankfurt. James first proved his ability by working with his older brothers transporting English goods supplied by Nathan from Manchester and London through the French embargo to their father in Frankfurt. Later he coordinated information and specie flow between London and the Landgrave of Hesse, working under the nose of Napoleonic agents who were looking for seditious nobility and their agents.[4]

In 1810 the family business was officially renamed "Mayer Amschel Rothschild and Sons." A printed circular announced the new partnership of Mayer Amschel and his three sons: Amschel, Salomon, and Carl. James was promised a share when he reached his majority; a separate agreement with Nathan, who remained in England, was drawn up at this time. By the terms of this agreement, Mayer Amschel controlled shares valued at 370,000 gulden, Amschel Mayer and Salomon were each given shares worth 185,000 gulden. Carl was given shares valued at 30,000 gulden and James was promised shares of an equal amount. According to the partnership agreement, only Mayer Amschel was permitted to withdraw capital, hire and fire, and his sons could only marry with his consent. Though Mayer Amschel died in 1812, the agreement was not modified until 1818.[5]

James was restless in Frankfurt; his first big opportunity came in 1811 when his father was able to secure a passport and letters of introduction to French treasury officials for him. Mayer Amschel replied to the request of the Grand Duke of Frankfurt, Archbishop von Dalberg, for a loan of 80,000 gulden with a promise for the funds and a request to secure a passport and introductions for his youngest son. The Archbishop headed for Paris to attend the baptism of the Roi de Rome, the baby boy born to Napoleon and Marie Louise of Austria, while James went to Paris to assist Nathan, who was secretly providing funds to Wellington's forces in Spain. At risk of being caught by spies working for Napoleon, James informed the French treasury minister, François Mollien, of his own activities and convinced the minister that transferring gold out of England would actually benefit the French government. James also established ties with leading French bankers Guillaume Mallet and Jean-Conrad Hottinguer, both Protestants of Swiss origin. In exchange for English gold, these established bankers supplied James with bills drawn on Spanish and Portugese banks that Wellington could cash and use to pay his troops. Between 1811 and 1814 James was at the nexus of an operation involving the entire family that transferred approximately twenty million pounds to Wellington and to England's allies on the continent.

James did not return to Frankfurt at the time of his father's death in 1812; perhaps he feared that he might encounter difficulties reentering Paris, where his activities had attracted the attention of the authorities. He lived frugally above his first office at 17 rue Le Peletier, part of the new Chaussée d'Antin district in the second *arrondissement*. Here, near the Bourse, most of the important bankers and financiers lived and worked. James kept to himself, entertaining only his brothers when they came to Paris. Socially, he remained a Frankfurt Jew, deferential, his French still rudimentary and heavily accented. Eager to join high society, James did not seek out connections in the French Jewish community whose elite were Sephardic, Ladino-speaking Jews from Bordeaux, living in the third and fourth *arrondissement*. Instead, he tried to make connections with Protestant bankers and with the nobility.

In 1814 the Allies defeated Napoleon; Louis XVIII, who had lived in exile in Buckinghamshire, prepared to assume the throne of France and wished to do so in as regal a manner as possible. Nathan Rothschild, happy to be of assistance to the restored monarch, offered him 200,000 pounds. At the same time, Nathan informed the new king that his brother James, whose business was listed in the Paris trade almanac of 1814 as Rothschild Frères, was ready to be of continued assistance to the monarchy. However, James and Nathan were not the only bankers eager to assist in the Bourbon restoration. In 1815, when the allies met at the Congress of Vienna to arrange for French payment to the victorious allies, the Rothschild family bank was at first only able to play a minor role compared to the more established Protestant banks.[6]

In 1818 the Rothschild brothers met in Frankfurt to renew the agreement that regulated their business relationship. The new agreement stipulated that each of the five partners was entitled to 4% of their share per annum, and that lump sums spent on legacies for children, houses, or landed estates were to be deducted from their share. With the new policy in place, James would have no difficulty buying property in France. His brothers, who lived under Austrian jurisdiction, however, were still obliged to seek imperial dispensation before they could do the same. Twenty-six-year-old James was free to act without any family interference in his personal or financial affairs. In December 1818, he bought the hotel at 19 rue d'Artois (renamed rue Laffitte in 1830) for 500,000 francs. The house had been built by the banker Laborde before the French Revolution and was occupied during the Empire by Hortense, the daughter of Empress Josephine, who later became Queen of Holland. James lived in the main wing, between the forecourt and the garden, and set up his offices in the subsidiary wings framing the forecourt.[7] He was now properly, even lavishly, installed in the new neighborhood, Chaussée d'Antin, whose main street was the lively Boulevard des Italiens, the most modern quarter of the capital. His neighbors were the financial leaders of Paris: Jacques Laffitte, Joseph Périer, Gabriel and Benjamin Delessert, François Davilliers, and Jean-Conrad Hottinguer. A group of artists also inhabited the neighborhood: Horace Vernet, Paul Delaroche, Ary Scheffer, Gericault, Delacroix, and the singer Béranger. Mlle Mars, Mlle Duchesnois, and Talma, all famous theatre personalities, lived in the Chaussée d'Antin. Pauline Viardot, the singer, and Marie Taglioni, the famous dancer, were also James's neighbors. Unlike the aristocratic neighborhoods of the *faubourg* Saint-Germain on the left bank and the *faubourg* Saint-Honoré on the right, the Chaussée d'Antin was welcoming to self-made men and women. Like many of his affluent neighbors, James also had a summer home in Boulogne-sur-Seine with a three-acre garden that he purchased in 1817.[8]

In short order James was able to attract guests from the more fashionable *faubourgs* to his home and to his business. Salomon, whose connections with the Austrian court, particularly with Metternich, were growing, was able to secure titles of nobility for all the brothers. From 1817 the brothers, their families and descendants were permitted to use the particle "de" or "von" to indicate their noble status. Only Nathan in London refused this honor. Amschel, Salomon, Carl and James agreed on a coat of arms and a motto: "Concordia, Integritas, Industria," reflecting the family belief in the importance of collaboration, honesty, and hard work.

A few years later James applied to be appointed Consul-General of Austria to France. The Emperor asked the treasury department to review the application. Ritter von Stahl, who had met James on the latter's recent visit to Vienna, responded with favor. He pointed out that James was a young man who is intimately acquainted with several members of the Polytechnical Institute in Paris, and with members of the Conservatoire des Arts et Métiers as well. In addition, James knew many of the most cultured French manufacturers and businessmen. He concluded his report: "I can not suggest a more suitable person for his Majesty than the head of the Paris House, James von Rothschild."[9]

In 1821 James was appointed Consul-General of Austria in Paris and Nathan received the same appointment in London. For James, this was a very important step to social respectability, for now he would be invited to a variety of events because of his title, events that had been closed to him as just another successful banker. James was invited to official state functions and was allowed to don his red consular uniform for ceremonial occasions, such as the coronation of Charles X in Rheims, which James attended in 1825. In 1822, Metternich helped the Rothschild brothers to ascend the social ladder one more rung by arranging for them to be granted the title Baron, and also by ensuring its inheritability. Amschel in Frankfurt, Salomon in Vienna, Carl in Naples, and James in Paris used this title. Nathan decided against using the title, hoping to be accorded an English title of nobility instead. In addition to the Austrian honors, James received medals from the Grand Duke of Darmstadt in 1818, and James and Salomon both received the Order of St. Vladimir from the Tsar during the Congress of Verona in 1822; the same year James was granted the French Cross of the Legion of Honor.[10]

Armed with financial success and resplendent with the titles and honors, James was determined to penetrate the social world of the French society. His first great success was a ball given on March 3, 1821, attended by the diplomatic corps, several ministers, a large number of distinguished foreigners, as well as the powerful of the court, the city, and the army. Comtesse Juste de Noailles, niece of Talleyrand, drew up the guest list. Louis Martin Berthault, who had organized balls for the Comte d'Artois (later Charles X) before the Revolution and had redecorated Compiègne for Napoleon I, erected a neo-Gothic ballroom overlooking the garden, and supervised arrangements. Each lady at the ball received a diamond ring or brooch as well as a bouquet of flowers. More than 1500 people attended.[11] The *Gazette de France* carried a story of the triumph of the ball. The Maréchal de Castellane recorded, "Great lords mock him yet are delighted to visit his house, where he entertains the best company in Paris." But a more telling commentary was recorded by Henrietta Mendelssohn, sister of the Berlin salonnière Dorothea Mendelssohn-Veit, who lived in Paris while working as a governess for the daughter of Count Sebastiani. She described the event as follows:

> For the past two weeks nothing has been talked about in the world of the great and rich here, save a ball which Herr Rothschild finally gave yesterday evening in his new and magnificently decorated house. As yet I have no details as to how it went, but I can scarcely believe that it was other than I have heard for more than ten days—I do not exaggerate—from people of every age and class: that 800 people were invited and at least as many besieged him with visits, letters and pleas in the hope of getting an invitation . . . As I am presently feeling—for whatever reason—daily more miserable and peevish, I did not make use of my invitation to this ball, though it was sent by Herr Rothschild with the most courteous billet ever written.[12]

With this ball and the many small dinners that preceded it, James tried to establish himself in the world of Parisian high society. When Metternich visited Paris James gave a large dinner party for the Prince that was attended by all the chief diplomats. Prince von Württemberg and Prince Esterhazy, who in Germany would not have shaken a Rothschild hand, attended along with everyone else. In an effort to please his titled guests, James no longer served kosher food, having decided that it would be a discourtesy.

As Consul-General of Austria and a leading member of the banking community, James was likely to receive invitations to homes that had been previously closed to him. But entrance was not acceptance. In the complicated world of Restoration society, nobles who had emigrated during the vicissitudes of the French Revolution and those whose titles dated to the Napoleonic era were not on the same social level; they inhabited different quarters of the city, and were recognizably different in terms of their style of dress and their readiness to open their homes to newcomers. James, whose early education did not train him for society, made several faux-pas as he tried to establish connections in this highly ritualized world; but still, he persevered. He subscribed to the theater and variety reviews, *Courrier des Spectacles* and the *Journal des Théâtres*. He started going to concerts. He took a box at the Chantereine Théâtre and a table at the fashionable Ledoyen. In the 1820s he retained an artist, Allard, for five francs per month. And he made his first major artistic purchase, Greuze's *The Milkmaid*. James also began to purchase horses and carriages of style and elegance. His *daumont*, a barouche with four dapple-gray horses and two postillions liveried in blue and gold, created a sensation at Longchamp.[13]

Between 1820 and 1825 James made important renovations to his mansion on rue Laffitte to accommodate his lavish receptions. He hired Louis Martin Berthault, a society architect and designer, to widen the stairway, build a ballroom over the garden that could hold 3,000 guests, and create game rooms, including a billiard room. Berthault built the ballroom and also acted as a social organizer for several balls, filling anterooms with flowers and placing rare plants on every step of the stairway leading to the ballroom. Gold-fringed drapes adorning an enormous bay window became the talk of society. Bronze consoles and blue and gold stools were the simple furnishings that allowed the eye to concentrate on the paintings on the walls and ceilings, and on the opulent costumes of the guests. Following Berthault's death in 1823, James hired Pierre-Luc-Charles Ciceri, considered the best designer of the day, and the painter François-Edouard Picot, to complete the transformation of the mansion into a palace.[14]

Despite James's efforts to dazzle society, the Restoration court of Louis XVIII and later, the court of Charles X, were not impressed. The Bourbons would do business with James, but they never forgot his lower social status. A Jewish banker from Frankfurt, no matter how successful, could not reach the heights of the old aristocratic families who were intimates of the Court. Eager to prove the enduring correctness of his political vision, Louis XVIII reintroduced rituals that had been discarded during the French Revolution. The King received the nobility at the Tuileries several times a week. The most significant reception day was Sunday, when nobles of all ranks were permitted to visit with the King after mass. Dressed according to rank, individual nobles waited to be greeted by the Sovereign. Additional receptions on Monday at 12:30 P.M. for the men and at 8 pm for the ladies ensured a continuous round of visiting by the nobles at the royal court. Ambassadors had a standing invitation to come on Tuesday evenings and during those visits, the hierarchy among the British, Austrian, Russian and other ambassadors was visually evident to all in attendance.[15] The Court also took the lead in throwing lavish balls and other smaller parties, restricted to ladies who had been presented to the Court and to gentlemen on the Civil List and Ambassadors.

In this rigid hierarchy, James played a minor role. But the Bourbons were not the only party-givers at Court. The Duc d'Orléans, later to become King Louis-Philippe, lived in the Palais-Royal, where he frequently entertained a wider circle of people who came to be called *le Tout Paris*. In addition to large monthly gatherings, Louis-Phillipe gave excellent concerts and dinners. These occasions attracted a mixed guest list of aristocrats, diplomats, foreigners, and liberal members of the Senate and the Chamber of Deputies. It was here that James Rothschild felt more at ease. When Betty joined him in Paris, she too was ostracized by the Court but well received by the Orleans family. Marie-Amélie, the wife of Louis-Phillipe and the future "Queen of the French" was especially welcoming to the young bride from Frankfurt.[16]

When Betty arrived in Paris in the summer of 1824, following a brief honeymoon in Switzerland, she was the beneficiary of all of James's efforts to establish himself in French society, and she rapidly became a strong asset in his effort to win social acceptance. Betty started her life in the capital as Baroness James de Rothschild, the bride of a successful banker living in a mansion on rue Laffitte previously owned by Queen Hortense. James continued to work tirelessly to acquire and build his financial empire. In his view, continued success depended on his relations with the French aristocracy. Betty shared that view and became a vital partner in the endeavor to be socially accepted. James had bought her wedding gifts of clothing and jewels to ease her entry in to the homes of French aristocrats; Betty set to work at once learning her new role.

Because she arrived in the city in summer, when society ladies were in their country homes or visiting spas, she had a few months to observe other aspects of Parisian life. Under her windows on rue Laffitte the streets teemed with peddlers of all sorts: box sellers, umbrella hawkers, cleaners who removed stains from garments, herb tea sellers, pastrie makers from Nanterre, flower girls, and water sellers. On the nearby rue Taitbout was the famous Café de Paris with its red velvet curtains and mirrored walls and its regular patrons: Alexandre Dumas père, Alfred de Musset, and Dr. Véron. Across the street was the Café Tortoni, famous for its ices and also known as the little Bourse because of the traders who gathered there to discuss stocks, shares, and loans. The Théâtre Français, the Théâtre Vaudeville, three opera houses, and several concert halls were all in the neighborhood.[17]

In addition, green pastures were never far from the city streets in the 1820s; wells and fountains abounded with gossiping laundresses; strolling musicians and acrobats crowded the narrow walkways. Open-air cafes gave the streets of summer an air of constant festivity. This intoxicatingly free world lived in close proximity to the fashionable and glamorous new boutiques of the covered passageways where one could find elegant stationery at Susse, tea at the confectioner Marquis, libretti at Frères, and cakes at Felix, where the clientele was very chic and very English.[18]

Betty adjusted rapidly to her new life and was soon attending and giving parties. The first witness to Betty's entry into the Parisian world of high society who left a record was Lady Granville, wife of the British Ambassador, and one of the most successful hostesses of the day. Lady Granville was keenly aware of the high priority Parisians of her social set placed on style, and she thought

Betty had a natural flair. In a confidential letter to her sister Lady Granville explained the Parisian mentality:

> My dear, French people are . . . extremely civil and *prévenants,* but there is a *fond* of ill-breeding, insolence, conceit, and pretension *qui se fait jouer* through all their countenances, manners and attention . . . I believe the exquisite set into which it is my good fortune to be admitted is the worst specimen of its kind . . . They begin by thinking themselves *ce qu'il y a de mieux au monde.* Their conversation is all upon dress, the Opera, Talma. There is not as much mind as would fill a pea-shell . . . They are pedantic and frivolous, with the most *outré* consideration of rank.

> *"Vous aimez* Paris." *"Vous vous plaisez parmi nous."* Neither as doubt or as question. *"Lady une telle est bien: on ne la soupçonnera pas d'être Anglaise."* *"Vous avez des enfants: vous êtes bien heureuse de pouvoir les former à Paris."*

> . . . the truth is they have an aplomb, a language, a dress *de convenance,* which it is as impossible for me to reach as it would be for one of them to think for five minutes like a deep-thinking, deep-feeling Englishwoman.[19]

This complex world was the one in which nineteen-year-old Betty de Rothschild was determined to achieve success. Having been the victim of unhappy social experiences in Vienna, Betty wanted to make her salon a place for people from different backgrounds to enjoy good food, good conversation, and musical entertainment. As Lady Granville observed, she gave the impression of having natural skill for this role. Certainly, her fluent French and her many years of studying literature, music, dance, and painting had prepared her for her new responsibilities. But, as Lady Granville explained to her sister, there were many shoals in French society that had to be navigated. Even the charming Countess Apponyi, wife of the Austrian Ambassador, cried when she revealed the pain she felt because she was not loved by the French. She told Lady Granville that she was heart-broken and that she wished she could leave Paris. Lady Granville confided to her sister Lady Carlisle that the French feel physical repulsion when they chance to meet with English partners in a quadrille.[20]

Despite the chilly reception that sometimes greeted them, James and Betty entertained regularly, hosting at least four dinners—with between ten and sixty guests at each gathering—per week. The Austrian Ambassador Apponyi described a sumptuous meal at the Rothschilds in April 1826. All the ambassadors of the great powers were in attendance as well as Metternich, the Duke of Devonshire, the Russian Prince Razumovski, and a small galaxy of French aristocrats: the Duc and Duchesse de Maillé, the Baron de Damas, the Duc de Duras, and the Comte de Montalembert. The table was dominated by an immense silver-plated platter in the form of a candelabrum—worth at least

100,000 francs; the food was prepared by Carême, who had previously worked for the Prince Regent and Tsar Alexander.[21]

Betty adjusted to living at rue Laffitte, which was not only her home but also the center of her husband's expanding financial universe, and she soon had to adjust to motherhood as well. On May 6, 1825, Betty gave birth to Charlotte, twenty-one months later she gave birth to Alphonse, and two years after that to Gustave, all before she reached the age of twenty-five. Her last two children, Salomon and Edmond, were born in 1835 and 1845, respectively. Children did not interrupt the lively social schedule maintained by Betty and James. On November 9, 1827, Betty and James entertained, as was their style, an eclectic group of distinguished guests at dinner. Before dinner was served, two and a half-year-old Charlotte de Rothschild was asked to sing to entertain the celebrated Rossini and the other guests: Lord and Lady Granville; Pozzo di Borgo, the Russian Ambassador; the Duc de Mouchy and his brother and sister-in-law the Vicomte and Vicomtesse de Noailles; Comte and Comtesse de Flahaut; Comte and Comtesse Alexandre de Girardin; the Comtesse Alexandre de Laborde and her daughter Mme Gabriel Delessert; Baron Gérard, the famous painter; Salomon von Rothschild; and the Maréchal de Castellane.

Late in the evening Betty entertained the assemblage with some songs. Maréchal de Castellane commented about her performance in his diary: *"Elle a bien chanté, en tremblant beaucoup; son accent allemand est désagréable."* Castellane continued, describing James, *"*James Rothschild is thirty-two-years-old; he is small, ugly, and proud, but he gives parties and dinners; the grand seigneurs mock him but they are none the less charmed by attending his parties and dinners where he gathers the best company in Paris."[22] Betty and James did not restrict their dinners to the old nobility. They invited nobles of all ranks, those newly created and those of ancient lineage, as well as musicians, painters, and actors. They also served the best food and drink in Paris. Their struggle to be accepted and to feel accepted was won only gradually.

Lady Granville may have perceived Betty as *née coiffée,* but only Betty's childhood confidant Charlotte could understand the difficulties facing a young married Rothschild woman in the capital of Europe. Letters from the early 1830s reveal that Charlotte, now married to Betty's brother Anselm and living in Frankfurt, was a frequent guest at Betty's homes in Paris and Boulogne and that the women sometimes traveled together to spas and other vacation destinations during the summertime. These childhood friends shared many interests—music, art, religion, children, and family. They both struggled to create a new role: that of a Jewish woman who was actively engaged in secular society. In Charlotte's company, Betty could express her true feelings without fearing the disapproval of family elders.

The winter of 1830 was an especially harsh one in Paris, prompting Charles X to provide extra funds for fuel and food for the poor. The aristocracy followed the King's lead with a plan to raise funds by holding a charity ball. The newspapers announced a ball to be held on February 15th at the Opera on rue Le Peletier. *La Mode* printed a picture of the uniform to be worn by the *Dames Patronnesses* of the ball: a white gown with a blue sash worn over the shoulder. The ball was a great success, attracting 4,352 people and leading the Duchesse de Maillé to comment: *"Tout le monde à sa place . . ."*[23] (everyone in his place).

But there was no place for Betty de Rothschild among the Dames Patronnesses for this ball. The Patronnesses included the inner circle of court elite: the Duchesses of Maillé and Guiche, the Princesse of Léon, the Comtesse de Girardin and the Comtesse de Noailles. A second tier of those attached to the Orleans family were included: the Comtesses de Montjoie and Mollien, the Duchesses Descazes and de Massa, the Marquises de Caraman and de Dalmatie. Ladies who had been attached to the Imperial Court were made Patronnesses: the Duchesses d'Albufera, de Raguse, and d'Otrante were in this group. Even the wives of the leading Protestant bankers: Mmes Davilliers, Hottinguer, André, Delessert, Périer, and Alphée Bourdon de Vatry, were all named Dames Patronnesses.[24] Despite Betty's friendship with some of these women, Restoration society was unwilling to welcome her; this was about to change.

The following summer, in July 1830, while most of elegant Paris was at the summertime resorts of Dieppe or Aix, the Bourbon Monarchy was overthrown and the Orleans Monarchy of Louis-Philippe was installed. James, who had considerable financial dealings with the overthrown monarchs, was taken completely by surprise by the July Revolution. Fearing the worst, he rushed to bury his bonds at his brother's country home at Suresnes. When he recognized that the revolution had been successful, he quickly broadcast his support for the new monarchy by donating 15,000 francs for the care of those wounded in street fighting. Betty dressed up three-year-old Alphonse in a miniature National Guard uniform.[25] James had been friendly with Louis-Philippe for ten years; Marie-Amélie had always been cordial to Betty. Now that Louis-Philippe had become King of the French and Marie-Amélie Queen, the Rothschilds would know no barriers to their social acceptability at Court. James became a member of the King's inner circle, and Betty associated with the women who attended the Queen and her daughters-in-law.[26]

Despite the coronation of a new Monarch, Legitimists who remained loyal to the deposed King were openly hostile to the Orleans family and to their friends, Betty and James. Their anger was displayed at a party given by the Rothschilds in February 1832. That evening, the guests at rue Laffitte included Legitimists as well as the young Duc d'Orleans, son of Louis-Philippe. The Duc de Rohan, a critic of the new monarch, referred to the King's eldest son as *le poulet*, the popular caricature of Orleans as a chicken that appeared in the opposition press. Those loyal to the King demanded an apology; none was forthcoming. Only the determined intervention of the King prevented a duel of honor. Marie-Amélie and her sister-in-law Madame Adélaïde were distraught, and several memoirists commented on the fact that the Duc d'Orleans stopped coming to parties at the Rothschilds.[27]

Despite this unfortunate event, the Rothschilds continued to invite aristocratic guests who often did not meet each other elsewhere; meanwhile, the friendship between the royal family and the Rothschilds remained strong. This was especially notable in the friendship that developed between Queen Marie-Amélie and Baroness Betty de Rothschild. While the Duchesse d'Angoulême (niece of Charles X) refused to receive Betty, Marie-Amélie not only met with her privately, but also embraced her in public. In 1837 the Queen and her children were the first to ride the eleven-mile railroad from Paris to Saint Germain financed by James Rothschild. When she descended from the train, Marie-Amélie embraced Betty before the waiting crowds. Memoirists of the period noted this moment as marking Betty's arrival in the inner circle.[28]

During the July Monarchy the Rothschild social calendar was set by French court customs. The Parisian season of balls and dinner parties started in November and lasted until Lent (forty days before Easter). During the season the King and Queen hosted eight balls along with frequent concerts and gala dinners. Every other Sunday there was a royal reception at eight in the evening where guests included aristocrats, military officers, and a host of bourgeoisie who wore blue frock coats and white pants, replacing the knee breeches and silk stockings of the prior regime. National Guards in uniform circulated throughout the rooms. Louis-Philippe, eager to create a more egalitarian image, dispensed with the blue and silver livery, eschewing the antiquated dress of the Bourbons; servants wearing black frock coats were sometimes indistinguishable from guests. Gone also were the elaborate toilettes of the Restoration ladies, replaced by simple bonnets and shawls. Guests no longer approached the throne to be formally presented to the monarchs. Instead the royal couple strolled about accompanied by an attendant who asked each person his name.[29]

Some of the royal guests were not pleased with the new ways. The Duchess de Dino, for example, missed the exclusivity of the earlier royal gatherings:

> Yesterday, I was at the great evening reception at the Tuileries, the Queen having sent word to me that I might come and go by the private apartments, so as not to have to wait for my carriage. It was the last Court of the season, and I took my daughter-in-law, Mme de Valençay. The palace, when lit up, is really superb, and many things look well—in contrast to many others. This applies to the black coats scattered here and there among the uniforms, the elaborate dresses of some women and the bourgeois caps of others. There was nothing like disorder, but there was no distinction of rooms or places. There is no procession; the Court makes its entry when all the company is assembled and makes a tour of the ladies, after which the men present file past by themselves. A little man in uniform preceded their Majesties and asks each lady her name, a proceeding which in the case of three-quarters of

them seems absolutely necessary . . . They were very gracious to me, and I think they were pleased that I went on the day of one of the great receptions which may well be called "public." They feared that I would restrict myself to special audiences. That, I think, would have been in bad taste. I might prefer not to go at all, but when one is pleased to see people in private, it does not do to hide one's self and repudiate them in public.[30]

The Duchess of Dino was not the only one who commented on the court of Louis-Philippe; but where the duchess saw a lack of decorum and etiquette, others saw too much similarity between the court of Louis-Philippe and that of the deposed Bourbon monarchs. These critics wanted more inclusiveness and fewer privileges for the nobility. It was Louis-Philippe's policy to create a *juste-mileu* by erasing the distinctions between aristocrats, old and new, and the upper bourgeoisie. He was aided in this effort by the social skills of Betty and James Rothschild, who invited the widest variety of people to their balls and parties. At rue Laffitte, the old nobility, the new nobility, and the financial elite mixed freely with a wide variety of foreign guests and artists.

The complementary personalities of James and Betty as host and hostess are evident in an anecdote told by Rodolphe Apponyi, the nephew of the Austrian Ambassador. Rodolphe was a lively member of the younger social set in the early 1830s. James was fond of him and promised to provide a dance floor and music for Rodolphe and his friends whenever they wished. Apponyi, counting on this promise, arranged to meet at the Rothschild home with a dozen young men and women and twenty-four dancers following an opera performance. Everyone showed up: "the ladies dressed for a ball looked ravishing; they were the most beautiful women in Paris. With large bunches of camellias in their hands, they looked joyous, lively, and even more, graceful."[31] But Apponyi, noting that rugs covered the floor, realized there would be no dancing that evening. James knew that all the prominent houses in Paris were not making merry because of a recent attempt on the life of the King. However, seeing all the well-dressed and lively young people, James was inclined to flout etiquette and roll up the rugs. Recognizing that Betty might think otherwise, he consulted her. Betty reasoned since no other house was hosting dances, if the Rothschilds were to have a dance the newspapers would report it and the family would be held up to public ridicule. James concurred with his wife's reasoning; his impulsive manner was tempered by Betty's concern for social correctness. There was no dancing that evening, but concerts were offered to the group as alternative entertainment.

In January of 1837, Betty's parents Caroline and Salomon gave a ball that attracted considerable attention. *Le Bon Ton* reported on the opulence of the costumes and jewels of the participants. The Princess Dolgorouki, for example, came in a white dress, embroidered with velvet dahlias; fresh dahlias were also woven into her beautiful black hair. Charlotte von Rothschild, visiting from

Frankfurt, wore a sprig of ivy connected to a chain of diamonds and rubies in her hair . The Comtesse de l'Aigle and the Marquise de Dalmatie likewise wore flowers woven into their hair held by diamond pins with pearl ropes threaded around their braids.[32]

Each season the Rothchild balls were designed to be more magnificent with larger guest lists than the previous ones. In 1843, a crowd of more than 1400 guests caused a traffic tie-up on rue Laffitte, which was closed off for the occasion. Sometimes hosted by Betty and James, sometimes by Caroline and Salomon, Rothschild balls attracted an eclectic set of nobles, artists, ambassadors, and financiers. Some came to be seen or to enjoy the renowned Rothschild hospitality; others came to see the growing collection of paintings. In the 1840s James and Betty acquired many extraordinary works, some formerly owned by royalty. Rembrandt's *The Standard Bearer,* previously in the collection of King George IV of England, was sold to James at the beginning of the decade. Jan van Eyck's *Chartreux Madonna* and Greuze's *Little Girl with a Bouquet* soon joined the collection. Van Dyck, Luini, Rubens, and Murillo were added. Betty selected A *Young Man* by Rembrandt, a Ruisdael, a Teniers, a Wouverman, and a Hobbema for her sitting room. For their bedchamber, Betty and James preferred family portraits and historical paintings like *Moses in the Bullrushes* by Paul Delaroche. In the grand salon, *Virgin and Child* by Luini, *Infanta* by Velázquez, *Portrait of a Nobleman* by Franz Hals, and an ensemble of six Nattiers, plus the other Rembrandt and the Greuze already mentioned were displayed. The collection was insured for ten million francs.

Following the lead of the royal family, Betty and James frequently held costumed balls. At the balls, the ladies sometimes dressed as Rebecca or Sarah, Old Testament heroines, perhaps in homage to their hostess. In contrast, Betty and her son Alphonse, in a salute to their guests, sometimes dressed as medieval lady and page. Mme Mollien, one of the Queen's ladies, thought that costumed balls add sparkle to the evening, as they permit the abandonment of strict decorum. She described one particularly successful costumed ball in which the Prince de Joinville arrived in Turkish costume carrying an enormous drum and making a tremendous noise.[33]

The *Carnaval* season of 1842 was a "fabulous" one according to *Le Bon Ton*. The final event, hosted by the Duc d'Orléans, was a magnificent costume ball. The men's costumes, designed by Gavarni and Charlet, famous for their theatrical costumes and sets, were ornate and fantastic; the ladies wore outfits made by the best dressmakers in Paris. *Le Bon Ton* noted a magnificent costume worn by Horace Vernet who came dressed as a Bedouin chief and bowed low to the King in "salam" style. Amidst the splendor of the evening, Betty and James Rothschild were singled out for the opulence of their attire. James wore a Louis XIII costume; his vest was decorated with ten jeweled buttons, each valued at 20,000 francs. Betty wore diamonds whose value was estimated at 1.5 million francs. *Le Bon Ton* went on to review the splendid costumes of the royal family, replete with their diamonds and emeralds, but the exorbitant cost of the costumes was mentioned only in the case of the Rothschilds.[34]

The revelry of costumed balls sometimes came at the expense of one of the guests. Rodolphe Apponyi reported an incident involving James at a ball in February 1844. Three to four hundred guests arrived in costumes at Mme Merlin's ball. One man arrived dressed as a Turk. A coachman followed him in to the ballroom demanding to be paid for his cab. The Turk claimed he had no money to pay the bill. Someone else called out, "But here is someone who has enough money for all of us. M. de Rothschild will pay the eighteen francs." The coachman then held out his hand to James. Apponyi noted, "Everyone in the room was convulsed with laughter, particularly since James found the joke in poor taste and became seriously annoyed with the prank."[35]

During the week of Lent, concerts and lectures replaced balls. The *promenade de Longchamp* marked the end of the Paris season sometime during April. In May, society leaders left for their summer residences where they continued to receive guests. Since school vacation started on August 15th and lasted until the beginning of October, summer holidays continued through this period. During the long summer season, some members of high society went to spas, a practice that became increasingly popular during the July Monarchy. Elegant spas were found in Cauterets and Bagnères-de-Bigorre in the Pyrenees, in Vichy and Mont-Doré in the Centre, in the eponymous city of Spa in Belgium, in Bade, Ems, and Wiesbaden in the Rhineland, and in Aix-en-Savoie in Piedmont. The cure typically lasted three weeks. These spas catered to the elite by opening casinos (except in France where they were illegal), and bringing in theatrical performances, lecturers, and musicians. In addition to spas, sea bathing became popular in the resorts built in Dieppe and later in Trouville and Granville. At these locales guests partook of walking and fishing, while concerts and balls provided the entertainment. October was reserved for hunting. Society leaders did not return to Paris until November.

Betty and James followed the rhythm of the social calendar of French high society—frequent entertaining during the season and summers spent in their country homes with additional trips to spas. At the same time, they observed Jewish customs and holidays throughout the year. Rosh Hashanah, often celebrated in September, found several members of the extended family in Paris or Boulogne celebrating with Betty, James, and their children. By Yom Kippur, a fast day ten days after Rosh Hashanah, the extended family returned to their respective homes. Sukkot, the Feast of Tabernacles, was often celebrated with family guests in the countryside. Chanukah seems to have already been eclipsed by the festivities associated with the end of the Christian year when the Rothschilds gave *étrennes*, elaborate New Years gifts, to their acquaintances and staff.[36] Purim, with its joyous masked celebration in the Judengasse, was replaced by masked balls at carnival time. Passover remained an important holiday, though unlike his observant brothers, James no longer refrained from working on the holiday. For Betty and James, Passover was a time for the extended family to gather and to have a meaningful discussion about their past and their connection to the Jewish community.

In the 1830s Betty and James did not take a leadership role in the Jewish community of Paris; they focused their efforts on becoming part of Parisian society. In 1829 James had himself elected to the Union Club, the most elegant club of its kind in Paris. He also joined the Grand Orient Lodge and later became a member of the Jockey Club. Betty began to make small donations to charities espoused by society ladies, and to work with them to collect funds. A letter from Lady Granville to the Duke of Devonshire from January 23, 1834 mentions Betty de Rothschild working at a charity bazaar alongside Mlle. Laborde, and Mesdames de Massa and Potocka. Mme Apponyi felt obliged to attend and to buy something: "Les jolies petites boutiquières! Irons-nous déposee notre petite offrande de dix francs?" Lady Granville, perhaps less sympathetic to French charities, refused to attend.[37]

Society life was at times interrupted by political crises, such as the overthrow of the Restoration monarchy and the frequent attempts on the life of King Louis-Philippe. Natural calamities caused by especially cold winters or the outbreak of disease also disrupted these rituals. During the spring of 1832, a cholera epidemic in Paris claimed 18,000 lives and closed many of the brightest homes. Betty and the children retired to the countryside along with many other Parisians of means. James had acquired a second country residence in 1829: Ferrières, a hunting estate, with a dilapidated chateau and 1200 acres for which he paid 2.6 million francs.[38] While Betty, the children, and their grandparents retired to the countryside, James stayed in Paris to tend to business.

During the July Monarchy, Betty's guest list expanded from the ambassadors and financiers she had invited earlier on to include people in the arts. Rossini, an early visitor, remained a close friend of the family and a frequent guest. His artistic rival, the incredibly popular Meyerbeer, was another addition to Betty's guest list. Urbane and well-educated, Meyerbeer, was the toast of the town for his wildly popular spectacular operas, especially *Les Huguenots* which premiered in 1836. Heinrich Heine, a friend of both Betty and James, was a regular guest and an ardent admirer of his hostess. Chopin performed frequently while Liszt occasionally played at rue Laffitte. Delacroix, recently returned from Morocco where he painted Jewish women, was a guest, as was the more established Gérard. But the painter who was the most frequent guest during this period was Ary Scheffer, the tutor of the royal children and friend of the Queen. James and Betty bought a historical painting titled *Ruth and Noemi* from Scheffer as well as some paintings inspired by the German writers Burger and Goethe.[39] He was hired to paint a portrait of Charlotte, Betty's daughter, and also became her teacher. James and Betty befriended Balzac who visited frequently. Dr. Dupuytren, the noted physician who tended to James after his fall from a horse, was often invited, as was

Letronne, the most celebrated Hellenist of his day. The actress Rachel, the Comtesse de Castiglione, and the Princesse de Lieven were also regular guests.

Betty developed a special relationship with Heinrich Heine, whom she met in Boulogne in September 1833. Betty showed appreciation for Heine's poetry and invited him frequently to her salon. He spoke of her support as the "angelic help of a beautiful woman . . . who is justly famous for her wit and knowledge."[40] In 1834 Heine sent Betty a copy of his book *Der Salon*, signing himself "Ihr ergebener Schulzling" (your faithful protégé). A year later, he described her to a friend as his earliest patroness in Paris. He spoke of her beautiful smiling face being constantly in his memory. He praised her in his articles as not only one of the best-looking women in Paris, but as one who is distinguished by graciousness and intelligence. He wrote to her about his life with the Princess Belgioso, whose chateau in the countryside provided a rustic retreat.[41] Betty remained close to Heine for more than twenty years. He continued to send her notes and sometimes books. One letter shows his appreciation for her aesthetic ability and intelligence:

> Since you have continuously shown great talent to appreciate beauty of form in art as well as in life (where it is called tact) you certainly will have an artistic interest in the problem of how a German poet can be translated into French. I am sending you a book today concerning this formal problem.
>
> These pages might present to your mind not a poetic but a purely aesthetic reward where the comfortable thought wrestles with the brittle language,— whether it is done victoriously that is the question whose solution I leave to your sharp mind to decide . . .
>
> I don't know whether you read the preface to the new edition of my book . . . Here I said quite a few edifying things concerning the parvenus of St. Simonism, those former *va-nu-pieds* who are now millionaires . . . [42]

Heine's letters also attest to Betty's lightheartedness. In a playful letter of May 1851, Heine wrote:

> You can't do a greater favor to the great than by enriching them and for this reason I take the liberty of sending you the book that will follow, one that I came across by accident.
>
> Though I know in advance that it will not get your approval, it might, nevertheless, give you some hours of entertainment and perhaps while bringing about a utopian point of view it will distract you from your daily annoyances.
>
> The author is totally unknown to me, and, at times, his book truly upset me. It is a very malicious book causing mischief not to mention the blasphemy that cannot affect us who are anchored in secure truth. But the book is

extremely attractive, exciting and of a horrible originality, the author deserves a beating and laurels, and in any case, I can't deny him the honor of
having described a female character you could not find any better in Sopho-
cles, in Shakespeare or on rue Laffitte. I am very sorry that my current condition won't allow me to hear a judgment about this character from the
mouth of a noble woman . . . [43]

Another of Betty's particular protégés was Frederic Chopin, who arrived in
Paris in September 1831 eager to be introduced to society. Betty invited him to
perform at one of her musical evenings, where he played for her guests a few
weeks before his official debut in the city. Chopin soon became Betty's private
teacher as well as the teacher of her daughter Charlotte and her niece Mathilde.
Betty graciously secured four influential protectors for Chopin—Maréchale
Lannes, Princesse de Vaudemont, Comtesse Apponyi, and Prince Czartoryski.
Chopin, who lived close by for many years, was a regular guest at rue Laffitte.

Chopin also invited Betty to his studio from time to time to listen to some
of his pupils. In 1842, he asked Betty to attend a recital by Karl Filtsch, a Hun-
garian prodigy he had lured away from Liszt and taken under his wing. Betty
attended the recital with Count Apponyi, Meyerbeer, and a number of ambassadors. They were thrilled with the young Filtsch. In January 1843, Betty
invited Karl to play Chopin's Piano Concerto in E minor with the maestro in
her home. Karl's older brother wrote home to their parents: "The soiree was
brilliant in every respect! LaBlache, Grisi, Mario, Pauline Viardot, Chopin and
Karl were the artists. About 500 persons attended the party. The room glittered
with gold, crystal, paintings, and tapestries. Ices were served and flowers were
plentiful and beautifully arranged."[44]

Chopin remained close to Betty during the eighteen years of their friendship, until his death in 1849. They had many friends in common: Heinrich
Heine, Ary Scheffer, George Sand, Eugène Delacroix, and for some years Franz
Liszt and Marie d'Agoult. Their friendship was testimony to the relative openness of French society during the years of the July Monarchy. Despite the long
friendship, Chopin harbored ambivalent feelings about Jews. In games of charades at Nohant with Sand and her children, Chopin frequently played a Jew or
an Englishman, both outsiders whom he ridiculed. In a letter to Sand, Chopin
complained that his journey from Nohant to Paris was ruined because of the
presence of a Jewess in the coach. Chopin's conventional anti-Semitism did not
impede his relationship with his Jewish publisher, Schlesinger, and he remained
close to the Rothchilds. Like the rest of French society, Chopin made room for
Betty and James in his circle, seeing them as aristocrats, and only secondarily as
Jews. He invited them to his home on Ash Wednesday in February 1847, along
with Prince and Princesse Czartoryski and Comtesse Delfina Potocka, for a
musical evening. Later that year he visited Ferrières several times, enjoying the
magnificent hospitality of the Rothschilds.[45]

Despite a life of great success as a composer and considerable success as a performer, Chopin spent more than he earned. The consumption that ended his life made it impossible for him to continue to give lessons. Betty visited him in his apartment on the Place Vendôme, bringing him 1,000 francs. Charlotte, following her mother's example, sent her old teacher a decorative goblet that he described in a letter home: "It had a silver-gilt saucer and spoon. The glass itself is crystal and had a silver-gilt stem." Though Chopin dedicated very few of his works, his appreciation for Betty and Charlotte was expressed by the dedication of his Waltz in C sharp minor Op.64 no.2 to Betty and the Ballade in F minor Op.52 no.4 to Charlotte.[46]

Another artist who was a frequent guest and who remained a friend of Betty and James for many years was Balzac. The writer first met James at Aix in 1832. Four years later, he dedicated *L'Enfant maudit* to Betty, and in 1846, he dedicated *Un Homme d'Affaires* to James and sent Betty the complete edition of his works. Many society ladies thought that Balzac was a poor conversationalist; like most writers, he preferred to offer amusing and long monologues while not allowing others to speak. His constant financial troubles were also the subject of criticism; nevertheless, Betty and James remained loyal to the garrulous and sloppy Balzac, recognizing his talents and helping him pay his debts.[47]

In addition to musicians and literary artists, Betty and James were fond of painters: Ary Scheffer was a frequent guest as was Delacroix. But Betty wanted Ingres to paint her portrait. In 1842, after finishing a portrait of the Duc d'Orleans, Ingres started work on the portrait that would have the place of honor in Betty's salon until her death, when it was moved to Ferrières as requested in her final letter.[48] This work was interrupted when the young Duc d'Orleans died tragically in a carriage accident in 1842. Ingres stopped his work on Betty's portrait in order to devote time to paint copies of the young duke's portrait and to create a stained glass window for a memorial chapel. Later, progress on Betty's portrait was slowed by Ingres's work on the celebrated portrait of the Comtesse d'Haussonville. In that work, Ingres appears to have used a particular perspective, most noticeable in the angle of the Comtesse's arms and head, which was also used to great effect in Betty's portrait. Ary Scheffer's recently completed portrait of Betty's daughter Charlotte provided another model for Ingres. In that work, Charlotte is seated, her hand near her face, in the same room with green damask wall hangings and deep red upholstery that is used in Betty's portrait. Betty was painted many times, but she singled out her portrait by Ingres as the "only one that she really liked."[49]

Ingres exhibited the painting in his studio in the summer of 1848. Théophile Gautier, a prolific critic, wrote the following appreciation:

> . . . The artist had to paint a woman of the world that bathes in an atmosphere of gold; he knew how to be opulent without being ostentatious, and he corrected the sparkle of the diamonds with the flash of intelligence and wit.

Mme de R . . . , dressed in a gown of lively and brilliant pink, has just seated herself amid splendid pleats and rich fabrics that still billow; one of her elbows rests on her knee; her right hand casually plays with a closed fan; the left hand, half folded, barely touches her chin. The eye sparkles, lit by a retort ready to burst from her lips. It is a spirited conversation, begun in a ballroom or at supper that is still going on; one can almost hear what the interlocutor is saying just outside the frame.

The headdress comprises a beret of black velvet that graciously accompanies a white feather. This Athenian of the rue Mazarine (Ingres) had the coquetry to place his grand style at the service of the fashion press, and this beret, which the milliner Mme Baudrand could sign, is, despite its exactitude, [rendered] in the most beautiful Greek style.

. . . Never before has M. Ingres made anything so bold, more lifelike, or more modern; to extract beauty from one's own milieu is one of the most difficult tasks of art.[50]

Betty's vitality and her spirited engagement with others was captured by Ingres for the ages. Louisa de Rothschild, Betty's cousin, captured those qualities in her report of a visit with Betty:

Yesterday we went to St. Leonards to see Betty. . . . [She] was as usual fascinating, eloquent—*tant soit peu exagérée et grande dame*. I found the afternoon's visit long enough and was not sorry to regain the comparative quiet of the steam carriage, for Betty's torrent of words and thoughts rather stunned me and made me feel even more stupid than usual. . . . [51]

In addition to following the lead of the royal couple in terms of keeping a very lively social schedule, James and Betty were influenced by them in their building projects. Louis-Philippe organized a major overhaul of Versailles, making it a museum of national history. He continually hired architects and artists to renovate and redecorate his other palaces for both family living and royal entertaining. In the early 1830s James hired Charles-Edmond Duponchel, an architect, designer, and theatre producer, to renovate and reconstruct the residence on rue Laffitte. Caroline and Salomon Rothschild, neighbors on rue Laffitte, engaged in a similar extensive renovation which cost 1.5 million francs. Soon Pierre-Luc-Charles Ciceri, who worked on the earlier renovation in 1823 and was now well-known as a designer and also worked with the Paris Opera, joined the project. The new décor of both houses combined extravagant decoration with the latest in modern comfort. This opulence was displayed to Parisian society during the winter of 1836 and attracted extravagant commentary from the guests and the press.

Heinrich Heine reported:

Fig. 3. Ary Scheffer, Charlotte, Baronne de Rothschild, 1842. Private collection.

Here everything comes together which the spirit of the sixteenth century could invent and the money of the nineteenth century could pay for; here the genius of the visual arts competes with the genius of Rothschild . . . One must admire the flair with which everything had been done, as much as the costliness.[52]

Fig. 4. J. Ingres, Baroness Betty de Rothschild, 1848. Private collection.

Delphine Gay de Girardin, writing under the penname the Vicomte de Launay and edited by her husband in *La Presse*, wrote:

The mantels are covered in gold-fringed lace antimacassars; the walls are concealed under marvelous embroidered, brocaded, spangled fabrics of such thickness and strength they could stand alone and, if needed, actually support what they cover, should the walls give way. The curtains are fabulously beautiful; they are hung double, triple, and all over the place . . . Each piece of furniture is gilded; the walls too are gilded.[53]

Apponyi added:

The paintings are on a gold base, executed by excellent artists, the fireplaces admirably carved. The chairs are of ormolu bronze, with very high backs, surmounted by figures holding the arms of the house of Rothschild in enamel. The carpets, the candelabras, the chandeliers, the fabrics of the draperies with heavy gold and silver tassels, everything is in the same style; there are clocks inlaid with niello and enamel on azure background, solid gold vases encrusted with precious stones and fine pearls. In a word, it is a luxury that surpasses all imagination."[54]

Le Bon Ton, the society magazine that reported on people and events of the season commented that both the house of James and Betty and the house of Salomon and Caroline were marvelous: "The two adjacent houses appeared to realize the tales of the Thousand and One Nights. Such luxury is awesome to those who do not have at their command the bourses of Naples, Paris and London."[55]

Another Jewish woman who rated attention in the society press was Rachel, the famous tragédienne. Born Elisa Felix, Rachel's talent was so extraordinary that she was able to overcome an inadequate education to play leading roles in classical French theatre. Rachel entertained at the Rothschilds and in other grand homes. The King, who had been absent from the theatre for three years, made his first appearance to see Rachel. Rather than commenting on Rachel's talent, Mme. de Girardin, who reviewed the performance in La Presse, tied Rachel's success to her being Jewish. According to Girardin, some felt that Rachel's victory was connected to her having a large and enthusiastic Jewish claque. Girardin went on to say that even if that were true, she for one applauded a nation that rallied to support its talented members like Rachel, Meyerbeer, and Halévy.[56] As Betty and James knew, public attention for Jews in mid-nineteenth century Paris came with the attendant risk of notoriety and thinly veiled anti-Semitism.

Ironically, the royal family and the Rothschilds shared both the pleasures of privileged living and the hazards of notoriety. From the beginning of his reign, Louis-Philippe was the object of satiric attacks in the press and of repeated attempts on his life. James also experienced attacks in the French press that grew in intensity during the last years of the July Monarchy. In June 1846 James staged a celebratory opening of the Northern Railway. 1,700 guests were invited to travel in first class cars to Lille for lunch and then on to Brussels for a lavish dinner. A cantata, composed for the occasion by Berlioz and Jules Janin was performed. The guest lists included Victor Hugo, Alexandre Dumas, Prosper Merimée, and Théophile Gautier, who described the festivities in La Presse.

Twenty-four days later a terrible accident on the line resulted in the deaths of at least fourteen people. Pamphlets attacking James for his callous disregard for life and concern for only monetary gain were laced with standard anti-Semitic barbs. Hostile journalist Georges Dairnvell charged in "The Edifying and Curious History of Rothschild, King of the Jews" that James had secured the contract for the Northern Railway only by bribing deputies with 1,500 shares. In his eyes James was "Rothschild I . . . the speculator monarch . . . a capitalist who enriches himself incessantly while the fathers of children lose all but their last crust of bread."[57]

The July Monarchy was overthrown in February 1848. For Betty and James, closely associated with the deposed royal family, it was a time of great uncertainty and fear. Like the royal family, Betty and the children fled to England to seek shelter from the Revolution. Suresnes, the country home of Betty's parents, was burned to the ground, as was Louis-Philippe's chateau at Neuilly.[58] James stayed in Paris and hurried to make an alliance with the revolutionary government; knowing that his business was highly dependent on government stability, he pledged to help the fledgling republic. When Louis-Napoleon was elected president in 1848 and later crowned Emperor of the French in 1851, James continued to work with the government, remaining an important financier of the Second Empire, despite his differences with the Emperor's chief financial advisors.

Though the end of the July Monarchy did not mean financial reverses for James's business, which doubled from 20 to 40 million francs during the reign of Louis-Philippe and was worth 150 million at the time of his death in 1868, it did spell the end of the brilliant period of French society life for Betty. Her salon remained dark for several years as Betty stayed loyal to the deposed Orleans monarchy. She maintained ties with Marie-Amélie, who was in exile in England, sending her fruit and remembering her birthday. As a sign of friendship, the Queen bequeathed to Betty the mittens and black silk coif she had worn during her flight to exile.[59]

Betty did not completely shun society, recognizing that it would be detrimental to family interests. Writing to her son Alphonse, who was visiting the United States in April 1849, she said: "I have finally broken the ice and have appeared in the salons of the Presidency, from which, without giving the appearance (and the pretension) of political intrigue, it was difficult to stay away any longer."[60] But Betty refused to be presented at court when President Louis Napoleon became the Emperor Napoleon III. James did not distance himself from the Emperor, but he never had the relationship with him that he had had with Louis-Philippe. Napoleon III turned to a younger generation of bankers, like the Péreire Brothers and the Foulds, who were more willing to speculate with public funds and whose actions were less prudent than those advocated by James.

No longer in the limelight, James and Betty began to focus more of their attention on Ferrières, the country estate purchased by James two decades earlier. In the thirties and forties James hired an architect to create some new rooms on the first floor of the castle—a bathroom, a library and a study, and several bedrooms on the second floor. Though the architectural style of the house was neo-classical, the décor of the bedroom suites was Renaissance with dark woods—ebony, mahogany, and oak; the central room was decorated with the weapons of war and armor. Sculpted furniture lined a long gallery with walls covered in Venetian leather and lit by stained glass windows.

Most of the modifications executed during these decades were to the exterior of the house. A sophisticated drainage system was put in place, pathways were traced, and massive plantings were added. A new park, designed by Placide Massey, manager of the Trianon nurseries and of the Versailles vegetable garden, adorned the grounds. Several annex buildings were built: an orangery, stables, sheds, pheasantry, and laundry. These buildings supported the grand scale of living which the Rothschilds enjoyed. The laundry facilities washed 80,000 pieces of laundry per year. A Dutch dairy, a merino sheep farm, and a bakery supplied the other residences as well. Ferrières also boasted splendid stables, a riding school, and a special riding track. Wood cut in Ferrières was used as firewood at rue Laffitte.

In 1853, James and Betty planned to spend more time in Ferrières with their growing family and their expansive collection of paintings. They decided to build a new chateau, selecting an English architect, Joseph Paxton, who had recently completed Mentmore in England for their cousin Mayer. Paxton was a modern architect, well known for the use of iron and glass in the Crystal Palace at the London Exposition of 1851. James intended to make Ferrières a symbol, a testimony to his power and glory. A modern architect was to his liking. Yet, as the project developed, James and Betty hired several additional architects who drew plans to create an impressive yet comfortable environment. While Paxton held primary responsibility for the architecture of the exterior, Eugène Lami, who had already worked for the family at Boulogne, and who had designed interiors for the Orleans royal family at Chantilly and at the Tuileries, was hired to create the interior.

Lami and Betty spent several weeks in Venice touring patrician palaces to find designs that would dazzle a new generation of guests. Lami made major changes to Paxton's plan for the interior, focusing on reception rooms and extravagant decoration. The resulting rooms were fewer and larger. Salons designed to accommodate lavish parties overlooked the park. The grand stairway designed by Paxton was further enlarged by Lami, allowing for the display of women's gowns. The immense great hall, covered with a towering glass ceiling, became the art gallery. Five private apartments for the family and eighteen suites for guests were also designed. The chateau could house 100 servants; the stables could house 80 horses. The final product was a symbol of the enormous financial success of the family. James's initials and the family crest were emblazoned everywhere; a huge escutcheon surmounted by a crown on the entrance porch announced that this was the palace of the Rothschilds. James even appropriated the symbols of the French kings: the crescent of Henry II and the sun of Louis XIV were both found on the ceiling of the family salon. In later years, Ferrières, the most magnificent of the sixty chateaux built by the Rothschild family all over Europe, came to embody what was called the Rothschild style. It was a style invented by Betty and James and Eugène Lami.[61]

Betty and James continued their lavish entertaining at Ferrières. Their guests remained an eclectic group of artists, writers, aristocrats, financiers, and government leaders. Some came to hunt, others to ride, others to enjoy the extraordinary food, wine, and company. The most famous guest was Napoleon III, who came to Ferrières by rail in December 1862, accompanied by his Minister of Finance, Fould; his Minister of State, Comte Walewski; the English Ambassador, Earl Cowley; the Austrian Ambassador, Richard Metternich; and Generals Ney and Fleury. The Emperor was met by James and his four sons, who came to the station in a coach, the lackeys all wearing dark blue gold-braided liveries. Louis-Napoleon, in hunting dress, walked across a green velvet carpet embroidered with golden bees that had been rolled out across the station platform to his waiting carriage decorated in the Rothschild colors of blue and yellow.

When the imperial party entered the grounds of Ferrières, imperial flags were hoisted on all four towers of the chateau. The rest of James's family, including representatives from the Frankfurt, London, and Vienna houses, were gathered in the main hall. The Emperor greeted the ladies, but he reserved his most formal greeting for Betty, who had refused to be presented at the imperial court. Triumphant in violet velvet, Betty received the Emperor's words: "Je vous remercie de votre bon accueil," with pleasure. She felt that he could not have been more polite if he were addressing the Empress of Austria. Napoleon stopped to admire paintings by Van Dyck, Velásquez, Giorgione, and Rubens, glass cases which contained valuables of all kinds, and artistic treasures from every part of the world. In accord with custom, the Emperor planted a commemorative cedar tree.

A lavish luncheon was served on the famous Sèvres china, each dish painted by Boucher. Afterwards, the men went on a hunt that netted a remarkable 1,231 head of game. The afternoon concluded with a buffet of the choicest delicacies. From the gallery surrounding the hall, a choir from the Paris Opera burst into a hunting song composed by Rossini for the occasion. The imperial party returned to the station, their way illuminated by keepers, huntsmen and other employees who held torches all the way to the station.[62] This party marked the apotheosis of Betty's career as a hostess.

In the waning years of the Empire, Betty and James continued to be invited to lavish receptions and balls. They attended a costume ball at the Tuileries to which the Empress Eugénie came as Marie Antoinette and Betty, accompanied by her daughter-in-law Leonora, came attired in a Renaissance costume covered with jewels. But Betty and James never felt close to those who surrounded the Emperor and Empress. Increasingly, the society pages reported the presence of Alphonse de Rothschild and his wife Leonora as well as Gustave and his wife Cécile at the major events of the season. James and Betty spent more time together in Ferrières, tending their garden and feeding their swans.

CHAPTER THREE

Matriarch

Evy tells me that upon comparing notes with her cousins of all ages she found that one and all loved their good, kind little aunt (Betty), better than all their other aunts. Children are certainly the best and most unerring judges of excellence of heart.
Charlotte (Lionel), Wildbad, to Louise (Anthony), Paris, August 1, 1849

So much tenderness, care and devotion given by my beloved spouse, Betty Baroness de Rothschild, amidst our fortunate years as well as in stormy times; the good direction this tender mother gave her children; the distinguished mind with which she raised them, both gently and firmly, toward knowledge useful in practical life; finally, the pious sentiments she inspired in them have filled me with love and gratitude.
James de Rothschild, Last Will and Testament, 1868

In 1812, Mayer Amschel Rothschild died leaving clear instructions in his will as to the disposition of his business. He withdrew 190,000 gulden from the firm and divided it among his wife and daughters; but the business was to belong entirely to his sons. His will emphasized the distinction: "None of my daughters and their heirs has any right or claim on the said firm (Mayer Amschel Rothschild and Sons), and I would never be able to forgive a child of mine who, against my paternal will, allowed themselves to disturb my sons in the peaceful possession of their business."[1] Twenty-four years later, in 1836, Nathan Rothschild died leaving young children and a very capable wife, Hannah. Like his father, he provided financial settlements for his wife and daughters. Following his father's admonition, he called on his sons to "carry on in harmony and peace the banking house founded by me and under my name in London." But breaking with his father's advice, he stressed that his sons were to work in consultation with his widow: "My dear wife Hannah . . . is to cooperate with my sons on all important occasions and to have a vote upon all consultations. It is my express desire that they shall not embark on any transaction of importance without having previously demanded her motherly advice . . ." He concluded:

> [It is my] earnest wish that the association between my firm in London, now carried on by my four sons, and the other Houses, which my four dear brothers direct, shall be allowed to continue . . . I therefore recommend to my sons, in their business, to follow willingly the advice and recommendations of my brothers.[2]

In fact, the brother whose advice was most heeded was James, as he became the head of the Rothschild family until his death in 1868. In his own will, James urged his sons to respect their mother, to cooperate with each other, and to adhere to the religious traditions of the family:

> My dear children, all of your lives be loving and respectful to your excellent mother, who is distinguished in every aspect of spirit and heart. Pay attention to her prudence, confide in her unlimited affection for you. Love her, respect her, follow her advice until the last days of the long life that God will grant for your happiness.

> I strongly recommend . . . to my three beloved sons, Alphonse, Gustave, and Edmond, to never forget the mutual trust and brotherly agreement that prevailed between my beloved brothers and me, and which became for us a rich source of joy in good times, and a shelter in trying times. This brotherly union alone, the last wish of my deceased, distinguished, and venerated father, was what made our strength and our protective aegis, while love of work and integrity were the sources of our prosperity and public trust.

> Again, I beg of you to never stray from the sound traditions of our fathers. It is a precious inheritance that I bequeath to you and that you shall transmit to your children. God's will granted man his religion at the same time as life; to obey this decree is our first duty; to leave its cult is a crime. Thus, love and serve with good deeds the God of your ancestors: may I be welcomed in his bosom and watch over you up in the heavens as I watched over you on this earth.[3]

In his will, James declared that he wanted to secure for Betty a position worthy of her. He returned to her the 1.5 million francs she brought as dowry and added the 750,000 francs he had given her in the marriage contract. In addition to the 2.25 million francs, which earned approximately 4% or 90,000 francs per year in the Rothchild bank for Betty, he added an annual gift of

350,000 francs for the rest of her life. James provided for her to continue to live in the family mansions on rue Laffitte, in Boulogne, and in Ferrières; he also added 100,000 francs per year to maintain Ferrières, as well as many additional gifts and rental incomes. Betty also inherited substantial sums from her father. No other Rothschild woman had ever inherited so much.

During the decades that elapsed between the writing of the Mayer Amschel's will and James's will, the role of women in the Rothschild family had undergone changes that accompanied the movement of the family out of the Judengasse and the modernization of European society. While Gutle Rothschild was an extraordinary wife and mother, her role remained strictly confined to the family. As family matriarch, Gutle enjoyed the respect of her daughters: Jeannette, Isabella, Babette, Julie, and Henriette, and her daughters-in-law: Eva, Caroline, Hannah, Adelheid, and Betty, in all aspects of family life. Her home remained the center of Rothschild family life long after her married children moved out of the ghetto and out of the city. Despite some petty squabbles among the sisters and sisters-in-law, this group of women remained loyal to each other and to the family. Betty, the youngest of this group, learned how to raise children and how to navigate society from this tight-knit community of women.

Eva Hanau, born in 1779, was the oldest of the five daughters-in-law. She married the most traditional of the brothers, Amschel, in 1796. To the despair of her husband, she remained childless; nevertheless, Eva played an important role in the family by assisting with the secular education of her nephews who spent years of apprenticeship with Uncle Amschel in Frankfurt. Eva looked after the continuing education of her nephews, hiring tutors for them and hosting them in her home.[4] She presided over large family dinners, especially at Sukkot, when the visiting family arrived to eat outdoors in the garden. Eva was the first Rothschild hostess to entertain members of the aristocracy, beginning with Prince Metternich, who supped with the Rothschilds in October 1821, precipitating the acceptance of Eva into new social circles in Frankfurt.

Caroline Stern, only three years younger than Eva, had the benefit of a broader education. The letter she wrote to her husband Salomon, calling on him to support Jewish civil rights in Frankfurt, proves that she was a woman who had concerns for civil and political issues. She understood the need for leadership in the Jewish community, which faced the possibility of the loss of rights that were won during the Napoleonic occupation of Frankfurt. Influenced by the reform-minded journal *Sulamit*, Caroline was emboldened to speak out about the future of her people. Echoing new ideas about childrearing presented in *Sulamit*, Caroline wanted her children to reflect on their emotions and to develop a sense of self. She wrote to her husband in 1820: " . . . for you know, dear husband, that it has always been my aim that our dear children should not conceal from us their true, innermost feelings; and I—or rather we—have achieved it."[5] Though Caroline included Salomon in this matter, it is clear that it was her influence that held sway in the area of the children's education. She hired tutors for Anselm and Betty; and she was proud that her son was the first Rothschild to attend university, studying science in Berlin and continuing his studies in Cambridge. Salomon was unenthusiastic about Anselm's higher education, concerned lest he lose interest in banking.

Hannah Cohen, Nathan's wife, held a pivotal position in the Rothschild family. Born in 1783, she was the well-educated daughter of a leading English Jewish banking family. Hannah's sister Judith married Sir Moses Montefiore, while her sister-in-law Henriette, Gutle's youngest daughter, married Abraham Montefiore. Hannah's knowledge of English customs and her family connections were of great importance to Nathan in establishing the English banking house. Hannah and Nathan had seven children, all well-educated at home by a variety of tutors; the sons also attended university. Hannah remained deeply religious and sought to inculcate a love of Judaism in her children. Hannah and Nathan entertained modestly and infrequently, a habit their sons lamented after visiting their more extravagant Aunt Betty and Uncle James in Paris.[6] Hannah was not inclined to go to spas during the long summers, preferring to visit family in Paris or Frankfurt.

Adelheid, Carl's beautiful wife, was born in Hamburg in 1800. An accomplished singer, she entertained influential business and political leaders in her magnificent Naples home. She also hosted a colony of young artists including Moritz Oppenheim, who spent weeks with the family as he painted the picturesque Bay of Naples. Adelheid and Carl had five children: Charlotte, the eldest of their children, married Lionel and moved to London where she developed a lively correspondence with Betty. Mayer Carl and Wilhelm Carl moved to Frankfurt, married Rothschild cousins, and took over the Frankfurt bank from Uncle Amschel. Adolph married a Frankfurt Rothschild and managed the Naples branch until his retirement and the closing of the bank in 1863. Anselm Alexander died at the age of nineteen.

Betty, daughter of Caroline and Salomon and wife of James, was the most influential of the group of Gutle's daughters-in-law. Like Hannah in London, Betty established an independent base of operation in Paris. Her influence extended to her own five children and the many nieces and nephews who spent weeks, months, and even years with Aunt Betty and Uncle James. Her position as a family matriarch lasted fifty years, beginning when James became the head of the family following Nathan's death in 1836.

As matriarch, Betty devoted herself to maintaining Jewish traditions while adopting a modern French lifestyle. She was aware that conversion to Christianity had affected some prominent French Jewish families, including friends like Adolphe Crémieux, whose wife and children converted to Catholicism. Betty was determined that her legacy be different. She wanted to be both French and Jewish, partaking of the best the modern world had to offer while adhering to her family's sacred tradition. In these goals she had her husband's respect and cooperation.

Betty gave birth to Charlotte twelve months after her marriage to James. A governess was hired for Charlotte at an early age and Betty and James enjoyed showing her off on all occasions. Charlotte showed talent in music and drawing and was given special tutors in both areas. As mentioned previously, Betty and Charlotte studied piano with Chopin for many years. The fact that Betty continued to study with her daughter was not unusual among aristocrats of the day. Queen Marie-Amélie also studied with her children. In addition to training her in the arts, Betty also provided religious instruction for Charlotte. During her visit to Frankfurt in 1836 she met Albert Cohn, a native of Pressburg, who was en route from Vienna to Paris. Cohn had studied oriental languages in Vienna and was hoping to continue his studies in Paris. Betty seized the opportunity to hire the well-educated Jewish scholar for her children. Cohn agreed to provide religious instruction for Charlotte, who was eleven, and later for Betty and James's sons, Alphonse, Gustave, and Salomon. In return, Betty provided Cohn with a letter of introduction that would help him get started in Paris.

Charlotte also studied drawing; one of her tutors was Flandrin, a pupil of Ingres, who also painted James's portrait. Betty, who took painting classes as a youth in Vienna, often returned to her easel, sketching alongside her daughter. Whereas Betty remained an amateur, Charlotte was a serious painter whose watercolors were exhibited in the annual Salon sponsored by the Académie des Beaux Arts starting in 1864.

In 1842, at the age of seventeen, Charlotte followed what was becoming a family tradition by marrying a Rothschild. She married her English cousin Nathaniel at Boulogne. Her wedding followed a time of family crisis over another marriage. Hannah Mayer, the talented and beautiful daughter of the widowed Hannah, married Henry FitzRoy in a church wedding in 1839. In the view of the Rothschild family, Hannah Mayer had betrayed them by marrying outside the faith. Nathaniel, the bride's brother, was the only member of the family to attend the wedding. The bride's mother, Hannah, devastated by her daughter's decision, accompanied Hannah Mayer only as far as the gate of the church.[7]

Hannah Mayer was strongly denounced by James for her action, but in characteristic fashion, Betty wrote a consoling letter to her sister-in-law Hannah, the mother of the bride. The FitzRoys, meanwhile, lived on the margin of the family for years; they were not received at rue Laffitte for a decade. The next Rothschild to marry was Hannah's son Anthony, who wed his cousin Louisa Montefiore in 1840. Anthony's sister Louise married Mayer Carl Rothschild of the Naples family in July 1842. Both of these weddings took place in London. Later that summer, the English Rothschilds traveled to Boulogne for the marriage of Nathaniel and Charlotte, the first Rothschild marriage on French soil.

Fig. 5. H. Flandrin, Baron James de Rothschild, 1863. Private collection.

Rothschild wedding ceremonies were beginning to take on the trappings of the aristocracy. Charlotte's wedding was certainly influenced by the style of the aristocratic weddings typified by the marriage cermony of the Duc d'Orléans and his bride, Hélène of Mecklenburg, who were wed in 1836. James and Betty, friends of the King and Queen, were probably present at some of the receptions for the young couple; but even if they were not in attendance, they would have read about the events. *Le Bon Ton* carried a vivid description of the arrival of the Hélène at Fontainebleu, and of several musical and theatrical performances that took place to entertain guests of the royal family. The marriage ceremony was described as solemn and moving:

> The princess looked calm and majestic, really worthy of the throne of France: one could not be any more gracious or noble. Her costume was magnificent: she wore a white dress with Alençon stitches, exquisitely worked. Her headdress was a garland of diamonds and the hat, orange blossoms. The trimmings, lifted and hooked, were held by bouquets of delicate flowers, fine white roses, white lilac and Spanish jasmine. The queen and all the princesses wore blue and were sparkling with diamonds. No one wore white, exclusively reserved to the bride.
>
> After the civil marriage, the retinue took a newly renovated stairway leading to the chapel under the Henri II gallery . . . to a gallery . . . expressly laid out for the marriage, following the Lutheran cult of the Augsburg confession. This brand new gallery is soberly decorated, and quite in harmony with the seriousness of the event. An altar was set up . . . M. Frederic Cuvier married the spouses. The pastor gave a remarkable sermon that impressed the audience, and he blessed the spouses.[8]

Le Bon Ton also provided a description of the costume of the important guests and a review of the fabulous trousseau that was admired by the court and their guests.

Much less is known about the marriage of Charlotte and Nathaniel Rothschild. Members of the English and French family gathered, representatives from Frankfurt, Vienna, and Naples were also in attendance. The ceremony was performed in a little temple erected for that purpose in the garden, the road to it strewn with rose-petals. After the ceremony, the guests remained to play whist, billiards, or walk in the garden. Champagne flowed and James toasted the King. In addition to the many gifts provided by the groom, Charlotte received 20,000 pounds from her grandfather Salomon. [9] The young couple had four children within a period of six years: Nathalie, who died shortly after birth; James Edouard; Mayer Albert, who died at the age of four; and Arthur. Charlotte suffered from ill-health throughout her life; nevertheless she maintained an active schedule supervising her children's education, supporting the philanthropic world pioneered by Betty, and developing her talent as a watercolorist. She died at the age of seventy-four.

Betty gave birth to Alphonse in February 1827 and to Gustave in February 1829. Both boys were welcomed into the Jewish community with a *bris* (ritual circumcision) that was accompanied by a small family gathering. Like their sister, Alphonse and Gustave were the recipients of attention and affection from doting parents. Tutors were hired to begin their education. Taillefert was an early tutor who taught both Alphonse and later Gustave. In 1836, all of the children—Charlotte, Alphonse, Gustave, and baby Salomon, accompanied Betty on an eight-day trip to Frankfurt for the marriage of Nathan and Hannah's son Lionel to his artistic cousin, Charlotte von Rothschild of Naples. Betty's retinue included servants and Taillefert.

Lionel and Charlotte were married on June 15th, but due to Nathan's unanticipated and serious illness, many of the thirty-six members of the family, including James and Betty and their entourage, remained in Frankfurt. To alleviate the tedium for her young sons, Betty sent Alphonse and Gustave, with Taillefert, to Metz, where the latter had a family home. The boys stayed with the Taillefert family for some weeks. Betty wrote on July 5th:

> My dearest children,
>
> I had the pleasure this morning of receiving M. Taillefert's letter; he sends me the most pleasant details about you, my good little children. I must admit that Papa and I had expected a quick word from you, my dear Children, whose every scrawl gives us the greatest pleasure because it shows signs of your loving affection. I hope you are keeping this pleasure for another day. I beg you to send us your lines, even if they are very poorly written, for your loving parents attach far more importance to what you reveal freely from the heart than to a well organized letter and well formed handwriting. However, you mustn't forget about either of those elements.[10]

Betty continued her letter explaining that she, James, Charlotte, and Salomon would leave Frankfurt for Creitznach, a nearby spa, where James could rest and yet still be in close touch with his seriously ailing brother Nathan. She explained that she is sorry the boys will not be with them, but hopes that they will continue to learn and develop and to rid themselves of "those little faults that often worry and harass us." Even during this family crisis, Betty did not miss the opportunity to guide her children.

The following summer, Betty again wrote to ten-year-old Alphonse and eight-year-old Gustave, who were spending time at her brother's home in Frankfurt, again accompanied by Taillefert. Betty was recuperating from an unspecified illness that left her very weak with lengthy periods of fatigue. Nevertheless, she wrote to her sons often. Alphonse and Gustave had developed strong friendships with Julie and Mathilde, the daughters of her cousin Charlotte and brother Anselm. Even at this early stage, their mothers may have been thinking of future marriage possibilities:

> Your last letter, my dear Alphonse, gave us a very real pleasure and I was immensely satisfied with the way your mind has progressed. I hope this trip will have completely fulfilled the purpose we had in mind and that it will

have contributed to expanding your horizons and developing your judgment and forming your character. Keep up your observations and widen your circle of thoughts little by little. How is good Aunt Charlotte and her delightful children? Has Gustave already gone back to his loving caresses with his little woman, Matty?[11]

In 1838, Betty and James embarked on a lengthy trip to Italy. James was in search of new spas and cures for his ailments; Betty wanted to show her artistic daughter Charlotte the beauties of the country. Alphonse and Gustave remained behind with their tutor; but three-year-old Salomon came along, as did Albert Cohn. On October 8, 1838, Betty wrote:

My excellent, dear Children,

I couldn't leave Genoa without sending you, my dear and good Alphonse, my excellent Gustave, a quick loving word particularly to assure you how much pleasure we got with each fresh reading of your delightful letters. Believe me, my dear and beloved Children, that among all the many distractions that we have found in the beauty of nature here, and among the masses of artistic riches there is none that equals that which your dear missives give us . . .

(To Alphonse) Your charming letter with all its details about the zoo greatly entertained us. I congratulate you my dear son; your success at this sort of composition was marvelous, for there's nothing so difficult as telling well what one has seen well, and you did it wonderfully. Salomon burst out laughing when he read about the lion falling over . . . I must also say to you dear Gustave that your last letter showed us a very marked progress that delighted us. I beg you to keep up the good work.

Betty went on to explain that she missed taking German and religion lessons with Alphonse and hoped that he was making good progress with his new tutor, the Judaic scholar Salomon Munk. She was clear in her goals for this education:

I hope you and Gustave will apply yourselves wholeheartedly and attentively to the lessons that concern the moral basis of our beliefs. It's only this way that they will become imprinted on your heart and your mind and make you worthy one day of bearing the name of your ancestors, renowned for their virtues. [12]

Betty asked Alphonse to write to her in German and from time to time to send a few lines in Hebrew as well. She reminded the children to pay attention to their dear grandparents, to their tutor Taillefert, and to their governess Josephine.

Betty studied music and drawing with her daughter, and she became a frequent companion in history and philosophy studies with her sons Alphonse and Gustave. The importance of the mother's role in assuring that children developed studious habits and became accomplished in several areas of knowledge was popularized during the July Monarchy in *Le Journal des femmes* and other women's magazines. Betty's participation in lessons with her children was a socially approved way to continue her own education. She was in her mid-twenties when she started attending lessons with her children and close to fifty when she stopped. These lessons provided Betty with access to continuing education at a time when advanced degrees for women were almost unknown.

Betty's next letter to Alphonse and Gustave was dated October 11, 1838, and was written from Leghorn. She wrote that she hoped their school lessons were going well. Both boys were attending the Collège Bourbon though they continued to live at home as did the sons of the royal family. Betty was informed that Charlotte and Anselm were visiting Paris with their daughters. She instructed her sons as follows:

> I am very happy that you are having such a nice time with your charming little cousins. Only, don't forget, my dear little boys, if the male sex is the most admired, the female sex is gentler and more delicate and is entitled to respect which the stronger sex must never forget or neglect. So I hope in your games with your little cousins you are sure to be gallant and nice as one could expect from two Frenchmen and troubadours like yourselves. [13]

Betty and the family spent the next few weeks in Naples with the Rothschild family at their sumptuous home, the Villa Acton, but she never lost sight of her responsibilities to her sons in Paris. She was well aware that Alphonse was struggling in his classes at the Collège while Gustave was doing quite well in his classes. She was overwhelmed with happiness that Gustave came in "first," making no errors in his assignments; she noted that his teachers were justified in having been strict since the results were so pleasing to all. Alphonse, who had had earlier successes similar to his younger brother, was finding difficulties in the more demanding work expected of him. In her next letter written on the 21st of October she concluded:

> It seems my dear Alphonse that you have a harder battle this year and that there are more good pupils and more who will try to claim first position. That is all for the best, my son, for there is neither pleasure nor honor in fighting where victory is easy, and at your age it is important to enjoy overcoming difficulties. [14]

The postscript to her letter echoes the ideas about close parent-child relationships voiced by Caroline to Salomon many years earlier:

I have just read your letter of the 14th, my dear Alphonse, that this week at school was not a happy one for you. I am so sorry for all the misery it is giving you, my dear child, for our part, we know it's impossible for you to maintain your high position all the time without expecting a little failure sometimes. But what gave us infinitely more pleasure than the best mark could have done, my Child, was the openness and sincerity with which you admit to it. I assure you, my dear little one, that that quality in your heart is worth at least the first place, and for me personality developments give me much more pleasure than those of the classroom. Cheer up then, and don't be upset about a fault you will soon manage to dispel and on a disadvantage that became a benefit for us.[15]

A few months later, on February 23, 1839, Betty wrote from Rome to tell the boys that the family would be home to celebrate Passover together. She reported that the warmth of spring sunshine in Rome was beneficial to their father, and that she had found the city very interesting. Rome, she wrote, is one of those cities that one greets on arrival like an old acquaintance and leaves like a friend to whom one has revealed the innermost thoughts of one's soul. "You will see it one day, my dear little ones, and I'll be very happy to be your Cicerone."[16]

Betty's enthusiasm for the city did not blind her to the plight of Roman Jews who were restricted to life in a cramped ghetto. During the visit, James was granted an audience with Pope Gregory XVI; with Albert Cohn at his side, he convinced the Pope to grant permission to establish a vocational school adjacent to the ghetto. This school is an early example of James's philanthropy; it also indicates the growing importance of Albert Cohn in advising James about philanthropic needs in the wider Jewish world.[17] Eight years later Betty remembered the Jews of Rome and asked her father Salomon to intercede on their behalf. Salomon, working through the Papal Nuncio in Vienna, convinced the Pope to abolish the humiliating duty requiring the city's rabbis to make an appearance at Carnival. For centuries the rabbis marched through the streets, dressed in grotesque outfits, as objects of derision while the crowd pelted them with rotten food. In addition, the pope also asked the College of Cardinals to improve the condition of Rome's Jews. [18]

When the family arrived home, Albert Cohn reclaimed his role of religious instructor for Alphonse's coming Bar Mitzvah. The Bar Mitzvah was held on Saturday, May 9, 1840, at the Rothschild home on rue Laffitte. Invitations were sent to a small number of relatives and friends. Following the Torah reading and the *moussaf*, the traditional obligations of the Bar Mitzvah, Albert Cohn quizzed his pupil on Jewish principles. Cohn had prepared Alphonse for these questions by writing a compendium of Jewish history, philosophy, and observances; copies of the booklet, entitled, *Examen d'un israélite à l'âge de treize ans,* were distributed to the guests. Cohn also addressed a sermon to Alphonse in which he called on him to remain faithful to his religion and to help his persecuted brethren. Two years later, on Saturday, April 23, 1842, Gustave celebrated his Bar Mitzvah; this time the guest list was numerous and Chief Rabbi of Paris Ennery was among them. In honor of the occasion, Cohn's Bar Mitzvah booklet was reprinted in French and German.[19] Gustave used the occasion to request pardon from his family and teachers for any unintentional sorrow he had caused them in his youth. The *Archives Israélites* added: "We don't doubt that the young sons of M. de Rothschild will always bring glory to their people and that they will one day work to insure their full equality."[20]

It is likely that Alphonse and Gustave also celebrated their birthdays with friends. The Rothschilds, striving for social acceptability, often followed the example of the royal family. In January 1834, Queen Marie-Amélie noted in her journal that she invited many pupils from the Collège Henri IV to celebrate the twelfth birthday of her son Aumale. Later, the children were taken to the Théâtre-Français.[21] Alphonse and Gustave probably had similar celebrations with their friends following the French social customs of their class, while continuing to receive a Jewish education created for them by tutors and their family, specifically by Betty.

In the early 1840s, Betty's work was aided by the appearance of a new book for Jewish children, *Les Matinées du Samedi,* by G. Ben-Levi. This book contained moral and religious tales for youth; its popularity can be seen by the fact that it was translated into English and was reprinted many times. The tales included a history of the Furtado family, friends of the Rothschilds, whose ancestors included a mayor of Bordeaux who presided over the first general assembly of Israelite delegates to Napoleon I; the Furtado patriarch devoted himself to the political emancipation of his people. It also included a biography of Rachel, the actress who was a frequent guest at rue Laffitte, emphasizing her empathy with the poor since she never forgot her own humble origins. Finally, the book included a history of the Frankfurt Rothschilds, specifically noting the modesty of Gutle, who never traded her humble abode in the ghetto for a mansion.[22] This book, along with the one authored for Alphonse and Gustave by their tutor Albert Cohn, prepared the young Rothschilds for a life of commitment to the Jewish community. Throughout their continuing education, Betty remained a constant companion and guide to the boys, as can be seen in the surviving letters.

In the summer of 1841, Alphonse, now a young man of fourteen, took a trip with his father accompanied by Léopold Thibault, another tutor, to Frankfurt. Alphonse's letter to Betty of August 20th, written in French in a flowing hand, is the first sample of his writing to survive:

My dear Maman,

We arrived yesterday in Frankfurt; we found the whole family as well as possible. Our Grandmother was very sick, but she has completely improved, thank God. Uncle and Aunt are also very well. And Aunt Anselme has never had such a healthy look. My cousins have all gotten bigger except Mathilde who is terribly pale. Natty has become very sweet, he has grown a lot . . . but how different he is from our little Salomon. Little Ferdinand came through a dangerous crisis. He lost teeth and was very sick and is still pale.

There, my dear Maman, is the state in which I found the family who so graciously received me. Frankfurt hasn't changed, it remains as it was three years ago. We are having as much fun as the weather permits. My dear Maman, I must tell you a little bit about the baths that we visited which pleased us much because of their gay atmosphere. There were a large group of society people. The princesses and others hadn't changed . . . We went to visit the chateau of the Duc de . . . which as you remember is in a picturesque spot and we rode horses . . . We passed some time at Ems and the next day we went to Wiesbaden, through Schwalback, where we stayed for only a few hours . . . There are beautiful mountains and hills with chateaux.

Papa has benefited enormously from his baths.

Adieu, my dear Maman, I embrace you . . . and my good grandmother, and my dear Charlotte, and my little Salomon.

And, I remain, forever, your very affectionate son, Alphonse.

P.S. I haven't received a letter from Gustave in a long time. I hope nevertheless to receive one soon . . . [23]

Betty's pleasure at receiving this charming letter was probably doubled when she read the letter sent by Thibault the next day:

Madame la Baronne:

Alphonse did not have time to tell you that last night Madame la Baronne Anselme hosted a ball that Prince Metternich attended and Alphonse got a chance to see him. I am profiting by this circumstance to add to Alphonse's letter all my expressions of satisfaction that will add to your pleasure. I can report that during the first half of our trip Alphonse was perfectly amiable, always interested in everything he saw during our rapid trips through each town, always good-humored during the delays caused by travel. He behaves very well for his age, with no affectations of seriousness or childishness . . . We work very little, but I trust that you will think that he has profited in more than one way from this enjoyable vacation which you had the goodness to give him; and I am certain that when we return to you we will quickly and completely make up for time lost. Mr. McCarthy from whom we separated with a lot of regret and who will be returning shortly to Paris will confirm, I trust, what I have written to you as well as my hopes for your complete recovery . . . I hope that Mlle de Rothschild recovers from her summer aches . . . she merits never having to suffer . . .

Please receive my homage . . .
Your very humble and obedient servant,
L. Thibault[24]

The following summer, Gustave was sent on a similar voyage with Albert Cohn. Betty's letters to her younger son are affectionate, but also didactic. From Boulogne she wrote:

> Be assured, my dear son, that all my happiness resides in my children, and that you can add significantly to it by sticking to the good promises you made me. I don't want to rake up the past, my dear Gustave, as the idea that you want to make me forget it with your future good behavior gives me so much hope that I am already quite happy about it . . . Do be sensible and do what M. Cohn says. His letter gave me much pleasure as he says he is very pleased with you. I hope it will continue and that you won't prove him wrong on his first impressions of his little traveling companion.[25]

Charlotte added a few words to her mother's letter asking Gustave to write his observations about nature; Alphonse also added a few lines and sent regards from Thibault. James added to this family letter, writing to Gustave in Juden-deutsch. The next day Betty wrote again: "You are already thirteen and at this age you are nearly a man."[26]

Alphonse, who was fifteen years old, spent the summer at home studying. A new tutor, Désiré Nisard, a journalist and writer, was hired to prepare Alphonse for the baccalauréate. Nisard later became director of the Ecole Normale and a member of the Académie Française. Alphonse ultimately earned a law degree. By virtue of his family's position in society and his attendance at an elite school, Alphonse was invited to several balls designed for young adults of the aristocracy. For these balls he was required to dress properly; he acquired a special wardrobe of costumes and fancy dress suits. Alphonse also acquired a variety of skills deemed appropriate to a young man of his background including drawing, dancing, riding, and fencing. At the age of eighteen, in 1845, he became a naturalized French citizen; soon thereafter he joined his father in the family business. Three years later, in 1848, with the outbreak of revolution, Alphonse was drafted into the National Guard. After serving briefly, Alphonse was sent by his father to America for an extended trip while Gustave was packed off to Frankfurt to work under the supervision of his uncles. Both boys were kept away from the vicissitudes of French revolutionary politics on the assumption that they would return with clean political slates when the upheaval ended. Alphonse's letters from America have not survived, but more than fifty of Betty's letters written between November 1848 and June 1849 have been found.

The letters combine maternal concerns, family news, political reportage about the events in Paris and to a lesser extent other European capitals, mixed with commentary on the economy, and notes on society. Betty wished to protect, inform, and entertain Alphonse during his long and lonely travels in America. These letters show Betty's mature political and social views as well as her deep affection for her children. On November 22, 1848 she wrote:

> . . . As far as the health of the house goes, the status quo continues in the most favorable conditions for everyone, God be thanked. Your dear father still copes as courageously as ever without being affected, thank Heaven, with all the outside turmoil. My health is getting stronger too from day to day; and as for the little dears, they are blossoming with childish grace and glowing colors. Only our darling Charlotte's suffering will not change . . . The poor child will certainly leave us on Wednesday the 28th to spend a couple of months far away from here. This absence, added to the one I had to go through at your departure will be cruel for me, but I shall, however, be calmer when I know that she is sheltered from the knocks that could still threaten us, than if I kept her with me. Her little children are truly delightful, and charmingly rebellious. As for Edmond, he is not backward in sweetness and grace. He has now got into the habit of taking my prayer book for his devotions. And yesterday, in one of his pious outbursts, what if he doesn't say, "I pray to our good Lord God for Papa and for the chemin de fer du Nord!" . . . You may be sure that brother Alphonse and his journey and the sea also find their place among his prayers . . . Speaking of Germany, I must say that things in that country are taking a turn for the better. The domination of the saber is soothing Viennese sensitivities as much as it is restoring peace. Even commercial transactions are beginning to recover . . . Anyway it's lucky and astonishing that the bad feelings between the troops and the bourgeoisie has calmed down like this without bloody conflict.

> But back to our own concerns here. Cavaignac's chances seemed to have increased over the last days, however, an incident which occurred yesterday in the assembly could destroy these false appearances . . . The explanations which were fixed for Sunday can't fail to be important and to herald a sitting which will be at least worthy of the presence of the political Gustave . . . [27]

Betty continued her reportage the next day, Thursday, November 23, 1848:

> Yesterday I was told of a conversation about our poor Louis-Philippe, and I must share some tidbits with you that were really very eloquent . . . (Louis-Philippe said) "France is a country I have ruled eighteen years. May the man

be my judge who can keep that up for a year longer than I!" The poor family is still in Richmond where, with the tightest budget, they are spending 100 francs a day without receiving any money from France. Isn't it shameful that the little Queen (Victoria) won't put a royal palace at their disposal? Claremont's poison (a polluted water well) is still running in the veins of our good Queen. She is getting weaker every day, and it is feared, not unreasonably, that she shall succumb to this latest trial. Poor blessed woman, what an angel on earth.

M. Lambert who really wants to take charge of my little parcels for you, dear, best beloved son, will bring you some cartoons from *Charivari* which I hope will give you some amusing moments. I have also given him some dainty little pâtés, which may be less common in America than in our sybaritic Europe. May you enjoy eating them, my beloved son, and in as fine fettle as my heart desires.[28]

On December 14, 1848 Betty received Alphonse's first letter from New York. She wrote in response:

. . . You must be completely stupefied by the new aspect which offers itself to your eyes now, and I don't doubt, dear Alphonse, that your observant mind will find there ample scope for exercise and development. What stories you will have to tell us one day. The long evenings at Ferrières will be filled with them and will seem too short . . . Your description of New York and your pertinent and profound observations concerning the habits and customs of this new country, while they give me great delight in satisfying my curiosity, have especially touched the proud side of my maternal love in the profound thoughtfulness and the penetration with which you judge and observe so many things . . . Later when a hard-working, business life chains you to your desk, or when the ups and downs of political life bring you into contact with men and opinions, you will rediscover the precious fruits of this experience . . . there where the poisonous corruption of civilization has not yet managed to infiltrate.[29]

About Paris, she added:

. . . So here we are, then, as satisfied in the republic as we were in the first days of the royalty of the barricades. Commerce has started up again, fine ladies dress up, and there is even some hopeful talk of balls at the new court. Anyway, we are fine—for how long, I still don't know, but I would swear that it isn't forever . . .

On December 27th, she continued her report:

Yesterday we had a delightful little dinner party . . . I am not going out this winter and intend to take advantage of the Republic at least to avoid the boredom of grand receptions. That way I often see friends and loved ones in an intimate group. [30]

And three days later she added:

. . . we will spend tomorrow evening (December 31, 1848) in the strictest limits of our family circle, in order not to be distracted from all the intimate thoughts which our hearts might wish to bring about those who, alas, are far away from us . . . But there will be no joy apart from that, as our wounds still hurt too much, and our sorrows are too bitter. I should have liked to send you a little loving present of the day, but industry has been brought to a standstill by the disasters of the year and has produced nothing new or elegant which would be worthy of crossing the vast deep . . . [31]

Betty subscribed to several newspapers for Alphonse, including the *Revue des Deux Mondes* and *Indépendence Belge*. She wanted him to keep up with French and European affairs so that he could be ready to resume his position in Parisian society upon his return to France. On the other hand, serious consideration was given to the possibility of Alphonse staying on in New York for a longer period in order to establish a new branch of the Rothschild bank. The Rothschilds had banking interests in New York run by August Belmont, a native of Germany who had worked for the Rothschilds since he was fourteen-years-old, starting at the bank in Frankfurt. He was sent to the United States in 1837 to handle the family business there. During the time Alphonse was in the United States, he raised the question of Belmont's loyalty to the family and recommended restricting his authority. Betty believed that Alphonse should stay on and establish a new House for the family. She offered to help Alphonse convince James and the English Rothschilds. Ultimately, after serious discussion with both Betty and James, Alphonse decided to return to France; Belmont continued to represent the Rothschilds in the United States for several decades.[32]

Betty's letters were also suggestive to Alphonse of his future role as leader of the French Jewish community. When Alphonse reported to his mother that he had attended a synagogue in New York she wrote:

I am over the moon, dear Alphonse, because you went to the New York synagogue. It's a good thing, my good son, not only out of religious feeling, but out of patriotism, which, in our high position is a stimulus to those who might forget it and an encouragement to those who remain firmly attached to it. That way you reconcile those who might blame us even while they think as we do, and make sure one has the high esteem of those who hold different beliefs.

She also played a role in encouraging Alphonse to be philanthropic:

> I understand, dear son, that you must often have many demands upon you, and that your civil list must be a bit fragmented. Also, dearest son, I very much want to have a part in your philanthropy and to this end I am putting three thousand francs credit at your disposal, and for which you will address me personally for your domestic drafts.[33]

Betty's letters informed Alphonse that James had visited Frankfurt for a family meeting to review the partnership agreement in the wake of the impact of the revolutions of 1848. A decision was made to postpone any changes in the basic financial agreement until October of 1849, but on the matrimonial front some decisions were made. Charlotte and Anselm's daughters, Julie and Mathilde, had hoped to marry Alphonse and Gustave. Though these four cousins had played together in childhood, and both sets of parents would have approved the matches, the boys were not interested in marrying their Frankfurt cousins. In November 1848, Mathilde, the younger sister, married Willy, son of Adelheid and Carl. Betty confided to Alphonse, "her heart fluttered for the ungrateful Gustave and she only resigned herself after shedding copious tears." She added that James informed Charlotte and Anselm that it would be unwise for Julie to wait for Alphonse and urged them to seek elsewhere for the happiness of their daughter. Julie married Willy's brother Adolph two years later.

Betty's letters do not focus exclusively on Europe; she shared Alphonse's enthusiasm for the natural beauty of the New World. On February 7, 1849, she expressed her satisfaction that Alphonse was able to enjoy the variety, grace, and originality of the cities of New York, New Orleans, and Havana. Her writing in this letter corroborates Heine's judgment of the superiority of her mind and her fine aesthetic sense:

> In the middle of our foggy atmosphere and political storm constantly overcast with clouds when not with dust, your delightful letter with its picturesque descriptions, lively piquancy and tropical heat, was like a delicious mirage for me and all the aspirations of my heart reached out to it, not so much to admire what the most lively imagination could never dream up, than to be near you for an instant, my darling, to benefit from your perspective above all else and then to place my satisfaction and my impressions in those which came from you flocking around my soul. It would have been there my sweet child that I would have wished to seek for happiness.[34]

Betty spent the last two weeks of February 1849 in England, visiting with her daughter in Brighton, seizing the opportunity to spend a few hours with the exiled royal family in Claremont. While the King appeared calm and resigned, the Queen still bore the traces of poisoning from a polluted well; in Betty's eyes, she was more saintly than ever. Marie-Amélie welcomed Betty with an affectionate embrace. She enquired with interest about the whole family, including the traveling Alphonse and wondered if he would go as far as California. Betty replied, "God be thanked, you were avoiding that mad epidemic (gold rush)."[35] She periodically sent baskets of fruit to the Queen in an attempt to ameliorate her position with an expression of enduring friendship. The lamentable condition of the exiled royals was a constant reminder to the Rothchilds of the fleeting character of good fortune.

In mid-March, Betty again responded to Alphonse's descriptions of his voyage:

> I cannot tell you how much your letter from New Orleans interested and delighted me, and how much I first devoured it with my eyes and then read it reflecting with both heart and mind. You must have seen, understood and learned so many things—what a school of experience, and that at the beginning of your life! What will you have to tell us and what we will have to ask you! May that sweet moment not be far off! Indeed, you must take pity on us here, our politics are so unstable, our institutions so faulty, our development so backward in comparison with what you see and foresee in the New World, that we must seem to be real pygmies swollen with pride and vanity.[36]

Though Betty was impressed with Alphonse's description of the New World, she never ceased to be concerned about his health and spiritual condition. She reminded him about the coming Passover holiday, hoping that he would find a way to celebrate with co-religionists in New Orleans. On other occasions she expressed concern about cholera, malaria, and feminine seduction. But her biggest concern remained the decision regarding the establishment of a new Rothschild House in New York to be headed by Alphonse.

On March 24th Betty overcame her reluctance to break with her traditional Sabbath observance to write to her son on this important matter. Betty had been conferring with James and her son-in-law Nathaniel, reviewing the perspectives of both the French and English families on the subject of establishing another house for which they would provide seed funds. The English house recommended leaving the existing arrangements as is, while removing Belmont and replacing him with Davidson, one of their agents. But Betty was ambitious for Alphonse and for her younger sons. She wrote:

> America's future appears so grandiose to those who choose to reflect on it that I hold fast to the thought with pride, I confess, that you, my son, will be the one to lay the foundations of a House which will bring honor to our name. In any case, it seems to me that it would give a point to your journey, and it would give your business there and your developing mind the chance

to take off. Once the House was founded, you could quickly come back to us, dear son, while at the same time overseeing the man who would come to replace you from afar.[37]

Despite her hopes for him, Betty was not happy about the prospect of a lengthy separation from Alphonse. She expressed ambivalence in her next letter:

I feel a lengthy separation from you, my charming child, would subject me to a trial I am not sure I could come through triumphantly, and yet, I would not want to jeopardize my good children's future by any selfish personal considerations. Anyway, dear Alphonse, take to heart the words I am writing to you today. Think hard about the serious question you have been asked; don't undertake anything beyond your mental powers; tell yourself that an establishment in America would demand a long exile of at least two years. Tell yourself, too, on the other hand your career will take off as a result of your action and you will leap to the head of a great House with one step. They take a dim view of this project in London; they are worried that Paris is getting too much out of it, and would rather see an agent there. But this agent could only be Davidson who works very much in their interest. You know Davidson, and you will be able to judge if he could possibly replace you until our dear Gustave is old enough to take the helm . . . Tomorrow we will have our big Passover dinner with her (Grandma). What a gaping hole in the place where I am used to seeing you, dear, beloved son! How sad and poignant the pain of separation becomes when we gather for religious ceremonies and intimate family life![38]

Betty also continued to inform Alphonse about events in Paris. She noted that she had finally broken the ice and appeared at President Napoleon's salon. Staying away any longer would have been construed as political opposition. The President received Betty with cordiality and expressed his regrets at her "prolonged illness" that prevented her earlier attendance at his events. She noted the presence of aristocrats of all parties—Legitimists, Orleanists and, of course Bonapartists. The balls went on in their usual way despite political unrest, and Gustave was starting to enjoy them. Betty confided in Alphonse: "He roams about among the handsome young women and his choice generally bears witness to his good taste." At home, Betty was still entertaining on a more intimate scale; friends came for dinner or after dinner to talk. In addition, Betty reported on two extremely successful theatrical events: Meyerbeer's opera *The Prophet* and Scribe's play *Adrienne Lecouvreur*, starring Rachel.[39]

On May 10, 1849, Betty informed her son of a death in the family. She wrote:

We saw this morning the sad news of the death of poor Grossmutter (Gutle). She fell asleep without pain in the bosom of God; we must thank

Providence for having granted her such a long and beautiful life, and for having made her last moments so peaceful. Her death will leave a great abyss in the family in Frankfurt, and poor Uncle will suffer a great deal . . . The knowledge that death has come to cut off the thread of life for someone to whom so many thoughts and so much affection were attached makes the event no less sad.[40]

But the French Rothschilds had little time to mourn Gutle. Continuing political and economic crises plagued the new-born Second Republic. A few days later in another letter to Alphonse, Betty expressed the fears of many: "Europe burns, socialism is invading France and overturning Germany, bringing uprisings and the threat of civil wars, and bringing instability. God knows how much time this state of affairs will last. We must get used to it, but it is not without anxiety and alarm."[41]

Betty explained to Alphonse how happy she was that he was sheltered from the continuing political fluctuations; she expressed concern that Gustave is too much affected by the political turmoil of the day. Betty also reported that James was moving toward liquidation of his property and was getting ready to leave Paris if there was any more trouble. The recent destruction of Suresnes and threats against James's life were unsettling to the family. On May 24, 1849, Betty urged Alphonse to stay in America until the outcome of the political upheavals was clear. Expressing fears that had been with her from childhood, Betty wrote: " . . . stay in the New World; if worst comes to worst, if the Old World should fall, which God will not permit, it would become a new fatherland for us."[42] By mid-June the crisis had passed, the Second Republic was on firmer footing, and Betty urged Alphonse to return to the family. Despite his chance to become head of a new branch of the Rothschild bank, the consensus of family opinion determined that Alphonse should return home. After his arrival in France, he was soon off again, this time to London to study the British railway systems; upon his subsequent return he was assigned an important role at the Chemin de Fer du Nord.

Now it was Gustave's turn to travel beyond familiar bounds. In 1851 he was the first member of the family to travel to Palestine. Only three letters from Betty survive from this adventurous voyage. On March 6, 1851, Betty refers to "savage rabble who threatened the dear and precious life of her child." Presumably, this happened somewhere in the desert, since Gustave had reported on his trip around the Dead Sea. The letters continue to describe "charm and local color." But when Gustave wanted to continue on to Russia, Betty urged him to return, for he had been abroad for a year and she missed him too much. She wrote:

At this time of year the Black Sea is very rough and stormy. And Russia is difficult to cross because of the thaw and ice breaking up . . . What is to be gained in a country where there are no historic sites nor arts and civilizations, and which offers none of nature's beauties? What is to be gained except reports of spy-police and autocrats? It would be real madness to risk fatigue, health, time.[43]

Gustave returned to France and spent some months with his father and Alphonse in the offices on rue Laffitte. In 1853 he was sent on another mission, this time to Italy, where he helped James secure a large loan. Ten letters from Betty to Gustave have survived from this period and their tone is definitely more light-hearted, yet the topics remain constant—family, local news, business, and Gustave's future. She addresses Gustave fondly as "dearest Cuckoo."

Gustave left Paris for Turin in January, missing the event of the season, the marriage of Louis-Napoleon to Eugénie de Montijo. Betty reported:

> . . . the ceremony itself left much to be desired in the way of solemnity and enthusiasm. There was a great crowd in the streets, but it was there to be present at the spectacle rather than to applaud. The church was full, but there too the impression was theatrical and was too much inclined to one's curiosity rather than to any other feeling. The august bride was no doubt beautiful but less beautiful than before her marriage; the excitement and worries of the build-up to it had tired her and made her pretty face pale. All that was told me in great detail as I didn't leave my hearth.[44]

Betty, still loyal to Queen Marie-Amélie, did not attend the ball at the Senate. But she was able to offer an accurate report to Gustave since James attended with Charlotte and Anselm who were visiting Paris at this time; several weeks later Betty also reported that Salomon attended a performance at the Court, benefiting from a ticket reserved for the traveling Gustave. Salomon, eighteen-years-old, attended with Alphonse.

Betty also confided in Gustave that James was talking about sending him to Constantinople on a business assignment. Betty offered to help Gustave in dealing with James on this matter, as she had earlier offered to help Alphonse with his decision regarding opening a branch in New York. As noted earlier, Betty frequently served an important role in steering social and family decisions nominally made by her husband. She urged Gustave to write to her about his thoughts on whether he wished to go on to Constantinople or not, remembering that he was not inclined to go when he left Paris:

> Write to me to tell me what you think and want without concealing a thing, and I shall be able to incline the decision to the preferred side willingly and with no difficulty. I confess that the thought of a greater distance between us and of a longer separation displeases me so the sacrifice will be hard and sad for me. But I will not hesitate to make this sacrifice if it coincides with your wishes and the business needs.[45]

The next letters report the family's great joy in Gustave's securing a major loan for the family, the Piedmont loan. For the twenty-four-year-old Gustave this was a great coup. Betty wrote:

> Here's another feather in your cap. I hear with joy and pride people around me who are in the know saying that the Piedmont loan was a chef d'oeuvre. Your father is walking on air. The thought that the Foulds were going to involve themselves in this business was hateful to him . . . We were in need of a little good times, and I am doubly pleased, dear son, that it is you we have to thank.[46]

In another letter she wrote:

> You can have no idea of the . . . satisfaction of your dear father. Demands have already tripled and our bankers . . . are coming one after the other, only too happy to have a few crumbs of the munificence and generosity of your father . . . But one must be modest at the same time as grateful to God, who allows good people to triumph, and confounds the proud.

The question of Gustave's going to Constantinople did not appear again. Instead, Gustave continued on to Rome. Betty reminded Gustave about the difficulties of travel in winter when snow-bound mountain passes and stormy seas presented great danger. When he arrived in Rome, Betty urged him to see the Pope:

> I think, dear son, you won't forget to plead, as you have already so ardently done, the cause of our poor co-religionists with the Pope. Since the Jews are not so vile when it is a case of borrowing their money, one might well be able to treat them as human beings when it's a question of their material existence. Anyway, I am already sure that you will do what you can in this matter, and already sure, too, that my heart blesses you for all that you will attempt along this way, however weak, however fruitless even, the result may be. God alone directs it (the outcome), but His goodness sees our actions, guesses our thoughts and records them in the book of great and divine justice.[47]

Gustave returned home to join Alphonse and James at rue Laffitte. Alphonse had become a truly fashionable Parisian; he was known to sup with the glamorous courtesan La Païva. Gustave soon joined him in the social whirl, engaging in a flirtation with the Comtesse de Castiglione, a favorite of the Emperor. Salomon, no longer a child, had also grown up to merit a desk in the office, but he was not yet part of the social circle of his older brothers.

Charlotte (Lionel's wife) thought Alphonse combined the extraordinary energy and vitality of James with Betty's facility for languages:

He reads a good deal, listens a good deal and observes a good deal, remembering all that he has read, heard and observed. He can converse on the topics of the day with an easy manner, without pedantry, but always in a direct, penetrating fashion. He cannot be relied upon for an opinion, since he never voices one, indeed, perhaps does not have opinions; but it is a pleasure to hear him, for he speaks without emotion in the most engaging and lively tone. [48]

As for Gustave, she thought him an excellent fellow with the best and warmest heart. She noted that he was deeply attached to his parents, brothers, sister, and relatives. She also noted that he had a strongly developed sense of duty and his obedience could serve as an example to all young people of his age. She continued, "Whether he is talented, I cannot, in honesty, say. He has enjoyed the benefits and advantages of a good education, but is, as he claims, stupid, easily intimidated and incapable of stringing ten words together in the company of strangers." Nevertheless, he reputedly had acquired considerable skill in mathematics. His figure was slim, his bearing easy and his manners those of the finest society. In sum, she concluded, "I should like to see his profile at the altar."[49]

Others, outside the family, recognized the accomplishments of the two young men. On December 6, 1853, an Imperial Decree authorized Alphonse and Gustave to wear the medals of the Order of Leopold of Belgium, of the Dutch Lion, of Saints Maurice and Lazare of Sardinia, and of Saint Joseph of Tuscany. Alphonse was also appointed Regent of the Bank of France in 1855, the first Jew to win this honor. The Jewish community also bestowed honors on the brothers. Alphonse was elected to the Central Consistory in 1851 and served as its president from 1855 until his death in 1905. Gustave was elected to the Paris Consistory in 1852, where he served as president from 1856 until his death in 1911.[50]

In July 1856, Betty wrote (in German) to Charlotte, Lionel's wife, who was to become her closest friend following the early death of Betty's childhood friend also named Charlotte. Betty reported on the happy news that her son Alphonse had proposed to Charlotte's daughter Leonora, known affectionately as Laurie:

The happy and so anxiously anticipated news that my beloved son yesterday communicated to us with the warmest effusions of his feelings cannot leave you, dear friend, in any doubt about our own feelings and about the rapturous joy that is permeating my dear husband and me. If I can express it to you only in weak words, I have the pleasant certainty that you, my precious, will recognize in your own loving motherly heart my warm and joyful echo. For a long time, it has been my husband's and my sweetest wish more closely to attach your precious daughter by a heartfelt and holy bond; therefore, my heart was striving toward the sweet girl with true motherly love, waiting ardently for the moment to embrace this delicate, dear daughter. If, up to now, I have not lent words to this dearest wish, the motive, surely in advance to be approved by you my dear, Charlota, was not to interfere by a precipitous rashness with my beloved Alphonse's sweet desire, also permitting nothing to weaken in him the blissful conviction of once receiving your precious Laurie's hand solely by gaining her heart.[51]

On March 4, 1857, Alphonse and Laurie were wed at Gunnersbury Park near Acton. *The Illustrated London News* carried a full-page picture of the ceremony under a *hupa* (wedding canopy) with the bridegroom about to break a glass. The reporter wrote, "The bride had lovely . . . liquid almond-shaped eyes, the sweet complexion of a tea-rose," and she was attended by sixteen maids of honor. A large gathering of family and other notables came to celebrate. Among the guests reported by the *Morning Post* were the French Ambassador Persigny, several Members of Parliament including the Duke of Bedford, Lord John Russell, and Mr. Disraeli, a special friend of the bride's mother. Disraeli toasted the couple: "Under this roof are the heads of the Rothschild family—a name famous in every capital of Europe and every division of the globe—a family not more regarded for its riches, than esteemed for its honor, integrity, and public spirit." Alphonse and Laurie took up residence on rue St. Florentin, the former home of Talleyrand that was purchased some years earlier by James. They were immediately a great social success, becoming part of Emperor Louis-Napoleon's inner social circle. They were invited to Compiègne on a regular basis where Laurie's beauty and her talent at charades and *tableaux vivants* made her a much sought after guest.[52]

A year later, Charlotte and her younger daughter Evelina made the journey to Paris to spend time with Laurie and Alphonse as they awaited the birth of their first child. Charlotte described being greeted by the wonderfully handsome Betty. "She wore a picturesque, beautiful and splendid costume, entirely composed of ruby colored velvet. A fine lace handkerchief à la Marie-Antoinette covered her shoulders and a cap to match the costume." She went on to describe the young couple's new home: "Alphonse's rooms are little museums, full of numberless curiosities, antiquities, rarities—gems and jewels of all periods, lands and climes . . . The most interesting of Laurie's possessions, however, is her Brazilian monkey." This intelligent, pretty creature with his good humor and good nature and ability to sing thoroughly charmed Charlotte and Evy.[53] Into this happy little family came Bettina de Rothschild, Betty's first surviving granddaughter. Betty was thrilled with the little girl as she wrote to Charlotte: "I can only talk with delight about our angelic Bettina. She is the most joyous child and is developing more every day. She is already beginning to talk to everybody and is quite stable on her tiny, cute feet. In short, she is our true joy and the bright ray of sun that lights up our circle."[54]

A few months later Betty wrote to Charlotte to inform her that Gustave would not be proposing to Evelina since he had fallen in love with Cécile Anspach:

> The happy event that has moved our family for some days has already come to your knowledge through our dear Laurie, my dear Charlotte, and consequently is no longer new to you. But I cannot but confirm to you myself the union of our beloved Gustave with Miss Anspach, already deeply convinced of your loving sentiments toward me and my family, not to count with happy certainty on your friendly, kind interest. Our precious son followed his heart's inclination in the choice he made. We are hoping to the All Benevolent that his future wife will build a life of happiness and give us a good, loving daughter. All that we have seen and heard so far about the young girl seems, thank God, to agree with our sweetest hopes.[55]

Cécile Anspach was the daughter of a member of the Central Consistory and Council to the Imperial Court. The marriage contract between Gustave and Cécile was signed at rue Laffitte in the presence of numerous notables from the worlds of diplomacy, finance, industry, business, and the arts. The marriage took place at the richly decorated Temple of Notre Dame de Nazareth Street. Le Monde Illustré printed a big picture of the synagogue and a partial guest list: Fould, Delangle, Delessert, Halévy, Ingres, Meyerbeer, and Jules Janin. Seventy-four Rothschilds attended the wedding dinner. The costumes of the women were dazzling. The Chief Rabbi blessed the couple and praised their parents, singling out Betty for her charitable work and the goodness of her heart.[56] Gustave and Cécile took up residence on avenue Marigny and continued the Rothschild tradition of lavish entertainment.

Unlike his two older brothers, Salomon seemed to have had trouble meeting the expectations of his father for sober business transactions. After repeated confrontations with James about his reckless approach to investments, Salomon was sent to Frankfurt and then to America. Regrettably, no letters from Betty survive from this period. Salomon's original letters have not been found. Salomon's trip notes, full of the beauty of the flora and fauna of the New World, were published, but we have no record of his personal thoughts.[57] When he returned to Paris in 1861, he joined his father and brothers at the bank.

Some insight into Salomon's personality can be found in Betty's letters dating from his childhood. While it is risky to assume too much based on these early comments, the letters of the thirties and forties reveal something about the young Salomon and his role in the family. In a letter from Genoa to Alphonse and Gustave dated October 7, 1838, Betty described Salomon, aged three and a half, as follows:

Salomon has grown a lot, and we often think of him as a little angel in the paintings we are going to admire. But he is very naughty and more capricious even than a pretty woman. This morning he persisted in refusing to kiss Papa because he claimed that yesterday when he went to say good morning to him, Papa turned away. A sound little punishment put him to rights a bit, but it makes no difference—it'll begin all over again tomorrow. He is so pretty, that he is often taken for a little girl, which vexes him very much. The other day, a man with a big moustache said to him, "Hello, my little demoiselle," and Salomon looked him up and down, and said, like some Spanish nobleman, "Hello, Madame." And then he turned to me and said, "Me said 'Hello, Madame,' because he called me 'Hello, Mademoiselle'." The fact is that he is very sweet, and one has to spoil him in spite of oneself.[58]

A decade later, Betty confided in Alphonse regarding her fears of upheavals in Paris accompanying the elections of 1848. She referred to Salomon and Edmond as follows: "Whatever happens, I shall get rid of the little ones (Salomon would be very humiliated if he were to read that) and I shall send them off for a fortnight in Belgium before the elections."[59] In 1848 Edmond was three-years-old but Salomon celebrated his Bar Mitzvah in March of that revolutionary year; he certainly would not think of himself as a "little one" any longer. Salomon's place in the family was unclear. Charlotte was the only girl; Alphonse and Gustave were close in age and shared many experiences; Salomon was six years younger than Gustave and ten years older than Edmond, who was close in age to his nephews, James Edouard and Mayer Albert. Salomon was a teenager during the tumultuous days of the Second Republic, a time when his older brothers were sent away to avoid the draft and political complications.

In March 1862, Betty and James accompanied Salomon to Frankfurt where he married his cousin Adèle, daughter of Louise and Mayer Carl. The Chief Rabbi of Paris performed the ceremony in the presence of government officials, representatives of the diplomatic world, and high society. In honor of the event, James Rothschild donated 27,000 francs to several consistorial charities and made handsome contributions to the Welfare Bureau of Paris.[60] The young couple honeymooned in Venice where they met their English cousin, Constance, who described Salomon as "genial, brilliantly gifted, but less addicted to steady work and habits of business than his brothers."[61]

In July 1862 Charlotte, Lionel's wife, wrote to Leonora and Leopold, her children, from Spa. She reported that Addy (Adèle) and her new husband Salomon were her guests at luncheon and dinner where they were extremely good-natured, indulgent, amiable and lively. At the midday repast Salomon gave her his opinion of Mentmore, the mansion built for Mayer de Rothschild by George Paxton in England in the 1850s. He considered it deficient in elements of amusement for visitors. Charlotte remarked, "France is so luxurious and the palaces, castles and chateaux of the rue Laffitte, Boulogne, and Ferrières are so gorgeously magnificent and replete with all the pleasures of the earth, that everything else must appear tame and almost poverty-stricken by comparison." Nevertheless, the young couple stayed in England for a few weeks. On August 12, Charlotte reported that all the cousins went to the Exhibition on Sunday and met all the princes of the House of Orleans. Salomon's restlessness and desire to pursue pleasure are also evident in a letter from Betty to Gustave, written while enjoying Ischl, a popular spa that Betty frequented in this period. Salomon had just joined Betty for a brief visit between trips to various towns in the vicinity. She reports: " . . . his youth makes him see everything as beautiful . . . The dear boy can't keep still here. So I have met his desires by tracing an itinerary that may calm his Alpine ardor a little. He is a nice companion who deserves the effort one makes to give him pleasure."[62]

Betty wrote several letters to Gustave and Cécile describing her joy of being at Ischl:

> I found the place just as I had dreamed of: a clean and spacious little chalet, far from noise, far from the world and in a picturesque position halfway up the mountains, surrounded by enormous meadows where one can wander at will, either in the pine forests which overshadow the slopes of the mountains, or on the edge of the terraces which trace the course of the clear Traun—and that one can do alone with one's own thoughts opposite the splendid panorama of the Tyrolean Alps and the Dachstein, their beautiful glacier. Surely that would be sufficient in the world if one could be with those one loves! You can't imagine the purity and lightness of the air one breathes here, nor the gentle sweetness of its caresses. It feels as though it makes one's mind and body grow wings, the way it seems to lift and rock you.

She signed the letter, "Farewell, my dear Cécile and my beloved Gustave. A nice kiss for Baby (six-month-old Zoé Lucie) and all my love for you."[63]

A few months later in September 1863 Charlotte (Lionel's wife), who was visiting Paris, wrote to her children, "Addy, the fair *accouchée*, is perfectly happy; her baby, Hélène, is really charming—fair, fat and at a fortnight of age, the image of Salomon." Charlotte went on to describe the exquisite gifts Addy received from her mother-in-law, Betty, and from Salomon. The happiness of this little family, however, was very short-lived. Less than a year after the baby was born, on May 13, 1864, Salomon died in London of a heart attack; he was only twenty-nine-years-old. The *Archives Israélites* reported his death as a loss not only to the family, but to the entire Jewish community of Paris. It referred to Salomon as one of the strongest pillars of the community and especially lauded his work on the Charity Committee. Salomon was buried in the family plot in Père Lachaise cemetery; his old tutor, Albert Cohn, read a eulogy.[64]

Special prayers were offered by the Jewish communities of Nice and Tetuan since they had been beneficiaries of Salomon's charity; alms were distributed in Paris and in Palestine. Salomon's sudden death was the cause of profound and prolonged mourning for Betty. Marie-Amélie, from her exile in Claremont, wrote a touching letter to her old friend.[65] In this tragedy, as in so many other areas of life, Betty and the former Queen shared a deep understanding. Marie-Amélie had suffered the sudden loss of her first born who was thrown from a carriage in an accident; she assumed an obligation to her son's widow and children. Betty would do the same for Adèle and Hélène.

Betty's youngest son Edmond was born in 1845 when she was forty-years-old and James was fifty-three. Though Edmond's siblings were so much older than he was, his nephews, Edouard and Albert, were very close in age and the three of them played together until Albert's death at the age of four. Edmond benefited from excellent tutors and attended the Lycée Bonaparte where he was a very successful student, exhibiting a strong interest in collecting lithographs. Léon Holendersky, one of his tutors, wrote a poem on the occasion of Edmond's Bar Mitzvah, attesting to the spiritual interests of his pupil. Edmond, unlike his brothers, was too young to benefit from the tutelage of his father in the family business. He was only 23-years-old when James died; alone among the brothers, Edmond contributed little to the management of the enterprise. Instead, he devoted his time to intellectual, artistic, and philanthropic pursuits. In 1870 he was a member of the Garde Mobile and took part in the defense of Paris. He wore a medal attesting to his bravery; it was the only one of his many decorations that he wore.[66]

In 1877, at the age of thirty-two, Edmond married his twenty-two-year-old cousin, Adelheid, daughter of Wilhelm Carl and Mathilde in Frankfurt. This marriage was similar in several aspects to the wedding in 1824 between Edmond's parents when the thirty-two-year-old James traveled from Paris to Frankfurt to marry the nineteen-year-old Betty. In both cases the groom's father was deceased and the groom's mother celebrated the marriage of her youngest son surrounded by many Rothschilds in their natal city. Though recently on opposing sides of the Franco-Prussian War, Betty's family and their Frankfurt cousins were pleased to reunite the family in this traditional manner.

The Parisian Jewish community took note of the wedding. *L'Univers Israélite* compared Edmond's journey to Frankfurt to seek a bride to the Biblical story of Isaac who traveled to find Rebecca and brought her home to meet his mother, Sarah. According to tradition, Rebecca became like Sarah. In like manner, the article continued, Edmond brought his wife to his mother's home where she became charitable like Betty.[67] In keeping with family custom, donations were made in honor of this occasion: Adelheid's parents, who observed Orthodox practices, gave 300,000 marks to establish a school for the Orthodox community. An additional gift of 200,000 marks went to the city of Frankfurt to support young people who wished to become artists. This amount was to be divided as follows: one-third for Catholics, one-third for Protestants and one-third for Sabbath observant Israelites.

The Rothschild family motto—Concordia, Integritas, Industria—was created to reflect the business principles of Mayer Amschel Rothschild and his sons. In fact, these values of family harmony, of dedication to a principled and productive life, extended beyond the Rothschild business partnership to the culture of the Rothschild family. Betty de Rothschild, by virtue of her long and productive life and her extraordinary energy and empathy, was in a unique position to carry these values from the founding generation to subsequent generations of Rothschild children and grandchildren.

CHAPTER FOUR

French Israelite

Jews should be denied everything as a nation, but granted everything as individuals. They must be citizens.

Count Stanislas de Clermont-Tonnerre, 1789

Everywhere, even in countries that still dispute their claim to the rights of man and citizenship, the Jews strive to prove that they belong to the same nation as those with whom they share the earth, and that they are Jews only before God.

Archives Israélites, March 1844

Betty grew up in the warm, familiar environment of the Jewish community of Frankfurt, surrounded by family who followed centuries-old observance. At the same time, she kept her eye on the world of high society for which she was groomed by tutors. As a young teenager, Betty accompanied her mother to neighboring spas where she practiced the social graces. In addition to studying Hebrew and Jewish history and customs, she took piano lessons, painting lessons, and learned to sing. Betty sometimes entertained guests in her parents' home, and in Vienna she accompanied her mother to the great homes where she observed ladies performing in socially approved roles as hostesses. The world of high society was important to her father Salomon, whose business dealings depended on the goodwill of those in powerful positions, but there was no easy entrée into society for Betty and her mother Caroline; both women experienced social discomfort in Vienna.[1] Betty and Caroline soon returned to Frankfurt, leaving Salomon to navigate the social waters of the capital alone. The challenge of combining the two worlds—the world of Jewish customs and traditions with the world of the larger society in which they lived—was a challenge that faced the Rothschild family and other affluent and enlightened Jews. The Rothschilds emerged from the Frankfurt ghetto into the palatial homes they were able to afford as a result of their financial success. Despite their lavish new surroundings they remained committed to the Jewish community, particularly to those who suffered poverty and discrimination. In 1817, Carl Rothschild in Frankfurt wrote to his brothers Salomon and James in Paris:

> I am proud that Nathan provided substantial help to the Jews of Corfu . . . It is the best thing to be able to be of service to the Jews. Our father did so and see how well we are recompensed. The situation here is very bad. I am going to send through the Danish minister who leaves for Paris all the printed books, for and against us, which were published here.[2]

Ten years later Salomon in Paris wrote to Nathan in London to ask for his assistance for another Jewish community. This note offers a different explanation for Rothschild involvement:

> I (Salomon) ask you for a great service which you can render to me. Enclosed is a letter from Eskeles in Vienna who writes concerning the Jews of Hanover where anti-Semitism is very bad. Try to do something. As we are the great ones among the Jews we have to look after this matter.[3]

The Rothschilds, committed to maintaining the traditions of their fathers, expanded their concerns, seeking redress from discrimination against Jews wherever it existed. Their global attitude toward Jews did not stop them from becoming loyal citizens of France, England, and ultimately Germany and Austria.

Issues of identity for Jews who wished to live in the larger society were not solved when they bought new homes and changed their drab ghetto dress for the more colorful costumes of the aristocracy. Jews who made it out of the physical ghetto soon realized that there were social and psychological barriers that remained. The French Rothschilds continued to observe Jewish customs and traditions, making them unusual members of the French upper class. Echoes of their beliefs can be found in their letters. For example, in 1848, Betty wrote to the departing Alphonse:

> May God, who reads our deepest thoughts, grant them at least, and guide you during this long crossing, lighten your soul in difficult moments, comfort your heart in moments of worry and be your guardian protector.[4]

Months later she confessed to Alphonse:

I gather that another steamer is leaving for New Orleans and in spite of my repugnance for breaking the holy laws of the Sabbath, my heart overcomes my conscience, and is putting my pen in my hand so that I can chat tenderly with my dear absent boy.[5]

Betty's Judaism was not only a personal matter. Like James and his brothers, Betty was always keenly aware of the conditions of Jews in other countries. Two weeks after writing the above letter, she again wrote to Alphonse to tell him about the upheavals in Germany surrounding the question of the election of the King of Prussia as the head of the German Empire. While concerned with the "disorganization" plaguing the Old World, in distinction to the promise she saw in the New World, Betty nevertheless, returned to the question of how this revolution affected Jews:

We Jews ought not, however, complain about this great movement and relo-
cation of interests. Everywhere emancipation has brought down the chains
of the Middle Ages, and has given back to these pariahs of fanaticism and
intolerance the rights of humanity and equality. We should congratulate
ourselves on this and hope that the intelligent populace will be able to jus-
tify this great display of conciliatory justice.[6]

Thus, Betty remained observant of Jewish customs and concerned with the fate of Jews while she was also determined to succeed in French society. When she arrived in Paris in 1824, her husband James had already established their home in the artistic and financial milieu of the Chaussée d'Antin, far from the then small Jewish community in the city. James was already using social engage-
ments as a means to increase business opportunities. Betty was eager to assist him in this endeavor, but she was interested in more than financial rewards.

For Betty, success in French society meant the successful integration of Jew-
ish life into the modernizing world of nineteenth century France. The wives of the English and Austrian ambassadors who were Betty's first acquaintances in the city were not concerned with learning to be French; after all, they expected to go home to the place where they were part of the majority culture. For Betty, there was no home to return to in which she could be both Jewish and a mem-
ber of the wider society. For this reason, Betty chose to define herself as a French Israelite, that is, a modern Jew with French culture.[7] Betty saw Paris as the cultural and artistic capital of Europe, and France as a land of opportunity for Jews. She worked to put down roots in the city for herself and her children and their children. With the exception of a brief period during the upheavals of 1848, Betty continued to see Paris, her home for more than sixty years, as a safe haven for herself and for her family.

Though well educated by the standards of her class, Betty continued to learn and develop her identity as a French Israelite during her first decades in

Paris. Betty learned from the constant stream of talented guests attracted to the Rothschild homes, some of whom were Jewish, struggling with problems of identity like hers. Among them was Giaccomo Meyerbeer, the celebrated composer of popular operas who spent an extended vacation with his family in Boulogne in November 1833.[8] Meyerbeer, the son of the well-known Berlin salonnière, Amalie (formerly Malka) Beer, spent much of his life in Paris where he raised his children. Betty and her family remained close to Meyerbeer for decades. In 1849, Betty wrote to Alphonse lauding Meyerbeer's new opera, *Prophet*: "It's a grandiose work, as is everything that comes from his genius."[9]

A cultivated and enlightened man, Meyerbeer expressed regret at his inability to create a meaningful identity that included Judaism. He gave his children freedom to choose their religion on the premise that as a good father and an honest citizen he could not do otherwise. But he later amended his view, concluding that a father has the duty to teach his religion to his children and leave them the freedom to choose when they reach the age of reason. He lamented his ignorance of Judaism. Knowing no Hebrew, nor Jewish history, and few religious practices, he had nothing to teach. He noted with some bitterness that though he had lost his Jewish heritage and had failed to pass it on to his children, he was identified as a Jewish composer and his music was frequently criticized for being "too Jewish."[10]

Unlike Meyerbeer, Betty had a good Jewish education and she was not ambivalent about teaching Jewish history, Hebrew, and religious customs to her children. As noted previously, Betty hired noted Jewish scholars, Albert Cohn and Salomon Munk, to provide modern Jewish education for all her children. As they developed into adulthood, she enjoyed watching the continuation of the tradition in the next generation. On October 17, 1861, Alphonse and Laurie inscribed the name of their new son at the *mairie*. Lionel James Mayer René de Rothschild was a French citizen from birth, but he was also inscribed in the registry of the Orthodox synagogue where he was given the name Nathan.[11] A few days later Charlotte, Laurie's mother, wrote from Paris to her son Leopold in London:

> The Orthodox ceremony (circumcision) took place this morning and I am happy to say that your poor little nephew bore it admirably well. There was a grand breakfast, very smart, with wonderful cakes and sweetmeats, but without fish, jellies, creams or ices. Laurie received wonderful presents— beautiful diamond earrings from Baroness James, enameled pins with brilliant stars from Charlotte, blue china parrots from Cécile.[12]

Despite the fact that Betty's education in both spheres, Jewish and secular, was more than adequate, she was not taught how to merge the two identities. Meyerbeer's disappointment was a cautionary lesson for Betty. It underscored her need to create an identity that would preserve her Judaism while allowing her to develop within French society. During her twenties and thirties, Betty took elements from the two spheres to fabricate an adult identity. She had few models for this construction. She was forced to make compromises that would sometimes offend others and that might have been difficult to reconcile personally. Betty followed the lead of her husband in some compromises with Jewish custom: for example, the Rothchilds adopted French cuisine as opposed to kosher cooking so as not to offend French society. On other matters, however, Betty held to Jewish traditions more strictly than James; she observed the Sabbath and Jewish holidays more devoutly than he did. But on the Day of Atonement, the entire family attended synagogue together and ended the fast with a splendid dinner at home. James always invited Jewish officers, resplendent in their uniforms, home for dinner.[13] Caroline and Salomon, Betty's parents, apparently approved of these compromises, as they adopted the same practices when they moved to Paris.[14]

As Betty's French identity emerged, her concern for Jews in need around the world remained strong. In a letter from Salomon to his brothers written from Vienna on March 6, 1847, he credited Betty for her deep concern about the Jews of Rome:

> . . . on the suggestion of my beloved daughter (Betty), I felt compelled to apply to the Pope, by leave of the Papal Nuncio here, and on behalf of the Jews of Rome; in response the Pope has been pleased to abolish the humiliating duty, since centuries to be raised on Lent Sunday from the Jews of Rome; moreover the Pope has asked his college of Cardinals to give serious consideration to and improve the most annoying conditions of Rome's Jewry. Would that I could give to you and foremost to you my best daughter some better news, regarding our brethren, that would be more gratifying for me than anything else.[15]

In an undated letter to Alphonse in London, Betty continued the family tradition of asking other Rothschilds to assist in a matter of concern to foreign brethren.

> I am sending the enclosed letter from my dear brother, which will make you understand the extent of the persecutions weighing upon our poor co-religionists exposed to Austrian domination. For a long time, I would have spoken in favor of this holy cause through the French press, had I not feared providing more fuel to the hatred of the blind and intolerant passions, aggravating further the condition of the poor victims. But restraint is no longer necessary in Anselm's view; he has asked for the help of publicizing the problems. Our friend Fourcade already gave us the support of his pen in the latest news . . . It's now your turn, dear son, to enlist the *Times* in civilizing and humane polemic. With the help of your dear mother-in-law, so

active in all questions relating to the advancement of justice . . . a good article in this purifying organ of the English press, and the barriers of the Middle Ages shall crumble under the formidable leverage of public opinion and civilization.[16]

In general, Betty adhered to the principle *"Tiens au pays et conserve la foi"* (be loyal to one's country and remain faithful to one's religion), which served as the motto of the first Jewish journal in Paris, *L'Israélite français* (The French Israelite). Enlightened French Jews who wished to be respected as modern French citizens shied away from the French word *juif* with its medieval connotations. For them the word Israelite was more acceptable. Like the other readers of *L'Israélite français*, Betty's fluency in French, her stylish dress and fashionable entertainment helped her to cultivate friends among French Israelite ladies as well as among the aristocracy, the financial elite, and those from the world of the arts.

The role of French Israelite was sufficiently malleable in the early 1840s to enable Betty to establish a public role in French life. As the wife of a wealthy banker it was socially acceptable for Betty to become a philanthropist. Protestant and Catholic French women of means had established the legitimacy of this role in the decades since the French Revolution. In the 1840s, Betty expanded the role of woman philanthropist to specifically include French Israelites. Betty was used to public scrutiny as a society hostess. Reports of her balls and parties, her costumes and jewels were frequently in the society pages, but she knew that a public role in which she championed Jewish causes was a bold step and might lead to less friendly comments in the press.

Betty's goal to become a French Israelite who functioned beyond the limited realm of society hostess was challenged by periodic anti-Semitism directed at members of her family. For example, in 1836, Michaud, a member of the Académie Française, published a book of French history asserting that Betty's father Salomon Rothschild, one of the richest bankers in Europe, had been baptized in Vienna, having as his godfather Prince Esterhazy. Salomon was furious with what he saw as a scurrilous attack on his integrity. He wrote a strong letter to Michaud stating that he had never changed his religion, nor had he ever thought of changing it, and he demanded that a correction be printed in the next edition of the text. Michaud replied to Salomon, begging his pardon for the error. Not satisfied with the response, Salomon ordered that both letters be bound into his copy of the book. On the frontispiece he wrote: "I command my inheritors and descendants to never abandon the religion of their fathers."[17] He also asked his family to safeguard the book in perpetuity.

Another example of the tenuous nature of Rothschild acceptability in France was visible in the reaction of the French press to the Damascus Affair of 1840. The events in Damascus focused on the disappearance of an Italian monk and his servant; many Jews were accused of murdering the two in a ritual. The

Jews confessed under torture and were thrown in jail; the case was debated widely in the Western press while French and English Jews rallied to the cause of their falsely accused co-religionists. This public expression of solidarity with Jews in other parts of the world raised questions in France about the loyalty of French Israelites. A popular Catholic newspaper, ironically titled *Univers*, was particularly incensed that Jews expressed a universal feeling for fellow Jews. The editors charged French Israelites with disloyalty to France.

> Judaism has reappeared as a power, as a nationality, thus justifying the prophecies which rendered it imperishable and giving the lie to those philosophical theories which in recent years sought to efface it within the uniformity of modern civilization—and, as such, it has held all of Christianity in check . . .

They reserved their particular ire for the Rothschild family, as James took the lead in demanding freedom for his co-religionists. The editor of *Univers* warned:

> On David's throne, once it is restored, there will sit that financial dynasty which all Europe recognizes and to which all of Europe submits; its inauguration will surely provide a scene . . . most worthy of the venal century in which we are living.[18]

Betty's identity as a French Israelite was also affected by the pervasive Christian belief that enlightened Jews should give up their ancient rituals and convert to Christianity out of the conviction that it represented a more evolved faith. The Comtesse de Gasparin, a society hostess and close friend of François Guizot, visited the Holy Land in 1848 and published an account of her trip when she returned to Paris. She expressed the view of many French aristocrats who admired Jews for their faith, but found them strange:

> Can I speak without repeating myself of this tribe's relentless faith, its obstinate and vain hope; the mystery of its rituals, its existence and its degradation? Ignored and despised in spite of their number, enclosed in a choked neighborhood and dark synagogues, chased from all sites consecrated by the Bible, the Gospel or the Koran, the sons of Israel sustain above all others the hope for the future and for a national renaissance. They come from all corners of Europe, strange-looking, with the instinctive regularity of migratory birds, to add graves to those of their ancestors. Their number is very high in comparison with their religious and political importance, which is nil.[19]

Betty, raised with the anti-Semitic imagery of the Frankfurt ghetto, remained sensitive to any depiction of Jews as different and strange. Part of her lifelong concern with being stylish and making certain that her children were *comme il faut* (properly turned out) was the need to distance her family from any stereotypic image of Jews such as that captured by the Comtesse. James was less concerned about the opinion of others, though he was no less sensitive to their ridicule and he was always aware of his thickly accented French.

King Louis-Philippe, more modern than many French aristocrats, was comfortable with the concept of French Israelite. He saw Jews as members of the French nation, rather than as the perpetual strangers. He wondered why other European countries did not adopt the French policy of giving citizenship to the Jews living in their midst. He shared his thoughts on the subject with Albert Cohn before the revolutions of 1848:

> I don't understand the difficulties that the foreign sovereigns oppose to completely admitting the Israelites as citizens, reproaching them with forming a state within a state; I find on the contrary, that the Israelites are, as much by their qualities as by their defects, French in France, English in England, Italian in Italy, German in Germany. They adhere to the nation's quarrels and express the popular passions with the same warmth as the other inhabitants of the different countries.[20]

Nevertheless, following the upheavals of 1848, most European nations, having temporarily flirted with the idea of universal male citizenship, rejected Louis-Philippe's approach to Jewish citizenship. Indeed, even in France, where Jews had long been citizens, the majority of Frenchmen were not accustomed to the concept of a French Israelite. For them, Jews were a distinct ethnic and racial community who were living in France but were not really French despite the fact that they had been granted citizenship decades earlier.

Some Jews were keenly aware that they were not really considered French by their fellow citizens. Ben-Levi, the children's book author and a journalist for the *Archives Israélites*, captured the contemporary discomfort with French Israelites in a column printed in 1842:

> What is the meaning of this senseless phrase: "He's a Jew"? I hear it said: M. Crémieux is a very distinguished lawyer, he's a Jew. M. Azevedo, the new Prefect of the Pyrénées, is an eminent administrator, he's a Jew. Who wrote the admirable music for *La Reine de Chypre*? Halévy, he's a Jew . . . When you tell me that M. Delessert is the father of the French savings bank, do you add that he's a Protestant? When you talk about M. Guizot, do you tell me that he belongs to the Reform Church? . . . it is an insult that implies the words Jew and eminent are somehow contradictory.[21]

Despite the disappointment voiced by Ben-Levi with the failure of the French to fully accept Jews into their society, Betty recognized that the emerging identity of the French Israelite provided her with a large platform on which to develop her personality and her ideas. Had she only seen herself as Jewish, it is unlikely that she would have connected with French women philanthropists, nor would she have recognized that she shared many of their goals. This connection served as an important catalyst in Betty's evolution. From French women, she learned to move out into the public arena, which allowed her to expand her maternal duties to serve the needs of the growing community of poor Jews living in Paris. Similarly, had Betty seen herself as an aristocrat with tenuous ties to Judaism, she would have tried to merge into the local aristocracy, as had the Jewish salonnières of Berlin. When Betty accompanied James de Rothschild to Paris in 1824, she gave up her place of birth, her native language, and close proximity to her parents and brother, but she maintained her Jewish identity. Gradually, she developed her sense of self to include elements of modern French life. The new identity of French Israelite allowed Betty to develop as a modern Jewish woman who was deeply involved both in the cultural and artistic world of her time and in the Jewish community.

The role of French Israelite was created at the time of the French Revolution: Jews were granted the right of citizenship, but the discussion of citizenship pertained only to men. Thus, French Israelites as citizens were thought of as men, while their wives were part of the family of each citizen, in a pattern analogous to the general discussion of citizenship. Later, the Consistory established by Napoleon referred to its members as French Israelites, again assuming an organization of men. During Betty's years in Paris, French Israelite men continued to work out the complications of their role, as is evident from Ben-Levi's comments above.

Men like Adolphe Crémieux found ways to be both French and Jewish in the public arena. Crémieux served the Jewish community during the Damascus Affair and later served as Minister of Justice in 1848. He remained affiliated with the Jewish community for decades despite the fact that his wife and children converted to Catholicism. Fromenthal Halévy was able to serve the Jewish community by composing songs for special occasions to be performed in the synagogue. Simultaneously, he enjoyed tremendous popularity as the composer of grand opera in Paris. Closer to home, James de Rothschild was noted for his financial successes, though he was also a major contributor to the Jewish community. Thus, part of the definition of French Israelite for men included a well-defined role in the secular world.

For women, there was no comparable role required, since there was little appreciation for public roles played by women, whether as Jews or as French citizens. This was not satisfactory to Betty who, within the Rothschild family, was accustomed to speaking out on matters of concern to Jews around the world. Betty was also keenly aware that Christian women of her social circle had already begun to pursue active roles in charitable endeavors. Slowly these women developed the belief that their maternal concerns, spread to the public arena, would improve society. This concept, sometimes called

"*L'Ange de la maison*" (angel of the house), would remain a central component of French ideology throughout the century.[22] For Betty, being a society hostess and raising her children to be good French Israelites was important but not sufficient. Like her mother Caroline, with whom she remained very close throughout her life, Betty felt the need to speak out and to take action to help those in need, particularly those in the Jewish community. The French Israelite identity for women allowed her to develop the role of modern Jewish woman philanthropist.

Betty's sisters-in-law, cousins, and nieces in London and Frankfurt were all involved in charitable works for their local Jewish communities. But unlike Betty, they followed more traditional paths, typically working with family members on shared projects. Betty, on the other hand, was influenced by French society ladies and had a broader vision of what could be accomplished by an organization of women working together for the public good. In several letters, Betty's female relatives commented on the elegance, intelligence, and energy they found in their French relative. These qualities served Betty well as she prepared herself for the tasks ahead.

One resource for Betty's continuing education was the burgeoning advice literature written for women. Fashion magazines, literary reviews, and children's stories provided guidance on acceptable roles. Magazines like *La Mode*, which circulated from 1829–54, provided coverage of the latest fashion trends; but more importantly for Betty's purposes, it included stories about the social events of the season and biographical accounts of the participants. Literary journals like *Le Citateur féminin: Recueil de la littérature féminine ancienne et moderne*, which began publishing in 1835, featured authors like Delphine de Girardin, a popular salon hostess and writer of poetry and stories. Girardin and others who contributed to this journal called for women to be serious and informed without betraying their feminine nature. The *Citateur* included biographies, poetry, and short fiction by women. It was published quarterly, featuring twelve authors in each issue, half of whom were Betty's contemporaries.[23] From them Betty learned how to achieve the goal of being both serious and feminine, an objective that characterized the struggle for women's rights in France.

Two other journals, *Le Musée des familles* and *La Mère de famille*, are representative of the journals addressed to mothers, emphasizing their maternal roles. These publications frequently contained stories addressed to young readers; they were to be read out loud by the mother to her children. The practice of mothers reading to their children and the idea of close relationships between mothers and children fit well with the family traditions Betty brought to Paris from the close-knit Jewish community of Frankfurt.

The magazine that most effectively promoted the French nineteenth-century ideals of womanhood was the *Journal des femmes*. Its prospectus, issued in 1832, stated:

This journal wants to keep away from the passion always involved when it comes to writing about women. It does not want to defend them but only claim for them a right nature has given them, that society contests and liberty must restore. Women must make themselves heard. They should be able to prepare themselves for the noble functions that are theirs and get new strength through a strong and "constitutional" education.[24]

Featuring stories by famous women writers as well as recipes and fashion tips, the journal was devoted to creating an educated woman whose social responsibility was clear: to educate the next generation of French citizens. In 1840 the editors noted: "Today women have developed a more serious character . . . she wishes to learn more."[25] This was a role Betty was prepared to accept as she had primary responsibility for the education of her five children. In addition to sitting in on lessons given to her children, particularly those in moral philosophy, she also routinely wrote to her children about hygiene, health care, and social etiquette, topics frequently discussed in the *Journal des femmes*. She encouraged her children to work hard so that they would be able to assume leadership roles alongside the scions of the French aristocracy and bourgeoisie.

While the women's journals provided role models for Betty as she sought to expand her maternal role to include public responsibility, a popular novel titled *La Juive* (the Jewess) portrayed negative images for a public all too inclined to believe them. The novel, written by Eugénie Foa and published in Paris in 1835, featured a downtrodden Jewish woman who defied her father by refusing to marry someone he had selected for her. The novel was to some extent autobiographical. Eugénie was the daughter of a prominent Sephardic family from Bordeaux who was forced into an unhappy marriage. In the novel, the main character Midiane is kept sequestered at home under the despotic rule of her father. Nevertheless, Midiane falls in love with André, a Christian, and she subsequently refuses to marry the Jew selected for her by her father. In revenge, the father curses her, locks her in her room, and burns down the house. With the help of her beleaguered mother, Midiane escapes the fire, finds her true love André and becomes his mistress. The tragic story continues as André dies and Midiane and her child, rejected by all, die in poverty.[26]

Foa, abandoned by her husband who had squandered her dowry, lived on the edge of poverty while bringing up two children. Nevertheless, she didn't portray the efforts of a hard-working Jewish mother to educate her children in her novel; instead, she chose the familiar image of the powerless Jewess living under the strict rule of a tyrannical father. This image was antithetical to that of the modern French Israelite: it assumed that Jewish women would remain backward while the larger society moved on without them. Years later, Foa, unable to imagine becoming a French Israelite, chose to convert.

Fromenthal Halévy, one of the most popular opera composers of Betty's day, wrote the music for a grand opera titled, like the novel, *La Juive*. Based on a completely different story, Halévy's *Juive* opened in 1835 to great acclaim and was performed regularly for decades. The opera is set in medieval Constance; the central characters of the opera, Eleazar and Rachel, are modeled on the literary stereotypes of Shylock and his beautiful daughter. These types were well-known in France through stagings and editions of Shakespeare as well as through more popular works based on this story, such as Scott's *Ivanhoe*, which was one of the most widely read novels in France in the later 1820s.[27]

In Halévy's opera, the heroine Rachel has a split identity: She is cared for by her father Eleazar and she grows up thinking that she is Jewish. At the end of her life she learns that she was actually Christian, rescued from death by Eleazar, her 'father,' at the very moment when his two sons were burned at the stake for being Jewish. Rachel's loyalty to Eleazar, as they await their death for refusing to convert to Christianity, is clear:

Eleazar: On thy brow they want to pour baptismal water,
        Is that what you want my child?

Rachel: Who? Me! A Christian? Me!
       The flames sparkle!
       Come on!

Eleazar: Their God calls you!

Rachel: And ours awaits me!
       I am inspired by heaven,
       I choose death![28]

Thus Rachel, motivated by love and loyalty, dies at the stake with Eleazar. In the eyes of many in the audience, this sacrifice confirmed a commonly held belief that the only good Jewess is really a Christian. Despite the fact that Halévy introduced some appealing images of the Passover seder in one scene of the opera, the overriding image confirmed the view that Jews and Christians were fundamentally different and thus not capable of being part of the same nation.

Despite the presence of these negative images of Jewish women in French popular culture, Betty was determined to create an alternative reality for Jewish women. Betty was aware that the ladies of her day were expanding their traditional maternal roles to include succoring the children of the poor. Following the Christian tradition of *caritas* (based on the Latin term for love), the advice in women's journals advocated concern for the wellbeing of the poor. Ladies of Betty's acquaintance participated in charitable endeavors, primarily focusing on the needs of children and mothers. Women who previously spent their time at home or in society began to address the needs of poor children, encouraging them to become good citizens and productive members of society. To achieve additional social legitimacy, many of the societies formed to address social welfare issues relied on royal or aristocratic patrons or on the church.

Ernest Legouvé, a liberal republican, wrote *Histoire morale des femmes* in 1849, arguing for new public roles for women; he advocated that women be given the right to practice medicine, to become teachers, prison inspectors, and factory inspectors. Legouvé argued that Christianity was the source for the amelioration of women's conditions. The reviewer in the *Archives Israelites* sharply disagreed with this assumption, pointing out that for eighteen centuries women's rights had been denied in Christian countries. He posited that it was the Enlightenment and not Christianity that encouraged new thinking about women.[29] Like the reviewer, Betty believed that progress for women was not predicated on Christianity. Although, on a practical level, she learned much from observing Christian friends as they worked in the philanthropic circles of Paris.

One of the most successful women's societies of Betty's day was the Société de la Charité maternelle, founded in 1788 under the protection of Queen Marie Antoinette, and presided over by Betty's friend Queen Marie-Amélie in the 1840's. The goal of this society was to influence poor women to stop abandoning their babies by assisting expectant mothers. Following a brief interruption in the activities of this society during the Revolution, it was reorganized in 1801 with Empress Josephine as Protectress. It continued under the Restoration and flourished during the July Monarchy.

During the Second Republic and later the Second Empire, the Société de Charité maternelle expanded its membership and its activities, becoming a national organization with chapters in forty-three cities in 1850; by 1870, eighty-two cities sponsored chapters. The scope of activities was also enlarged to include assistance to poor pregnant women, paying for the services of a midwife, and care for the mother and newborn for several months. In Paris, hundreds of society ladies visited the homes of their charges and dispensed funds to meet urgent needs. The ladies also met monthly at each others' homes to discuss protocols for home visits, payment for midwives, and the distribution of funds for fuel and food for mother and child. In this manner, Christian women worked outside of their own families, expanding their maternal roles to care for poor children and their mothers.

Betty's awareness of the activities of her society friends was a catalyst to her own philanthropy. Working with her mother Caroline and her daughter, Charlotte, Betty established a fund to provide layettes for poor Jewish women. Established in 1847, this fund also provided twenty francs in winter months and fifteen francs in summer to poor married Jewish women who had resided in Paris for at least two years. The layette included a woolen blanket, two pairs of sheets, and several infant suits. Starting by supporting forty women, the society expanded its operation each year, helping 100 women in 1882.[30] Queen Marie-Amélie and her daughters assisted the charity founded by Betty, embroidering clothing for infant Israelites, as Betty had contributed to their efforts to help Christian mothers and their babies.

In 1826 Mme Emilie Mallet, wife of the banker Jules Mallet and a regular guest of Betty and James de Rothschild, established a new society to provide nursery day schools (salles d'asile) for children aged two to seven. Mme Mallet was joined by the Marquise de Pastoret and Mme Gautier-Delessert in this new endeavor. In 1830, the Conseil général des hospices, which had been supervising the nurseries since the previous year, created a high committee for the nursery schools of Paris. Fifteen women were selected for this committee, which met monthly, received reports about the success of the schools in different parts of the city, reviewed requests to open new schools, selected directors, and raised funds.[31]

By 1837, there were twenty-four day nurseries in Paris and the supervision of their operations was transferred to the Ministry of Public Instruction. Minister Salvandy was very positive about the contributions of the nursery schools to the health and security of young children. He noted that they inculcate from early childhood the habits of order, discipline, and regular work; they also freed mothers to earn wages needed to support the family. Salvandy was so impressed with the results that he asked Mme Mallet to design a course of study for nursery school teachers.[32]

Emilie Mallet opened several additional nursery schools during the turbulent days of 1848 and more during the cholera outbreak of 1849 when she also opened dormitories for children with sick parents. These dormitories were taken over by the Sisters of Saint Vincent de Paul and became the Oeuvre des orphelins de Ménilmontant. Despite the separation of church and state in France, dating back many decades to the French Revolution, many charities continued to be supervised by the church. While Betty supported the efforts undertaken by her society friends, she understood that they were promoting Christian values as well as habits of sobriety, cleanliness, punctuality, and thrift. She studied these groups in an effort to learn how to raise funds and how to organize Jewish women's groups.

Additional models of charitable works led by women emerged during the revolutionary year 1848. In July 1848 the Oeuvre des faubourgs (neighborhood charity) under the sponsorship of the abbé Petitot, curé de Saint-Roch, and abbé Faudet, curé de Saint-Etienne-du-Mont, was established to respond to the needs of school-aged children. The objective of this project was to support students in existing public schools and to create new schools where they were needed. The members of this society focused their efforts on the educational needs of poor children while not neglecting their need for clothing and food. By May of 1849 this Oeuvre listed 132 women members, including members of the aristocracy. The secretary of the organization, Mme Hanriat, reported:

> The neighborhood of Saint-Marcel houses only profoundly miserable people. Their fury against society is appeased; the visiting ladies are received

everywhere as angels of peace. It is not just the help that is brought them that is appreciated, but the wellbeing brought on by their presence. The worker, until now so skeptical, has finally understood that Christian charity knows how to equalize the ranks of society without confusing them; they receive with gratitude the charity that is offered them with sympathy and love.[33]

This organization, working together with the municipality to fund schools and children's needs, had important results in ameliorating poverty and ignorance, and in inculcating values. The Oeuvre lasted until 1880, when it was taken over by the state. It is likely that Betty de Rothschild was familiar with the work of this society, as the Oeuvre included members who socialized in her circles.

Another organization that expanded women's horizons was established in 1815 as an all male society. The Société pour l'instruction élémentaire, which established schools, edited books for children, and provided textbooks and school furniture, opened their membership to women in 1831. This organization also awarded prizes for the best books and encouraged the creation of school libraries. The lady members—Duchesse de Duras, Marquise de Pastoret, Comtesse Delaborde, Maréchale Lobau, Comtesse de Salvandy, Comtesse Rambuteau, Mmes François and Gabriel Delessert—were Betty's friends and influential women, but the leadership of this committee remained in the hands of men.[34]

Contact with Christian society ladies inspired Betty to imagine a public role for herself: Jewish woman philanthropist. Betty knew that Parisian society held the belief that only Christians were charitable, that charity based on *caritas* was in fact a Christian virtue. The older Jewish tradition of *tzedakah* was invisible to Paris society. This tradition, based on the concept of justice, held that helping the poor was not an act of love, but rather the fulfillment of religious obligation. Traditional Jews fulfilled these obligations by distributing matzo for Passover, offering a Sabbath meal to those far from home, or providing new clothing for children for the New Year. In addition, Jews believed that charity should be anonymous. As a result, the possibility of a Jewish woman becoming a charitable leader was not considered. Despite the obstacles, Betty recognized in her new role a way to combine commitment to Judaism and belief in taking action to improve the conditions of those in need through education.

It wasn't until July 1848, following the revolutionary upheaval that left thousands of Parisians destitute, that an organization, L'Oeuvre de bon secours, opened its membership to women of diverse religious backgrounds. This charitable endeavor was founded months earlier by Eugénie Foa, working with the support of the abbé Beuzelin, curé of the Madeleine, and the Archbishop of Paris, Monseigneur Affre, who was tragically killed at the barricades. Eugénie Foa, aided by Mme Cousin and Mme de Lafayette-Lasteyrie, created the statutes of their organization, whose general principles were printed in the radical *Voix des femmes*. Foa's call to action was influenced by both the Christian concept of *caritas* and the Jewish tradition of *tzedakah*. She wrote:

> God has fashioned us (women) to be solace in this land of exile; to accomplish this mission, my sisters, we must come to the aid of those who suffer; alone we can accomplish nothing; together we are able to do everything: let us act together. I do not ask you for a gift, but rather a loan; I am not asking you for charity for our sisters, poor workers without work, it is work, bread (I ask for).[35]

In the article, Foa explained the rationale for the plan to create workshops to employ poor women and girls. She believed in the tenet *"En moralisant les femmes, on améliore les hommes"* (by improving the morals of women, one makes men better). This revolutionary idea was the opposite of the bourgeois plan to improve family life by providing work for husbands while wives remained at home. Foa, a single mother, was aware of the impracticality of such a plan.

Foa envisioned a national institute made up of twenty leading women, each one of whom would work in her own parish and its churches to complete a survey of those able to make loans to assist women in need. The funds collected would permit the establishment of sewing workshops for women and girls who needed employment. The ladies would place orders for clothing or linens, and the resulting sales would be used to pay back the loans, to create dowries for the best girls, to provide an infirmary for the workers and their families, and to pay the employees. The membership of Foa's organization included the financial and political bourgeoisie, but the rules for participation announced that membership is open to anyone who puts in an order for work, regardless of religion or beliefs.[36]

Betty was aware of the efforts of Eugénie Foa to organize bourgeois women to help poor women. Foa's sewing workshop was briefly established on the second floor of a building belonging to the Minister of Public Works at 16 rue de Rivoli, close to Betty's home on rue Laffitte. Eugénie's sister, the sculptor Léonie, was married to Fromenthal Halévy, a frequent guest in Betty's home. Léonie and Eugénie were part of a small group of Parisian Jewish women who, like Betty, struggled to create a coherent identity for themselves in the turbulent years of mid-nineteenth century Paris.

Julienne Bloch, the author of a remarkable column, *Lettres d'une Parisienne*, in *L'Univers Israélite*, was one of several women who offered an alternative to the Christian model of philanthropy. Julienne was knowledgeable about Jewish history and traditions, but she advocated reforming some traditions to meet the needs of the modern French woman. In March of 1855 Julienne urged her readers to become more vocal about their place in society:

> Women keep silent amidst all the debates of which they are the object. Newspapers and books discuss our rights and duties, our mission in the temple and at home, our liberation and our minority status, and we have nothing to say about such issues that concern us directly![37]

Julienne commented on the initiation rites established by the Consistory in 1842; she did not like the way Jewish girls were ushered into the faith. The ceremony was called an initiation; for Julienne this term recalled the ancient Egyptian cult of Isis with its initiations. She also did not like the German Jewish use of the term confirmation for the ceremony since it was obviously borrowed from Christianity. Julienne was searching for a modern ceremony that would reflect something that was authentically Jewish. In the end, she advocated calling the new ceremony a consecration since it marked the time when the youngster's inner sanctuary was opened up to the holy commandments. In addition, Julienne wished to change the practice of dressing all the young girls in white for this ceremony, wanting to differentiate the Jewish from the Catholic custom. She advocated pink, blue, or dresses of any other color.[38]

Julienne was not only interested in the initiation rite; she addressed her column to the education that preceded the ceremony. As a teacher, she was deeply concerned with the level of Jewish education. She wrote: "Our young Jewish girls have limited valuable knowledge and their education is too superficial."[39] In a later exposition of the subject she explained why the state of Jewish education in Paris was so poor: "Our co-religionists lack religious education. For most [Jews], the observance of traditional holy customs is seen as a weakness; for others, the total ignorance of sacred knowledge results in stupidity, which negates all that it does not know."[40]

Julienne's column strongly supported modern Jewish education for the whole community, believing that girls should be given equal opportunities in Jewish schools, synagogues, and the community. She also took up the cause of women who wished to sing in temple, arguing that there was precedent for it within Jewish tradition:

> . . . men and women in the Worms synagogue during the Middle Ages were separated by a wall four and a half feet high with only a few narrow openings closed by curtains; and since women could barely hear the cantor in the men's section, an educated woman fulfilled the cantor's duties among the women. And yet, today, the daughters of our cantors can sing at the opera, but are not allowed to do so before the Lord. Today, young girls are taught to sing in concerts and perform in theatres, but are not taught

the sacred songs and religious rituals to perform, if need be, in a holy gathering of sisters in Israel.[41]

Disappointed with the lack of progress for women in both the Jewish community and in French society, Julienne described with enthusiasm the young English Queen Victoria who visited Paris in September 1855. She rejoiced in the triumphant entrance of the Queen into the city: the loud cheering as she passed, the garlands of flowers, the dazzling banners. She wrote:

> I feel proud to see a person of the weaker sex receive such tribute, command such respect, cause such enthusiasm, and rule over men by birthright and by the power of her merit and virtues, in the country of Salic Law and the Civil Code, which is so uncivil when it states: 'The wife must obey her husband.'[42]

Julienne introduced an even more compelling image of woman in the column devoted to the biblical Queen Esther. Julienne's Esther was a powerful and benevolent queen, not an exotic maiden selected by an oriental potentate. She wrote:

> The holiday of Purim belongs especially to the women and girls of Israel, because God chose a woman to save His people. Esther is one of the purest diamonds of the Jewish crown. We admire her grace, charm, pious modesty, and saintly resignation, which shall forever shine like a star in the memory of every Jewish woman . . . Esther's external beauty reflected her holy and beautiful soul . . . Unlike the orgy under the first queen, the feast of Esther was an event marked by propriety, dignity, noble and delicate manners; and instead of enticing the populace of Suze to drink, which leads to all excesses, the King brought the country relief and distributed blessings: that was the wedding gift that Esther had asked for, that was the first influence of the Jewish Queen![43]

This image of a benevolent Queen Esther, a virtuous woman who stood up for her people in time of their distress, appealed to Betty.

In addition to Julienne Bloch, Betty was influenced by another prolific Jewish woman author of this period: Grace Aguilar, an English Jew whose writing was regularly reviewed in French Jewish journals. Aguilar, like Eugénie Foa, was of Sephardic descent. She died at the age of thirty-one in 1847, but managed to write several substantial works that remained in print long after her untimely death. Her novels, *Home Influence: A Tale for Mothers and Daughters* and *Mother's Recompense*, had considerable success. Her *Women of Israel* was a series of biographical sketches of biblical characters, intended to arouse in young Jews the pride in their heritage. She also wrote, *The Spirit of Judaism: In Defense of*

Her Faith and Its Professors, and *The Jewish Faith*, a series of letters addressed to a friend wavering in her religious conviction.

Aguilar explained to her readers that she felt obliged to write *Women of Israel* because other books on this topic had been published for Christian women, claiming that Christianity is the sole source of female excellence. Aguilar, like Betty, was determined to refute the notion that the law of Moses sank the Hebrew female to the lowest state of degradation, placing her on a level with slaves or the heathen, and denying her mental and spiritual enjoyment. Aguilar replied to this calumny with her pen; Betty would do so through her philanthropic deeds. Both women believed in taking action. Aguilar wrote:

> Simply to deny this assertion, to affirm that instead of degrading and enslaving, the Jewish law exalted, protected, and provided for woman . . . would not avail us much. The women of Israel must arise, and prove the truth of what we urge—by their own conduct, their own belief, their own ever-acting and ever-influencing religion, prove without doubt or question that we need not Christianity to teach us our mission.[44]

Aguilar admitted that centuries of persecution had affected Jewish behavior in Jewish history. Likewise, the amelioration of economic conditions in certain quarters resulted in an indifference to Judaism, but she was certain that indifference would be replaced by a stronger, nobler, and more spiritually enlightened people. Women, she affirmed, "must join this movement as daughters, wives and mothers, but also as witnesses of that faith which first raised, cherished, and defended them—witnesses of that God who had called them His . . ."[45]

Grace Aguilar believed that the women of the Bible were mirrors of contemporary Jewish women; she continued, "if the Eternal, in His infinite mercy, extended love, compassion, forbearance, and forgiveness unto them, we may believe He extends them equally unto all of us and draws comfort, and encouragement, and faith from the biographies."[46] Aguilar agreed with Betty that there was no need to wait for Christianity, or the examples of the females in the Gospel, to raise women to equality with men. Aguilar's history included a chapter about the Wives of the Patriarchs, including Eve, Sarah, Rebecca, Leah, and Rachel. It continued with a review of the Law and how it established certain privileges for women. The period of Kings was next, including sketches of Deborah, Naomi and Hannah. Aguilar summarized the dispersion of the Jewish people and its effects on women's role, and she concluded with a chapter on the current status of Jewish women, calling on them to fulfill their mission.

In the 1840s Betty answered that call, taking on a leadership role in the Jewish community of Paris, of France, and eventually of world Jewry. She agreed with Grace Aguilar: "Our existence is in itself a miracle: naught but the providence of God could have thus preserved us; a nation so completely apart, that, though for more than eighteen centuries scattered over the whole world, and found in every land, our identity has never been lost, our race has never mingled, our religion has never changed."[47] Betty believed that it was her duty to work for Jewish continuity as well as for the dignified acceptance of the Jewish people as members of the world community. Her vision and her dedication to its accomplishment were the twin pillars of her identity as a French Israelite.

CHAPTER FIVE

First Lady

The critics of our day compare the piety of our mothers and our grandmothers with the more worldly character of the French Israelite of our day. Without wishing to diminish the real merit of our mothers and grandmothers, we ask if charity has ever been more developed and has even dried the tears of the needy among us better? Has it ever come to the aid of the child who needs instruction or the worker who wants to earn enough through working or the young women in need of a dowry?

Albert Cohn, *Archives Israélites*, 1850

On the banks of the Red Sea . . . a young woman played an important role . . . Miriam, sister of Moses. Accompanied by musical instruments, she addressed the women who followed her and told them to "Sing to the Eternal." Today the women of Israel, remain faithful. They are dedicated to charity; they bring their sisters and friends to work with them . . . See how in the privacy of their homes the women of Israel prepare magnificent objects for the next welfare lottery while continuing to try to sell as many tickets as possible.

Archives Israélites, 1877

In the early 1840s Betty de Rothschild had achieved an important place in French society. As a friend of Queen Marie-Amélie and a member of exclusive social circles in the capital, she sometimes joined in the charitable endeavors that constituted part of the accepted role for society ladies. She had already modernized her identity when she moved from Frankfurt to Paris; now, as a French Israelite, she decided to develop a public role as a philanthropist. In 1843, Betty launched the Société pour l'établissement des jeunes filles israélites (Society for the Support of Jewish Young Women) devoted to the continuing professional and moral education of twelve-year-old girls.[1] This was an audacious act for Betty, requiring the energy, intelligence and elegance frequently noted by her family. Unlike Queen Marie-Amélie, who was the *protectrice* of the Société de Charité Maternelle, which had roots in pre-revolutionary France, Betty started an organization that had little precedent in the Jewish community.

Within the Jewish community, philanthropic leadership was traditionally in the hands of men; it was nearly unprecedented for a woman to take the lead in charitable endeavors. It is noteworthy that James did not join Betty in high-profile Jewish philanthropy until 1852, when he supported the opening of a new Jewish hospital in Paris. Betty's focus on the needs of girls for vocational and moral education was revolutionary. Her experience raising money with other society ladies gave her confidence in her organizational abilities; her sensitivity to the plight of poor Jews in the capital was keen; her commitment to social activism on their behalf grew naturally from her abilities and her interests. Through her tireless actions on behalf of the Jewish community of Paris, France, Algeria, Morocco, and Palestine, she became highly visible as a philanthropist. Some called her the Queen Esther of her day.

The Société operated under the umbrella of the Consistory, specifically its Charity Bureau, but it was an independent entity under Betty's leadership.[2] Its membership was composed of women who shared the bourgeois belief common in mid-nineteenth century France that a woman's nurturing role should extend beyond the family to the community. The *Journal des femmes* explained: "Women's mission on earth is not to shine and please, but to influence the regeneration of human kind."[3] The members of the Société shared this view, specifically addressing their attention to the Parisian Jewish community. The Société was built on a tradition of private endeavors of the Parisian Jewish community, often supporting the Consistory, to care for the Jewish community. In addition, the Société provided an opportunity for Jewish women to play a role in the French Israelite community similar to that played by Catholic and Protestant women in French charitable organizations.

The Parisian Jewish community had grown substantially since Betty's arrival in 1824, reaching about 10,000 in 1843—approximately 15% of the Jewish population of France. During the next several decades, immigration to the city increased; by 1870 30% of French Jews lived in the capital. Nevertheless, Jews made up only a tiny fraction of the population of the city. In 1843 they were less than 1%, and by 1870 they approached only 2% of the population. Jewish leaders were not yet affected by large-scale Jewish immigration from other countries, but they were challenged by a significant number of paupers: roughly 20% of the Parisian Jewish population depended on charity to survive.[4]

Services for the needy were the responsibility of the Consistory, established in 1808 to represent the Jews to the government and to receive and handle money destined for religious expenses. This hierarchical structure included the Central Consistory as well as local consistories in communities with populations large enough to warrant them. The Consistory received money at first from special Jewish taxes, later from the state, private donors, the sale of temple seats, fundraising campaigns, and taxes on kosher meat. They were responsible for organizing and running elections; building, repairing and enlarging temples; supervising the charities and *kashrut*; hiring, firing and paying personnel; regulating circumcision; and controlling burial procedures and cemeteries.

The Consistory was superimposed on an older system of community organizations, which continued to function: mutual-aid societies, burial societies, and prayer groups. In Paris, these societies were legally superseded by the Charity Bureau (Comité de bienfaisance), reorganized and more controlled under the Paris Consistory in 1839. The Charity Bureau was charged with handling aid to the poor, founding a Jewish hospital, and *régéneration*, that is, finding ways to encourage Jews to exercise useful professions.[5]

This last item was complicated by the fact that many Jews arrived in the capital with no skills and a history of working as either peddlers or petty money-changers. Leading Parisian Jews felt that it was their obligation to modernize the newcomers by providing opportunities for apprenticeships and training through trade schools. The issue was not without controversy since moving into skilled professions frequently entailed giving up religious observances; the Sabbath and Jewish holidays were not recognized by Christian employers in Paris. A society to promote the apprenticeship of young Jewish men had been established in Paris as early as 1823, but it soon failed because of objections from Orthodox Jews who feared that the new emphasis on vocational training would lead boys away from the traditional study of the Talmud. The problem of unskilled and poor immigrants was addressed in the twenties and thirties through the establishment of Jewish schools that taught secular subjects; however, the need for a program of vocational training for children beyond the age of twelve or thirteen remained unsolved.

The first Jewish women to engage in philanthropy in Paris were the Women Protectors of the Consistory Schools (Réunion des dames protectrices des écoles consistoriales israélites de Paris). Organized by the Consistory in 1821, these women were asked to raise funds for the boys' communal school, a modern version of the *heder*, where students learned to read and write in French and Hebrew, and where mathematics and later drafting were taught. The Women Protectors, sensitive to the plight of Jewish girls, decided to establish a girls' school, which opened in May 1822. This decision met with hostility from the Consistory, whose leaders were opposed to creating a second school as long as the needs of the boys' school were not met.

Despite the opposition of the Consistory, in December 1821, the Women Protectors hired Mlle Caroline Mayermax as the instructor for the girls' school.

Mayermax had studied at the Ecole Normale Spéciale and had specialized in mutual education, the most up-to-date teaching method of the day where older pupils acted as instructors for younger ones. The Protectors promised Mlle Mayermax a salary of 1,000 francs, which the Consistory leaders agreed to pay with some misgivings. A short while later the women hired Mlle Flore Dreyfuss as an assistant teacher and the school opened in a cramped space with fifty-two pupils. The Protectors were determined to provide better classroom space and decided to write directly to the Ministry of Religion, which supervised elementary education, to ask for assistance in funding more classrooms. Again the leaders of the Consistory were opposed; this time they wrote to the Women Protectors denouncing their independent letter writing as a cause of embarrassment to the community. The women replied that as they were all mothers of families, they were not accustomed to acting as minors under the supervision of the Consistory. The women had no intention of surrendering control of their accounts or of diminishing their rights to supervise the girls' school. They adopted a curriculum that mirrored the boys' school with the addition of sewing and they refused to allow members of the Consistory to attend their meetings, claiming their womanly modesty as the reason to forbid men from participating in their deliberations.[6]

Despite these controversies, the schools made rapid progress in attracting pupils and in teaching them. School inspectors commented on the excellence of teaching, especially in the girls' school, and noted that the Jewish schools spent more on books, notebooks, and ink than the French elementary schools. Classes were held from 9–12 every morning, and from 1–4 on winter afternoons and 2–5 on summer afternoons. School was open daily except on the Sabbath, on Jewish holidays, and on national holidays. Strict discipline was enforced, with monetary awards given weekly for outstanding performance. At the time that Betty arrived in Paris, the Women Protectors were still supporting their school, but in 1834, they started working under the supervision of the Consistory.[7] The schools continued to flourish, receiving quiet assistance from James and Betty, who were working through intermediaries.

Betty joined one of the remaining women's mutual-aid societies, the Dames Israélites de Paris. This was an unusual mutual-aid society since it used two-thirds of its income for charitable purposes beyond its membership.[8] The other eight women's societies in existence in Paris were funded to assist members in times of difficulty—illness, death, maternity needs. Though mutual-aid societies were discouraged by the Consistory as they tried to develop the capacity of the Charity Bureau, some of them persisted until the end of the century.

In 1842, the Consistory, in its continuing effort to reform its charitable functions, invited thirty leading women of the Parisian Jewish community to form a charitable committee, the Dames Patronnesses. Betty was invited along with the wives of all the leading members of the Consistory. The creation of this committee was the catalyst for Betty to take matters into her own hands.

Identifying the needs of twelve and thirteen-year-old girls as a priority for the new women's committee, Betty launched the Société pour l'établissment des jeunes filles israélites. The members turned their attention to supplemental Jewish education, apprenticeships, mentoring, and funding for the families of the apprentice. The Consistory was supportive of this endeavor in part because it included a commitment to raise funds through a lottery that would support several projects supervised by the Charity Bureau.[9]

Betty, like her grandfather, Mayer Amschel Rothschild, who funded the Philanthropin in Frankfurt forty years earlier to meet the needs of poor children, was determined to break the vicious cycle of ignorance, poverty, early marriage, and too many children born into poverty and ignorance. Reflecting a new sensibility, she focused her work on women and girls. The group of women she gathered around her shared her belief that by improving the conditions of girls, they would create strong and capable mothers who would in turn improve the conditions of Jewish families and of the entire Jewish community. In this belief, Betty presaged the view expressed a few years later by Eugénie Foa in the motto, *En moralisant les femmes on améliore les hommes*. Betty's earlier charitable endeavors were family ventures; this time she moved beyond her family to enlist a larger group of women in the cause of girls and women.

When the Consistory brought women together in 1842, they did not expect them to create their own Société in which women would define problems, design solutions, and raise the funds to pay for their plan of action. They did not realize that French Israelite women had observed the actions of Jewish women in various women's societies, and that they had gained experience in their own mutual aid societies. Many of the women attracted to the new Société had been active in mutual-aid societies, including Mmes Alkan, Cerfberr, Anselme and Gustave Halphen, Aron Marx, M-B Oppenheimer, Anspach, and Mayer Cahen.[10] These women, and the others who came to Betty's house on rue Laffitte to discuss plans for their new Société, were primarily the wives of male leaders of the Central Consistory, the Paris Consistory, the Charity Bureau, and the Portuguese Synagogue. Betty's husband James, on the other hand, still had no official role in any of these organizations. Nevertheless, Betty was recognized as the leader of the group from its first meeting. Her social prominence and energy gave the group visibility in the Jewish community and beyond. Later, James and her children would follow her lead, holding positions of influence in the major Jewish associations of the city.

The twenty-five ladies who gathered for the first full meeting in 1844 shared the middle class belief propagated in women's journals that domestic bliss was dependent on women. Like their Christian sisters, they wanted to move beyond their homes to bring order and values into the homes of the poor. They believed that they could teach young women to run their homes economically, and to guide them to maintain happy families. Since they agreed that happy families were an essential ingredient for the development of future generations of French Israelites, these Jewish women leaders were determined to succeed in their emerging plans to reform Jewish family life by educating future wives and mothers. Remarkably, the organization they formed in the 1840s survived for decades with a continuously expanding membership and a corresponding development of mission. Betty Rothschild remained the leading figure of this group until her death in 1886.

The organization they created, first called Société pour l'établissement des jeunes filles israélites, was briefly renamed, Hachnassat Callah, (literally, escorting the bride) and later Société des dames israélites de Paris. The name changes reflect some alteration in the mission of the group. The first name, which was in use for almost ten years, captures the modern emphasis of the organizers—vocational training for teenage girls. The second, which was in use briefly, reflected the Jewish roots of the philanthropy, whose ultimate objective was to establish stable marriages and families. The third name, Société des dames israélites de Paris, was adopted in the mid-1850s. This inclusive title reflected the fact that several smaller organizations devoted to child care, maternity needs, supervising wayward girls, and the lottery were now working together with the girls' apprenticeship project. The Dames Israélites continued to provide services through the First World War.[11]

The original Société was important for the significant role it played in the lives of poor Jewish young women and their families for more than half a century. It also provided opportunities for wealthy and middle class Jewish women to play significant philanthropic roles in their community. In this Société, Jewish women of Sephardic and Ashkenazic origins worked together. Women whose husbands were competitors in the business and financial world also came together to work for the Société. For Betty de Rothschild, one of the major philanthropists of her generation, the skills learned at the helm of the Société would serve her well for the next half century. It was Betty's personal experience with all the issues of the Société that made it possible for her to fulfill the additional philanthropic roles she undertook in Paris after her husband's death in 1868, when Betty became the executor of his philanthropic estate. The responsibility would have daunted a less competent and less confident woman. Betty had experience in delegating administrative responsibilities dating back to her work with Albert Cohn. Later she hired Mme Fabre to distribute funds to individuals in need.[12]

The guiding principles of the Société remained in place for decades. The organizers pledged to accept any girl who had completed the initiation ceremony, adopted for all graduates of Jewish schools in 1842, and who was prepared to complete an apprenticeship program as well as a course of religious and moral studies. Each young woman was promised supervision by one of the ladies who were members of the Société. Membership dues in the Société was established at five centimes per month or any greater sum, opening the opportunities of membership to a large group of women.[13]

The founding members of the Société numbered about twenty women. They included: Mme Coralie Cahen, vice president and later secretary of the Société, wife of Moïse Cahen, who served as vice president of the Paris Consistory; Mme Isidore, also vice president of the Société, the wife of the Chief Rabbi; Charlotte, Betty's daughter, married to Nathaniel de Rothschild, who was a member from the beginning and ultimately replaced Betty as president in 1886; Mme Mathilde Cohn, Albert Cohn's wife, who replaced her husband as treasurer after his death; and Mmes Anspach, Bloch, Furtado, and O. Halévy, whose husbands were members of the Central Consistory. Mmes Joseph, Gustave, and Leopold Halphen, as well as Mme A. Israel, whose husbands were members of the Paris Consistory, were also present at Betty's home for the first meeting, as well as Mmes. Benoît Cohen, Jeramec, and Oppenheim, whose husbands were officials of the Portuguese Synagogue. Many of these women belonged to the same mutual-aid society as Betty; they had already worked together to make decisions about the distribution of charity.

When the group gathered at rue Laffitte for its first general meeting on March 31, 1844, Betty presided. At her side was Albert Cohn, whom she had hired eight years earlier to tutor her children, and who was now serving the family as advisor on philanthropic matters. Cohn held the title of secretary/treasurer of the organization from its inception until his death in 1877. Cohn was the only man to play a role in the Société; his presence reassured the leadership of the Consistory since he held important positions with the Charity Bureau during those decades as well. Cohn was, in fact, the only man ever permitted to attend meetings of the Société; after his death women assumed the roles of secretary and treasurer.

At the March meeting, Albert Cohn, reported to the assembled group:

Ladies,

In gathering you today for the first time in a general meeting, you probably wonder if the Société you intended to establish follows the path you traced for it, through which it could produce in the future the results you had in mind . . .

Education that develops so many seeds in the mind and heart of young children usually stops early in the [social] class whose progress you wish to protect. You would find few twelve-year-old girls still in school, and almost none older than thirteen; and yet a thirteen-year-old girl's education is not complete, and a young girl at that age cannot be expected to behave according to all the rules of propriety and morality. But necessity screams; hunger is not tolerable. Parents too poor to feed their children try to profit as early as possible from their labor, unlikely to be the most honorable trade.[14]

This report was published in the *Archives Israélites*, demonstrating to the larger Jewish community the purposes of the new Société and its independent structure.

The article set forth the conditions for acceptance into the program and the financial benefits for the families of the girls who participated. Girls were eligible for admission upon completion of their schooling and their religious initiation ceremony. Those who accepted agreed to take a course in religion and morals during their apprenticeship. Another feature of the program included individual mentoring of each girl by a member of the Société who would be responsible for finding a suitable apprenticeship, and would meet periodically with the mistress of the workshop to inquire about the progress and behavior of the particular girl. The Société was able to provide apprenticeships where the girls would be able to observe Jewish holidays and the Sabbath. In addition, to assist the parents of the young apprentice, the family would receive a monthly stipend throughout the training period totaling six francs. Finally, the Société promised to assist the young women in finding appropriate positions when they finished their apprenticeships and to provide a limited number of dowries for those who excelled in their studies and in their work.

Perhaps sensing that the readership of the *Archives Israélites* needed reassurance about the new public roles for women, Cohn pointed out that the plans of the Société were in accord with Jewish religious tradition. Assisting young women to reach happy marriages was recognized as a good deed on a par with charity and study. The ladies, led by Betty, were eager to unite their modern French ideas about family life with their traditional Jewish ones. Their work also reflected the growing acceptance of preventive charity as opposed to the random distribution of funds to the needy; their goal was regeneration, not simply providing alms. Cohn's approval in the *Archives* article gave the Société an endorsement from a prominent community leader.

In the Société's first year of activity, only nine girls requested support, reflecting the community's initial reluctance to allow girls to receive additional education and training. The girls who were accepted were apprenticed to dressmakers, seamstresses, a music copyist, and a boot-stitcher. These artisans, perhaps hired at times by the members of the Société, agreed to allow their apprentices to observe the Sabbath and holidays. The girls were required to continue their education during the year, attending classes in religion and morality. The ladies of the Société wanted the girls to learn how to become good Jewish mothers in addition to learning a vocation. Betty and her committee struggled to find ways to prepare poor Jewish women to become French Israelites fit for a life that would be both productive and observant of Jewish tradition. To encourage the girls to work hard at their apprenticeships and in their studies, as well as to win the approval of the parents of these young women, the Société created two annual 1500 francs prizes to be used for dowries.

Girls who qualified by their good behavior were eligible to participate in the drawing for a dowry. In 1844, only one girl was disqualified from participating in the drawing. The two winners announced in the *Archives* that year were Julie-Joseph, a dressmaker, daughter of Joseph Abraham and Henriette Lion;

and Henriette Salomon, a cap maker, daughter of Samuel Salomon and Eve Enerdinger. Five of the original group of nine continued to be supported as apprentices. In subsequent years more and more parents agreed to allow their daughters to become apprentices.

Albert Cohn's report was also designed to show the larger community the financial independence of the Société. He explained that the total income for the year reached 7,603 francs. This income was primarily from annual membership dues, but also included some additional contributions and some interest income. Expenditures for the year totaled 3,282 francs, with the majority of the funds being spent on the dowries. The Société completed its first year with a balance of 4,321 francs.[15]

Many community members who read the report in 1844 must have been aware that there was no similar apprenticeship program for boys. A program for boys had been tried and abandoned twenty years earlier because of controversy between Reform and Orthodox leaders. Since the Charity Bureau was still convinced that boys should be provided with vocational education and apprenticeships, it responded to the creation of the Société by announcing the creation of the Société des jeunes gens de Paris (Society for the Young Men of Paris) in 1846. This group was modeled on the Société pour l'établissement des jeunes filles Israélites and its first president was Alphonse de Rothschild, Betty's oldest son. The vice president was Dr. Mayer Cahen and the treasurer was Albert Cohn. Betty's son Gustave was also a member. Having many other opportunities to meet, the men did not use this society as a way to socialize as the women did. Nor did they practice one-to-one mentoring relationships with their apprentices. They did, however, provide a library for their apprentices that became a model for its type in Paris.[16]

It is somewhat ironic that societies supporting Jewish apprenticeship developed in the 1840s just as the traditional artisan economy began to decline, slowly replaced by a more industrial one. Nevertheless, apprenticeships continued to play an important role in the modernization strategies of the Jewish leadership. Seeking to provide an improved image of the poor Jew, often vilified as a dirty beggar, these new societies sought to prove that Jewish men and women could take their place in the modern work force and at the same time remain Jewish. Bourgeois Jewish leaders and progressive French civil servants agreed on the importance of teaching the values of productive citizenship to French Israelite youngsters. These leaders believed that French national consciousness and Jewish religious practices could live side by side in harmony. Unable to afford secondary schools, thousands of young people were given the benefit of a subsidized education through apprenticeships. The Société des jeunes filles israélites continued to provide additional classes throughout the remaining decades of the century.

One unanticipated consequence of the creation of the Société was that it also provided meaningful work to several generations of French Israelite women of means. To fund the Société's work, the ladies decided to organize an annual lottery, a device used by French society women to raise funds for Catholic charities. Starting in 1844, annual lotteries were held to benefit the Société and the Charity Bureau. As early as May 1844, the *Archives Israélites* lauded the fundraising efforts of the Société. An article describing the new lottery explained that a group of ladies had come to the aid of the Consistory in its effort to raise additional funds for the destitute.[17] The ladies collected 820 items as prizes, including some spectacular gifts: silk and velvet cushions, splendid baskets and screens, an ebony table, sachets, and dressing gowns. The prizes were donated by the most notable women, including Betty Rothschild, her daughter Charlotte, her mother Caroline, Queen Marie-Amélie, her sister-in-law Mme Adélaïde, and her daughters-in-law the Princesse de Joinville and the Duchesse de Nemours. The ladies sold 10,000 tickets at 1 franc per ticket; several additional donations resulted in a total of 23,000 francs, more money than was ever before raised for the Consistory.

Betty's active involvement was critical to the success of the first lottery. Her personal gifts and the gifts she solicited from her family, including 5,000 francs from her brother Anselm in Frankfurt, and gifts from the royal family, were important to the endeavor. Committees of volunteers led by Betty or her daughter or one of her daughters-in-law sold tickets to the annual lottery through the end of the century. Soliciting prizes, selling tickets, and organizing the display of prizes kept many ladies busy. Elaborate bookkeeping was developed to account for the number of tickets sold by each lady, the lists of donated prizes, the thank you notes to donors, and additional thank you letters to ladies who sold large numbers of tickets. These lists and letters are testimony to the activity of Société members.[18]

In accord with the agreement between Betty de Rothschild and the leaders of the Consistory, a portion of the funds raised always went to the Société des jeunes filles, while the balance went to fill other needs of the Charity Bureau. The Consistory was required to file a request annually with the Ministry of Religion for permission to hold the lottery and to seek a suitable space to hold all the objects for viewing by the general public. The display lasted a week and became a popular attraction for many levels of Parisian society. Each year the number of tickets sold increased and the funds raised grew, propelling Betty de Rothschild to prominence in the Jewish community.[19] Indeed, her association with the lottery was frequently cited as the reason for its success.

This kind of high profile philanthropy was new to the French Israelite community, which was accustomed to charity being given anonymously. James de Rothschild's donations to Jewish charities were handled by an intermediary through mid-nineteenth-century, but by 1850 this practice began to change. One indication of this change was the fact that James agreed to have his name and the names of other family members listed in the annual Jewish almanac, *Annuaire Officiel du Culte Israélite*, as donors in 1856. Ben-Baruch Créhange, the editor, noted that the Charity Bureau had given him permission to list the names of contributors to the Rothschild Hospital and that he would like to be able to list the donors to all the major Jewish institutions in France. While he agreed that keeping the donors anonymous for private gifts was a beautiful idea, he countered that it was important to publicize gifts made for the public good. Good examples, he believed, are a stimulant that should not be minimized. His view on this topic gained ground; every subsequent issue of the *Annuaire* listed donations by name.[20]

The increase in funds realized through the lottery and the steady donations accorded to the Société des jeunes filles israélites were welcome support as the Société continued to attract more and more girls who wished to learn a trade. The May 1846 issue of the *Archives* summarized the April 6th meeting of the Société, presided over by Betty de Rothschild: The activities of the ladies for the past three years had achieved significant results. The first two young women who won dowries were married in 1846 and there were thirty-five girls in apprenticeships, of whom twenty-three were still receiving monthly family allowances, while twelve were now able to meet their own needs. Some additional occupations were added to those previously mentioned: gold embroiderer, porcelain painter, tailor, flower maker, novelty designer, and polisher. Three young women won dowries that year: Jeannette Blum, father deceased, mother a bonnet maker; Fanny Isaac, daughter of Samuel Isaac and Rachel Mayer, seamstress; and Rosalie Mayer, father deceased, mother R. Ganol, no occupation. The *Archives* also reported that some of the earlier beneficiaries eventually joined the Société, able to make modest contribution to the needs of others.[21]

Reflecting on the growing need for funds, Albert Cohn, the treasurer, appealed to the ladies to create an endowment whose interest would be used to meet the needs of the Société. The Rothschild family had previously endowed several funds to benefit the Jewish community. The *Annuaire* of 1856 listed the following Rothschild endowments: The Dames de Rothschild fund provided 3,500 francs annually to provide for the needs of women during childbirth. The Nathalie de Rothschild fund, named for the stillborn first child of Charlotte and Nathaniel, provided 5,100 francs a year to pay for the rent of poor and aged members of the community. The Betty de Rothschild fund provided six savings accounts for children in elementary school, producing 300 francs each year. The Albert de Rothschild fund, named for Charlotte and Nathaniel's son who died at the age of four, provided 3,450 francs annually for clothing for children in orphanages. Finally, the MM de Rothschild Fils fund provided 700 francs a year for the orphanage. The establishment of endowed funds to provide for the Jewish community was not yet a common practice in Paris, but it was a Rothschild tradition carried from Frankfurt.

Reviewing the balance sheet of the Société, it appears that the ladies adopted the recommendation to endow their project. In their third year of existence, the expenditures were 6,620 francs, leaving them with 14,213 francs to carry forward, earning interest income for the following year. The policy of endowing the Société had Betty's support, though it was viewed with concern by some Jewish leaders who were more focused on current needs. Betty, on the other hand, was concerned about community continuity and was determined to ensure support during good years as well as difficult times by having a perma-nent fund in place.

An editor of the *Archives Israélites* disagreed. He cited the needs of a young woman who had been helped by the Israelite Relief and Enhancement Committee, a subcommittee of the Charity Bureau. He reported that as a girl, she was sent to the Consistorial school and later was apprenticed. Her needs were provided for until the moment when, as a worker, she could take care of herself. Now, an appropriate match was found for her. The suitor, knowing her circumstances, only asked for the minimum furnishings of a workingman's humble abode. But the funds needed for the dowry were not available from the Relief and Enhancement Committee. Nor, according to its regulations, could the Société offer funds to this needy young woman who had not been one of their charges. Ultimately, the author revealed, the dowry was provided pri-vately by Baroness de Rothschild, the worthy president of the Société "who is as inexhaustible as her charity."[22] Betty, while leading others towards modern philanthropic methods, was also ready to provide personal support for individ-uals in need.

Betty continued to work tirelessly to bring annual funds to the Société through membership dues and lottery tickets, but she also urged those who could to donate large sums for the endowment. While there are few financial records of the Société extant, it is clear from the number of girls who were assisted during the ensuing decades that she established a sound financial base. Requesting members of different means to contribute at different levels broad-ened the base of membership and permitted friendships to form among Jewish women of varied backgrounds. The Société became a model for similar groups in other French cities; the *Archives* reported the creation of similar groups in Strasbourg, Bordeaux, Metz, and Nancy. "All of the distinguished ladies, all those who are devoted to the public good, have the honor of belonging to this Société. They are inscribed on the list of donors and belong to the group of patronesses who organize with devotion an annual lottery which brings great advantage to the poor among us." [23] Thus, Betty's work was multiplied all over France. Characteristically, she made personal contributions to some of the groups in other cities.

Following the revolution of 1848, in which attempts to address the issue of employment and wages on a broad national scale ultimately failed, the *Archives Israélites* again summarized the successes of Betty's women's group in Paris. On March 24, 1850, the members met in Betty's home to discuss a report by their secretary Albert Cohn. [24] By this time, 133 young women had been aided by the

Société: forty-seven were apprentices, seventeen had received dowries and married, two were married by workers without dowries, one died, three were dismissed from the program, and sixty-three were currently employed in their vocational field. Those working were able to support themselves and aid their families. Albert Cohn added his praise for strict standards maintained by the Société for those permitted to compete in the dowry lottery. "You are not only seeking to help them to marry, but rather to establish families based on honesty and the highest morality with the aim of enriching the community."[25] Of the twenty-nine young women who wished to participate in the lottery in 1850, eleven who did not meet the high standards were eliminated. The two young women selected for dowries were: Mélanie Meyer, father deceased and mother, a brass polisher, and Pauline Créhange, daughter of a dressmaker.

The women reviewed their financial situation in the pages of the *Archives*. Revenue for the previous year included interest (1,125 francs), the lottery (2,554 francs), and membership dues (3,066 francs). Expenditures totaled 6,559 francs. A list of subscribers and their donations was included in the article: the Furtado family donated 210 francs, the Halphens gave 545 francs, and the Rothschilds 660 francs. The Ecole de jeunes filles, the exclusive girls' school directed by Mmes Mayermax, Cerf, Hirz, and Moch, contributed 595 francs; apparently, the leaders of the school collected funds from their privileged pupils to help Jewish girls less fortunate than themselves. Cohn noted that the work of the Société had narrowed the gap between different classes in the Jewish community. He expressed hope that the poor would acknowledge the gifts they have received by the supervision they would give to their children, providing them with the means to become self-sufficient adults. As for the rich, he hoped they would know the happiness that results from intelligent philanthropy.[26]

This Société, created in the waning years of the July Monarchy, continued to exist through the revolutions of 1848, the brief Second Republic, and the two decades of the Second Empire. In 1862 it was renamed Société des Dames Israélites de Paris. The Société survived the Franco-Prussian War and the Paris Commune. It continued to provide support for young women and their families through the beginning of the Third Republic. By creating this Société, Betty did more than provide funds for apprenticeships; she also created the first modern French Jewish women's organization.

By 1862 several additional women's groups had followed in the footsteps of the Société des Dames Israélites de Paris. Mme Joseph Halphen, a member of the Société des Dames, founded the Comité de l'oeuvre des femmes en couches (committee for maternity support). Mme Emile Oulman, also a member of the Société des dames, presided over the Comité des dames de la section de surveillance morale (prison inspection committee). Leonora de Rothschild, Betty's daughter-in-law, presided over the lottery committee in 1862. Two additional women's committees were formed to inspect the two child-care centers supported by the Consistory. Five years later an additional committee to inspect the refuge created for girls in trouble was chaired by Adèle de Rothschild, another daughter-in-law. The work of these committees was disrupted by the Franco-Prussian War of 1870 and by the Paris Commune of the following year.

In 1872, the *Annuaire Israélite* shows a consolidation of all the women's committees into one organization, Société de Patronage des Dames Israélites. Following the disruption of war and revolution, the membership of the organization was reduced to fifty-eight; Betty de Rothschild was selected president of the consolidated group. In the subsequent five years, under her leadership, membership nearly tripled, reaching 149 in 1877. In the *Annuaire* of 1880, the structure of the Dames Israélites is depicted as an umbrella committee with several sub-committees reflecting the scope of women's philanthropy: maternity support; inspection of schools, orphanages, and homes for delinquents; the girls' apprenticeship program.

Betty, now a grand lady of seventy-five, no longer presided over the entire group; she only retained her chairmanship of the apprenticeship committee, formerly the Société pour l'établissement des jeunes filles Israélites. In keeping with the growth of trade school opportunities for girls, this committee funded several girls who excelled in grammar school to go on to the recently established trade school for Jewish girls. By 1883, 1500 young women had benefited from the organization founded by Betty forty years earlier. A report of the activities of the committee prepared in that year noted that several girls had excelled in the trade schools while some had become teachers and assistant teachers. During the six-year period preceding this report, the committee on apprenticeship earned 72,000 francs and expended close to 69,000. Fortunately, the income from the lottery continued to expand as well. In 1870 the lottery raised 75,000 francs, it grew to 100,000 francs in 1878 and by 1881 it reached 125,000 francs.[27]

As noted earlier, Betty was the first French Rothschild to play a leading role in philanthropy. By the 1850s James de Rothschild, who for decades was a behind-the-scenes donor to Jewish charities, stepped forward to join his wife in Jewish philanthropic causes. The Rothschilds, still recovering from attacks suffered by the family in 1848 and wary of the new government, lacked confidence that French schools, prisons, and hospitals would adequately serve the Jewish community. Witnessing a rise of Catholic fervor in response to the secularism imposed by the revolutionary government of 1848, Betty and James decided to put greater efforts into Jewish philanthropy. Their first big joint effort was the founding of a hospital in 1852. The Consistory had long wished to increase its capacity to serve Jewish patients; the donation made by James de Rothschild, for whom the hospital was named, allowed the creation of a modern establishment on land donated by the family at 76–78 rue Picpus. This new structure was both a hospital and a refuge for the elderly; it also included space for orphans. It was known from the time of its inauguration as the Rothschild Hospital.

The inauguration of the hospital was a noteworthy event in the history of the French Rothschilds. While the British Rothschilds had long been associated with the Jewish Free School in London, the French Rothschilds had kept a low profile, with the significant exception of Betty's work with the Société. In recognition of James's financial importance to the state, several dignitaries attended the inaugural celebration: the Minister of Religion, the Prefect of the Seine, the Mayor of Paris, and leading members of the Consistory, including the Chief Rabbi, were in attendance. Speeches were read and a marble bust of James de Rothschild was unveiled. The comments of Moïse Cahen, president of the Consistory, referred to Betty's work and to that of her eldest son, Alphonse:

> There is a lot of misery and hunger for mothers and their babies. A woman, a mother, the Baroness de Rothschild, heard that suffering and established a fund to help mothers in need. Newborn babies will learn to bless her. When the children grow up they will need an education . . . The Rothschild family opened schools and shelters for 600 children. Alphonse de Rothschild is at the head of a trade school. The young girls are under the protection of the Baroness. They are placed in apprenticeship and given a dowry on the day of their marriage . . . Among the innumerable donations of the family to our Charity Bureau are: funds for wood, for unleavened bread, for food distribution, for rent for the indigent.[28]

Albert Cohn, the philanthropic guide for the Rothschild family, also paid special homage to Betty. Addressing James he said, "God by an infinite act of benevolence placed on your side your noble companion, who, with a particular and natural gift, knows how to give with grace, listen with kindness and answer with affability." He continued, addressing Betty directly, "Your house deserves without any doubt the title of first house of Israel . . . and you deserve the title, first lady of the Jewish people of our era."[29]

The Parisian daily *Illustration* carried an entire page celebrating the architecture and modernity of the new hospital and the good deeds of its founding family. The author wrote that the Rothschild family name was associated with every endeavor aiming to assist and morally uplift the needy in Paris, London, Naples, Vienna, and Frankfurt. He pointed out that the sons of Mayer Amschel Rothschild had built a hospital in Frankfurt dedicated to the memory of their father. Nevertheless, the author did not share the views of Betty and James about the need for a hospital to serve French Jews. He restated the views espoused in 1789 by Clermont-Tonnerre: "We must grant rights to Jews as individuals, but refuse them everything as a nation! They must form neither a political body nor an order in the state, they must be citizens individually."[30] In point of fact, the Consistory had developed social services for the Jewish community since its creation in 1808 reflecting the fact that the idealism of revolutionary rhetoric was not immediately carried out in state policy. Nevertheless, the author of the article about the Rothschild Hospital clung to the belief that specialized services for the Jewish population were unnecessary in France:

> We are among those who cheer at the civil and religious emancipation of Jews in France; we are among those who wish for total liberation, the rehabilitation of this unfortunate and resigned race, oppressed and trampled on by barbaric prejudices in the four corners of the world, with total disregard for modern civilization . . .

> We believe that there is something that can effectively help destroy these monstrous prejudices, it is the total and sincere merging of the Jewish race with the greater French family. In our eyes, all the efforts of enlightened Jews should be directed toward that goal . . .

> We believe that the Jewish community would have acted more wisely had it given the care of its sick and elderly over to public welfare, as it is entitled to do . . . [31]

Betty, James, and their children, despite their personal successes in French society, did not share this belief, nor did they wish the "merging of the Jewish race with the greater French family"; they wished to remain French Israelites. Furthermore, they knew that while they were able to secure first-rate medical care, that was not always the case with their poor co-religionists, forced into charity hospitals frequently run by Catholic orders. To protect them and their Jewish heritage, they continued to fund the expansion and modernization of the Rothschild Hospital for many decades.

The hospital building, large for its day, replaced the old house of the Parisian Jewish community with its fifty beds for the sick and a shelter for forty elderly residents; no longer would patients and the elderly have to go to hospitals and shelters where they could not practice their religion. The new facilities were soon too small to shelter the sick and needy who asked to be admitted. In response to additional needs, new funds were provided primarily by the Rothschild family, with general assistance from the rest of the community; new buildings were regularly added.

In 1857, Betty turned her attention to a new orphanage designed to meet the growing needs of Parisian Jewish children whose families were not able to care for them. The new orphanage was made possible by funds designated by Betty's parents, Caroline and Salomon Rothschild, both recently deceased. A beautiful two-story building was built next door to the Consistory schools on rue des Rosiers and connected to them by a spacious courtyard, adorned with busts of the founders. Built in accord with hygienic rules and with care for the comfort of the children to be served, the building accommodated classrooms, dormitories, a kitchen, and bathrooms. The inauguration ceremony was a chance to welcome Leonora, daughter of Charlotte and Lionel

Rothschild and Alphonse's bride, to the French Israelite community. The *L'Univers israélite* reported that when "[Leonora] . . . arrived in Paris, her first visit was not to the splendors of the capital, but for the orphan's house, for the children of the poor . . . The sweet and pious image of the Baroness Salomon de Rothschild seemed to say: 'here is the one who will replace me among you!' "[32]

During the first eight years of its existence, the orphanage admitted eighty children: forty-nine boys and thirty-one girls. These children attended a Jewish nursery school and later primary school. Trade schools and apprenticeships were provided for the older children. The success of the children in learning trades and going into commerce was noteworthy, yet soon the building could not house all of the children in need. In 1869, Betty, recently widowed, decided to build a new orphanage that would accommodate more children. She used money left by her husband to pay for the construction of the new building, which opened in 1874 on land donated by Betty on rue Lamblardie, adjacent to the hospital. Able to house 100 boys and girls, the new orphanage adopted progressive pedagogical techniques and continuing professional education. Betty assumed the presidency of its Inspection Committee. In the Exposition of 1878, the orphanage won a gold medal for skill exhibited in sewing from patterns.[33]

The operational needs of the hospital and the orphanage began to occupy a lot of Betty's attention and time. During James's lifetime, he was president of the hospital and he continued to meet its annual deficits. The *Univers Israélite* lamented in 1861 that members of the Consistory were negligent in supporting the hospital and that the Rothschilds were therefore obliged to keep adding funds.[34] In 1865, special rooms were added for sick children, rooms for nurses and for women in labor, and private accommodations for contagious patients. In 1866 a section of ten beds destined for the terminally ill was added in memory of Betty's son Salomon; two years later thirty-four more beds were added to this section; and in 1877, an adjoining building was inaugurated in memory of both Salomon and James to serve the needs of the incurably ill. In time this building developed into a modern hospice.

Betty and James also funded a nursing home that opened in 1853 with thirty-four beds. Need quickly outgrew availability and in 1868, using funds acquired from James's's will, Betty donated 50,000 francs to enlarge the nursing home. Additional funds were again needed in 1882. By the time of Betty's death, the home served eighty-three people.

Betty's work on all of these facilities and her continuing supervision of their operations called on the skills she had learned during her decades of philanthropic work. Her son Alphonse assumed the presidency of the hospital after James's death. Gustave and Edmond chaired important committees, assuring that the Rothschild facilities would provide the best care for indigent members of the Parisian Jewish community.

While they focused on Paris, the Rothschild family was also engaged in worldwide Jewish philanthropy. At mid-century, building on the model institutions they had created in France, Betty, James, and their children began to direct substantial amounts of their money beyond the French borders. As early as 1842, the French Rothschilds responded to a request for pledges to build a hospital in Jerusalem. Dr. Ludwig Philippson, editor of the *Allgemeine Zeitung des Judentums*, alerted his readers to the misery of the Jews in the Holy Land. He was particularly concerned with the lack of a hospital to care for the largely poor and sick population. The Rothschilds pledged 100,000 francs to build a hospital as well as a modern secular school. The Jewish community of Jerusalem, largely Orthodox and fearful of secular studies, rejected this offer. At the same time, Moses and Judith Montefiore replied to Philippson's appeal by sending Dr. S. Frankel to Jerusalem to set up a pharmacy and to care for patients.

Dr. Frankel, who arrived in Jerusalem early in 1843, became the first Jewish physician in the city. He arrived at a time when missionary activities were on the increase. Caroline Cooper, the financially independent daughter of an English physician, arrived in Jerusalem in 1848 where she joined Elizabeth Finn, wife of the British Consul, in starting a sewing school for Jewish girls. Called the Sarah Society, this school sought to convert their pupils. The following year, the Jewish Hospital was opened on Mount Zion, staffed by Anglican missionaries; it attracted many Jewish patients. In 1849, cholera broke out in the Holy Land, eliciting appeals to establish a hospital supported by the Jewish community in the *Jewish Chronicle*. Moses Montefiore, who was in Jerusalem at the time, carried the appeal of the community back to Paris.

In 1853, Gustave de Rothschild, traveling incognito on behalf of Betty and James, visited Jerusalem in the company of French officers. He reported home that Jews in the city were suffering from poverty and disease, that there was no Jewish hospital in the city, and that Anglican missionaries had seized the initiative to establish a hospital with the aim of converting Jews. He returned with a plan for a hospital provided by a leading member of the Ashkenazic community. Though Montefiore had proposed establishing a hospital using a bequest left by Joseph Truro of New Orleans, Betty and James decided not to wait until his plans could be put into motion.

Albert Cohn was sent as an emissary of the French Rothschilds to Jerusalem in 1854, carrying 50,000 francs to turn a long held dream into a reality. Cohn stopped en route in Austria, where he sought Austrian protection for his venture. In Jerusalem, acting on instructions from Betty and James, he paid 20,000 francs for a house which had been previously used as a school by the Sephardic Community. Assisted by Michel Erlanger, who came with Cohn from Paris, Cohn set up eighteen beds, nine for men and nine for women. One room became the pharmacy, another a synagogue, a third became the kitchen. On the lintel above the door to each room was a Hebrew sign indicating the function of the room. At the foot of each bed was a plaque with the name of a member of the Rothschild family or the Montefiore family. One plaque carried the name of Mathilde Cohn, Albert's wife and Betty's friend. The synagogue was large enough to accommodate patients, staff and others living in the neighborhood. Above the entrance to the building was a sign in Hebrew and French: Rothschild Hospital.[35]

Following the instructions of Betty and James, Cohn also established a broad range of philanthropic endeavors aimed at improving the conditions of Jews in Jerusalem. He started a fund for interest-free loans using 25,000 francs sent by Amschel Mayer Rothschild in Frankfurt. In addition, Betty contributed funds to establish a maternity program to provide medical help and financial support for new mothers and babies. The annual report for this fund was published by the *Archives Israélites*. The project supported 120 women each year. Betty's sons also established a fund, which provided occupational training and continuing education for forty youngsters. Betty's cousin Charlotte established a school for girls, carrying the name of her recently deceased daughter, Evelina de Rothschild. The school taught both secular and religious subjects as well as handiwork. Three hundred students enrolled the first year. Cohn also established a fund to distribute bread to the poor of Jerusalem.

Montefiore believed that Betty was the moving force behind the Rothschild endeavors in Palestine.[36] It was on her instructions that the hospital was named for Mayer Amschel Rothschild, the founder of the family. The dedication, attended by rabbis and other community leaders as well as the Austrian Consul Pizzamano, the English Consul Finn, the Prussian Consul George von Rosen, and the representative of the French Consul Lequin, took place on July 26, 1854. In 1856, following a second trip to Jerusalem by Cohn, this time accompanied by Alphonse de Rothschild, James donated an additional 280,000 francs for the hospital's expansion and upkeep.[37]

The staff of the hospital included a doctor, a surgeon, two pharmacists, one or two assistants, and a bookkeeper. The first doctor was Dr. Bernhard Neumann, who had resided in Jerusalem for several years before the opening of the hospital. Equipment and medicine were ordered from Paris. The daily menu of the patients was soup, meat, rice, bread, chicken, fruit, eggs and milk. The hospital library included books in Hebrew and several European languages. During the first decade of operation, between 560 and 712 patients were admitted yearly. Malaria, inflammation of the eyes, and dysentery were the most common ailments. The budget in the early years was 14,500 francs: a third for salaries, a third for operations, a third for medicine. Patients were treated in the hospital gratis. Three times a week the doctor received outpatients, regardless of religion or ethnicity, and dispensed free medicine. Home visits were charged a fee, but it was waived for those unable to pay.

In 1862, Dr. Neumann, who had developed eye troubles, left Jerusalem. Dr. Benjamin Rotseigal replaced him, but he succumbed to cholera along with 800 members of the community in 1865. Dr. Benjamin London from Vienna came to Jerusalem to replace Rotseigal. He not only supervised the hospital, but during his tenure, he was also responsible for the other Rothschild philanthropic activities in Jerusalem.

The Evelina de Rothschild School was expanded during this period. Originally, the school taught only reading, writing, arithmetic, prayers, and arts and crafts. In 1870, additional subjects were added and the language of instruction changed to French. During the 1870s, 240 pupils studied in this school. Dr. London established a prize for girls who stayed in school three years and reached the age of sixteen before marrying.

In 1875 Dr. Yitzchak Schwartz replaced Dr. London. Schwartz wrote to Alphonse de Rothschild recommending that a new hospital be built outside the walls of the Old City. Alphonse agreed; land was bought and a foundation stone laid in 1887. The building on Rehov ha-Neviim was one of the biggest and most beautiful of its day. The sign above the entrance read: "Mayer Rothschild Hospital" in Hebrew, French and Arabic.

While continuing to make contributions to fulfill Jewish needs in Palestine, Betty and her family also sent funds to Algeria, which had become part of France, to assist Jews there, whose needs for education, vocational training, hospitals and synagogues were pressing. Betty's growing philanthropic activities clearly necessitated clerical and accounting assistance. From the few extant records it is clear that she began to employ women and men to support her in these endeavors.[38]

The prodigious philanthropy of the Rothschild family was the subject of commentary in the press. The *Univers Israélite* reprinted an excerpt from "Letters of a Good Young Man," which appeared in the popular *Le Figaro* on December 28, 1856. The author explained that Baron James deducted a tenth of his annual income to donate to the poor. To meet the demands for funds he set up a special office where a staff of assistants open and file letters according to the type of request. One file is labeled 'red face' since the petitioners all start with, "It is with red face that . . ." Another file is labeled, 'honest bankruptcies.' A third is 'suicides,' referring to the letters that commence, "by the time you read this letter I will be no more." A fourth is from pregnant women soliciting layettes. The readers of *Le Figaro* also found out that Mme de Rothschild always answers the requests from pregnant women and a great deal of the others as well.

The annual donation of the Rothschilds to support Parisian Jews grew from an estimated 27,000 francs in 1850, to 65,000 in 1858, and reached 300,000 francs at the end of Betty's life.[39] Betty's personal involvement can be gleaned from account books detailing her expenditures in 1872 and beyond. Though the records are fragmentary, the purpose of these books was to allow Betty to reconcile her expenditures with her annual income. There were apparently separate accounts for regular household expenditures, for gifts, and for donations. The most complete record is for 1872, though only a summary for the months of January through June remain.[40]

Betty donated 30,764 francs through her assistant Mme Fabre in the first six months of 1872. During the same period, she donated funds for the construction of the orphanage that would open in 1874. She donated 47,000 francs to this project during the first half of 1872 and contributed 1,000 francs to the Orphanage de la Seine as well. Betty also continued to support the lottery, buying 800 francs worth of tickets in April and 11,800 francs worth in May. She made separate contributions of 881 francs through Dr. Cohn to support the family's work in Jerusalem, as well as 1,271 francs to aid the Jews of Smyrna, and 500 for the Jews of Poland. Additionally, Betty continued to fund the Rothschild Hospital in Paris, giving 1000 francs in May. She donated 2,000 francs on the anniversary of her son Salomon's death. Mme Ratisbonne, a member of Betty's Société, received 1,000 francs in April to help a poor person, and M. Bara received 225 francs per month for assisting the poor. Betty sent 949 francs to support the Stern family of Frankfurt and also gave 3,000 francs to the Fondation de l'institution des jeunes filles. During this six-month period she donated a total of 102,965 francs.

Though the vast majority of Betty's correspondence with individuals seeking financial support and other assistance has been lost, Betty's personal involvement with those she supported can be gleaned from a series of letters involving the troubles of Esther Schweitzer. The first letter, dated December 21, 1879, was addressed: "Chère Madame la Baronne" and signed "votre protégée." In it, Esther recounted how Betty listened patiently to her story on a visit to Boulogne and how she had shared the suffering of the young woman. The cause of the distress was a 400,000 francs debt incurred by Esther's husband Albert, who had bought wheat futures for clients; the investment proved very lucrative, but Albert was cheated by the sellers and as a result, he owed his clients a vast sum of money. Esther wrote plaintively, "I can't decide what to do and need your advice, ma chère protectrice." Esther concluded the letter with reference to her little girl, Josa, who wore a medallion given her by Betty, "may it be a talisman that protects her."[41]

Six weeks later, on February 8, 1880, Esther again wrote to Betty, informing her that all the creditors but one had agreed to wait for payment. Esther asked Betty to intervene with Michel Ephrussi and ask him to also wait for payment. Betty's reply was written three days later from Cannes. She did not respond directly to Esther; she wrote instead to her assistant Jodkowitz with instructions to invite Esther to come to the house in order to inform her that it is impossible for Betty to do as she asks. "Tell her to finish with the creditors as best she can and urge her to convince her husband to find a salaried position."[42] Betty concluded her letter by noting that she regrets not being able to help the interesting and courageous Mme Schweitzer.

A few months later, on September 1, 1880, Mme Schweitzer again wrote to Betty who was in Paris. She sent her greetings for the Jewish New Year and says that she had hoped to be allowed to pay a visit during the previous few months.

She wanted to be able to show Betty how her little girl, Josa, had grown. Esther concluded, "I await your summons."

One week later, having apparently received no reply, Esther wrote to Jodkowitz asking for leave to visit Betty and to bring her daughter. Albert was in Italy searching for business prospects. Esther offered to send him to meet with Jodkowitz in a few days so that he could report on business details from the beginning of the year. Three weeks later, apparently having received no invitation to visit Betty, Esther wrote again to Jodkowitz:

> I think now that we may not have to become expatriates since business is beginning to pick up slowly. I was thinking of taking the family, including two small children, to Trinidad. In either event, whether we go or stay, we'll need some help. I hesitate to write to the Baronne as she is ailing and I don't wish to distress her.[43]

The following week, on September 29, Esther asked Jodkowitz to request 3,000 francs from the Baronne to help the family meet their bills until the end of the year. She reported that business affairs in the U.S. were improving and that her husband had made some small commissions. A week later, Esther thanked Jodkowitz for having facilitated the needed assistance. She reported that Albert would visit him the following day.

On December 24, 1880, the correspondence resumed. This time Esther wrote to Betty, who was once more in Cannes, to report that her husband had definitively given up the grain trade and she requested that Betty have Jodkowitz recommend Albert for a position at a bank in Paris or Vienna. She concluded the letter, "protect me in my distress."[44]

The final letter in this series was from Betty to Jodkowitz, dated December 30, 1880. Betty noted that she was attaching a letter from Mme Schweitzer. She reminded Jodkowitz that last spring, when Esther told Betty that Albert had been offered a job working for Reinach for 10,000 francs, she urged him to take the offer. Regrettably, he did not. Betty again instructed Jodkowitz to ask Esther to call on him, and to tell her that Betty cannot guide her with regard to resettling in Vienna, that only Albert's parents, who live in Vienna, can provide that kind of assistance. Betty concluded, "If she decides to go, I authorize you to give her some thousand franc notes to help her."[45]

This letter to Jodkowitz continued with reference to a second letter enclosed, this one from a physician who had been ill for several months and had not paid his rent and faced eviction. He asked for 450 francs. Betty instructed Jodkowitz to reply on her behalf, explaining that she is in Cannes and cannot reply to his needs from a distance. She further instructed him to meet with the physician and to take care of his problem.

The last item in Betty's account book is dated October 1886. The entry is for 1,365 francs to pay for a curtain to cover the Torah scrolls in Temple Israelite in Nice, near the new home she had constructed in Cannes. Betty died one month before the item was posted. She died as she had lived: a devoted French Israelite. As such, she contributed to her community, to the poor of France, and to Jews in need throughout the world.

 CHAPTER SIX

Betty in War and Peace

*Paris is really extraordinary! This population, keen to know everything, is not com-
municating and yields to a great silence; these inquisitive people accept learning nothing and survive on what's at hand; these gourmands live off horses, and eat donkeys,
elephants, cockatoos, rats, dogs and put ostein from animal bones in their sauces . . .
these sybarites have become national guardsmen; these fops have become soldiers and
live in the mud and cold at the ramparts and in the trenches; these night owls go to
bed at nine o'clock, and walk around with lanterns because the city is no longer lit
up, thanks to the lack of charcoal; these pleasure mavens content themselves with
boredom; these merchants can no longer show off their merchandise, no longer make
sales or export anything . . . It is wonderful!*

Juliette Adam, Mes Illusions et mes souffrances pendant le siège de Paris

*One day the old Baronne James de Rothschild called on me at La Jonchère. Her
patriotism refused to entertain the idea of anything but a French victory. I ventured
to suggest that perhaps it might be well to prepare for an occasional reverse, but she
scouted the mere idea of such a possibility. 'France will beat Prussia and will be victorious all along the line,' she declared indignantly.*

Pauline Metternich, My Years in Paris

In March 1866, Betty learned that Marie-Amélie to whom she had been a loyal
friend and subject for four decades had died. She wrote to the Duc d'Aumale, the
new head of the Orleans family, expressing her profound sorrow: "My soul is so
troubled by the death of our beloved and saintly queen that I cannot find strength
to be resigned. I hope that divine goodness will help you Monseigneur to soothe
the blow, so big and deep, that struck you."[1] A few months later, in June, Betty
again wrote to Aumale to console him; this time it was for the loss of his son,

Louis Prince de Condé. The young man died of typhoid fever while traveling in the Far East. Betty, still greatly pained by the loss of her own son Salomon two years earlier, wrote: "Only a few months ago you experienced the most saintly pain; today your noble heart is ripped by the biggest, the most intense grief that God could have sent you. Nobody more than I can understand the despair of the parent who cries for a son so tenderly loved, nobody can share with more sympathy your immense pain."[2]

Finally, in December 1869, a year after Betty's husband of forty-four years died, Betty wrote once more to the grieving Aumale. This time the occasion was the death of his wife: "It happens, sadly, very often in life to endure a phase of pain where all the attachments of the heart seem to break one by one and those cherished beings, those we have loved the most, leave us." A month later, Aumale sent Betty a token of the friendship between the two families. Betty sent a note to thank him: "It is with deep tenderness that I received the precious souvenir that your royal highness deigned to offer me in memory of Madame the Duchesse d'Aumale. This ring, inscribed with such a touching legend, has already its own place among the pious relics of my heart, and it will remain for me an eternal and vibrant souvenir of the deceased who wore it, and of her exquisite kindness."[3]

Though Betty suffered many losses in the late sixties, she did not remove herself from the social life of the capital for long; she maintained an active schedule, giving balls and attending a wide array of events. She enjoyed taking fashionable rides in the Bois de Boulogne, seeing the social leaders of Paris and being seen. On one occasion when Betty was escorting one of her young Frankfurt nieces in her carriage, the Emperor passed in his carriage and graciously saluted the women. Betty was so nearsighted that she was unable to recognize the Emperor; she searched for her *lorgnon*, but was not able to find it in time. In a show of general affability, Betty assumed that the gentleman was a friend and called out "*Bonjour! bonjour! bonjour!*" as she would have greeted any young friend. When she finally retrieved her *lorgnon*, she was so mortified by her breach in etiquette that she retired to her room for days.[4]

A brief review of Betty's correspondence from this period illustrates her continuing sociability. Charles Garnier, director of the Paris Opera, wrote to thank Betty for the sample of drape "that seduced him in her Arabian nights' palace."[5] His letter commented on her gracious qualities as a hostess and took note of the marvelous works of art exhibited in her home; most of all, Garnier and his friends were charmed by the *baronne*'s good nature and by the ease with which she entertained her friends' requests.[6]

As was her custom, Betty continued to attend sessions of the Académie Française, asking friends like the Baron de Viel Castel to help her secure tickets to the open sessions. At the sessions of the Académie, Betty sometimes enjoyed the company of Princesse Mathilde, the Emperor's sister and a leader of cultural and artistic Paris. The Princesse, who was also a friend of Alphonse and Laurie, praised Betty for the wonderful evenings she organized at rue Laffitte.[7]

Though Betty had lived in Paris since her marriage in 1824 and had close connections at the highest levels of society, she was not a French citizen. Having left Frankfurt at a time when Jews were not accorded citizenship, she was not a citizen of any country. She remained an Austrian baroness by virtue of her late husband's appointment. By July 1870, Betty's immediate family (Charlotte and her two grown sons, James Edouard and Arthur; Alphonse and his children Bettina, Beatrice, and baby Edouard; Gustave and his children Zoé, Aline, and newborn Bertha; and Salomon's daughter Hélène) had all become French citizens. Betty was the only member of the French Rothschild family without official status in France. Nevertheless, she thought of herself as French; as the talk of war with Prussia reached a crescendo during the late spring of 1870, she elected to remain in Paris during the crisis.

Laurie and Alphonse were visiting family in Frankfurt in early July. They hurried home to Paris when it became clear that war was near. Trains were already being stopped by the military as they made their way back to France. On July 15th at Kehl, near Strasbourg, the border station was closed. Alphonse and Laurie proceeded in a horse drawn carriage past troop trains full of exuberant Prussian soldiers going westward. Laurie was convinced that they were all drunk. Upon arriving home, Laurie voiced her feelings and probably those of the French Rothschilds in a letter to her mother in London:

> I need not tell you how sad and disgusted we are and in fact all reasonable people must be at the prospect of war. Our mad Empress was I am afraid greatly in favor of it. She sends her only son, who is only fourteen, to see all the butchery with the Emperor. You know how enthusiastic French people are about military glory.[8]

Laurie, fearing for the safety of her children, left for London. In a re-enactment of Betty's voyage of 1848, Laurie gathered up her three children and boarded a packet to the Isle of Wight, from which they crossed the Solent to Southampton and took a train to London. Alphonse remained in Paris.

On August 7, 1870, the Empress returned to the Tuileries from her chateau in St. Cloud and issued the following proclamation:

> Frenchmen: The beginning of the war has not been favorable to us; we have been repulsed. Be firm in this reverse, and let us make haste to repair our loss. Let there be one party among us, that of France; one flag, that of national honor. I come into your midst, faithful to my mission and to my duty. You will see me first in danger, ready to defend the flag of France. I adjure all good citizens to maintain order. To produce disturbance will be to conspire with our enemies.

> The Empress Regent. Eugénie.[9]

Betty and her children responded to the war effort with patriotic zeal. Alphonse resigned his post as consul for the North German Confederation. He and his brothers subscribed for fifty million francs of the August war loan. Edmond and James-Edouard served in the Garde Mobile, while Alphonse guarded the ramparts of the city on the eve of the Prussian siege. On August 12, 1870, Betty addressed a letter to the Minister of War placing her estate at Boulogne-sur-Seine at his service for treating the war wounded; she also allowed a twenty-bed hospital to be erected on the grounds. Later she permitted the wounded to be treated in the courtyard of her home on rue Laffitte. Meanwhile, surrounded by the English Rothschilds, Laurie remained in London throughout the month of August, reading of one Prussian victory after another.

On August 18th, General Trochu entered Paris to govern the city for the duration of the war. Echoing the concerns of the Empress, Trochu called on Parisians of all parties to restrain the overzealous, and he cautioned against outlaws who saw in public calamity opportunities to satisfy their "detestable propensities." A law was issued ordering all those of German nationality to leave France. An estimated 30,000 Germans resided in Paris. An American physician, Dr. Robert Sibbet, reported that gendarmes went from street to street in the latter part of the month to round up the "hated Teutons" and send them off to the railway stations.[10] At the same time, a Soldiers' Aid Society was organized and several hundred thousand francs were collected to help care for the wounded and sick. Sibbet noted that the Sisters of Charity and women of eminence in the capital took the lead in this work.[11]

While some Parisian women focused on aiding the wounded, others assisted Empress Eugénie. The Duchess of Malakoff and Mme Pollet, both close to Eugénie, gathered the crown jewels, wrapped them in newspaper, stowed them in a cardboard box, and delivered them to Pauline Metternich, wife of the Austrian Ambassador and friend of Eugénie. Fearing the worst, they asked her to find a way to send the jewels to London. A few days later the Count de Montgelas deposited the jewels in the Bank of England. Pauline Metternich soon joined the women heading to London.[12]

On September 2nd, Laurie, still in London, read about the defeat of the Emperor at Sedan. Her cousin Constance de Rothschild wrote in her diary that Laurie's face was red with tears. She felt humiliated for the defeat of her adopted country; she also feared that after the defeat of the Empire radical forces would take over France. Constance observed, "She was dark crimson with excitement and her voice trembled so that she could hardly speak. After a few minutes her children came screaming and shouting into the room. They were allowed to make a fearful noise."[13]

On September 4th, the Empress Eugénie, aided by Prince Richard Metternich, escaped to England. A few days later Pauline Metternich arrived in London carrying a gift for the exiled Empress: the *Book of Hours* that had once belonged to Marie-Antoinette, given to her by her mother the Austrian

Empress Maria-Theresa. This small volume, overlooked by Eugénie as she fled the palace, was retrieved by Richard Metternich. He saved it from the revolutionaries and sent it to his wife to return to the Empress.[14]

The Republic was declared at the Hôtel de Ville on the same day. General Trochu was selected President and Commander-in-Chief while Jules Favre was selected Vice President and Minister of Foreign Affairs. Paris became a military camp. All business stopped except for the defense of the city. The sound of the bugle, the roll of the drum, and the tramp of soldiers were heard from early morning until late at night as troops marched back and forth through the city. The word "Imperial" was removed from the front of theatres, opera houses, museums, and libraries, and replaced with "National." Valuable collections in the numerous art museums were boxed up, shipped off, buried, or hidden in the catacombs under the city. At the same time, everything that could be useful during a siege was brought into the city: grain, hay, straw, wood, charcoal, peat, vegetables, farming tools, cattle, milk cows, sheep, swine, and fowl poured into every open space. The braying of donkeys, the lowing of cattle, and the bleating of sheep became familiar sounds in Paris.[15]

On September 18th the last railroad line was taken and the last telegraph line was cut; Paris was now cut off from the rest of France. Like Betty, the painter Berthe Morisot decided to stay in Paris. In a letter dated September 18th to her sister Edma she explained her decision to stay in Paris:

> I have made up my mind to stay, because neither father nor mother told me firmly to leave; they want me to leave in the way anyone wants anything— weakly, and by fits and starts. For my own part I would much rather not leave them, not because I believe that there is any real danger, but because my place is with them, and if by ill luck anything did happen, I should have eternal remorse . . . I have heard so much about the perils ahead that I have had nightmares for several nights, in which I lived through all the horrors of war. To tell the truth, I do not believe all these things. I feel perfectly calm, and I have the firm conviction that everything will come out better than expected . . . I am stupefied by this silence. I certainly wish I had news of you—though I dare not hope for an answer to this letter—and of poor Tiburce, from whom we still have not heard.[16]

This evocative letter from Berthe Morisot to Edma, living in the countryside of Mirand, sheds light on similar issues facing Betty and her family during the siege of Paris. Berthe's concern for her brother Tiburce, who was in the Guard, mirrored Betty's concern for her sons and grandson who were also in uniform. While Laurie and her children were in London for several months, it is unclear where Cécile and her children were staying. Since Cécile gave birth in July 1870, it is possible that she remained in Paris or Boulogne with her children during the siege. Betty's concern for those members of her family who did not leave Paris contributed to her desire to stay in the city. Betty shared Berthe's sentiment that "everything will come out better than expected." Unlike Berthe, Betty was able to assist others by providing medical attention to soldiers and to citizens in need. She was also increasingly conscious of her loyalty to Paris, the city that had been her home since 1824.

Betty may have thought about taking refuge in Ferrières, but the Prussian high command soon commandeered her fabled chateau. On September 19th, King Wilhelm moved into the private apartment of Alphonse de Rothschild, Count Bismarck took over the suite previously used by Baron James, and Field Marshal von Moltke took over Betty's suite. The King brought his own cooks and the estate was forced to supply fruit, vegetables, and flowers; however, Wilhelm ordered that the antiques and art treasures were not to be touched. Over three thousand men and twelve hundred horses were quartered on the grounds. Though the King and his immediate entourage soon moved to Versailles, the troops remained at Ferrières until August 1871.[17]

At the end of September 1870, the Rothschild Hospital put 100 beds at the service of the military. This unit was referred to as an "ambulance," a word used to indicate a hospital ward as well as a temporary unit set up in a private home to care for the sick and wounded.[18] Little is known about the two ambulances set up in Betty's courtyard at rue Laffitte and another in her country residence at Boulogne, but the work of the Rothschild Hospital ambulance is well documented. The building in which this ambulance was placed was new, having been constructed by Betty the previous year to function as a hospice for the elderly, but had not yet been occupied. The ground floor had six large rooms housing fifty beds; the first and second floors each had twenty-five beds in twenty-five private rooms. As a result, it was possible to keep patients with severe wounds as well as those with contagious diseases in isolation from the others.

During the long and frigid winter of 1870–71, despite the difficulty of securing fuel in the city, the Rothschild Hospital ambulance was warm and ventilation was adequate. But food was in short supply everywhere in the city; by the end of December, horsemeat, long a staple, was being replaced with chocolate, wine, and coffee from the Rothschild cellars. Fresh and dried fruit and vegetables remained available at the Rothschild Hospital long after it ceased to appear elsewhere in the city. The Hospital admitted a total of 482 soldiers and 50 national guardsmen from October through January. The biggest health problem was typhoid fever. Fifty-six wounded soldiers were treated; ten died of their wounds, eight from infection and two from tetanus.[19] Commenting on the generosity of Betty de Rothschild in offering the use of the Rothschild Hospital for soldiers, the journalist Maxime du Camp wrote: "Israel flew the Red Cross flag and didn't spare its energies."[20] He added that James's widow contributed large sums to help workers pay their rent during the cold winter of 1870–71.

On September 25th Berthe Morisot wrote to her sister again:

> We write to you every day hoping that out of all of these letters some will reach you, but we have nothing new to tell you. The victory of Friday has raised the morale of many. Would you believe that I am becoming accustomed to the sound of the cannon? It seems to me that I am absolutely inured to war and capable of enduring anything.[21]

Mme Morisot, Berthe's mother, also sent letters to Edma. On October 18th she wrote:

> Each day we hear the cannonading—and a great deal of it. All the fighting is taking place near us—so far without any important results. It is impossible to keep still; Berthe and I got as wet as water spaniels when we went to see where the fighting was taking place, and we almost fainted when we saw a body on a stretcher, the victim of a fire near the viaduct. There are often disasters of this kind. For instance, two chemical plants across the river blew up only a short time ago.[22]

Like the Morisots, Betty adjusted to the steady boom of the cannons and to seeing the wounded and dying near her home. She was not alone in offering assistance to victims of the Germans; 243 ambulances were installed in private residences in Paris by mid-November. Women of all classes, dressed in black with white aprons and the Geneva armlet, made their way through the battle-weary troops, carrying cups of warm soup or steaming chocolate. The government estimated that there was still sufficient food in the capital to hold out an additional 105 days.[23]

On December 15th Mme Morisot described the situation as follows:

> We see no reason why this should end; Paris will not yield as long as it is possible to hold out. The people are beginning to suffer, but are so courageous, and those who advocate capitulation are but a small minority. The general opinion is that we could indeed go on in this way for another two months.[24]

But December was a cruel month for Parisians. While those with enough money bought elephant and camel meat, recently taken from the zoo, to celebrate Christmas, others were forced to rely on the more meager rations of the soup kitchens established in each *arrondissement* of the city. It was estimated that 500,000 people, 25% of the population, were relying on food provided by the government to survive. In addition to the abnormally cold winter, Parisians faced a sharp rise in communicable diseases. Close to 500 Parisians a week died from smallpox, bronchitis, pneumonia, and typhoid fever. On December 23, 1870, Alphonse de Rothschild sent a letter to the mayor of Paris:

In view of the cold of the season, so severe and persistent, we have thought that the best way to aid those needing assistance would be by a distribution of warm clothing. I have consequently the honor of addressing you, as much in my own as in the name of my brothers and my nephew James Nathaniel Rothschild, concerning goods to the amount of 200,000 francs, which we gladly offer for the use of men, women and children. We beg you to kindly distribute these among the people of the twenty wards of Paris, in proportion to the number of persons needing assistance through the bureaus of charity in each ward.[25]

A few days later, in early January 1871, Betty organized a sale to benefit a group of women workers, the Oeuvre de Travail des femmes, at the railway station built by her late husband. Juliette Adam, a journalist who worked to raise money for women workers, commented on Betty's talent for philanthropic endeavors. "Her goodness and her generosity," Adam emphasized, "was immense even taking into consideration her vast fortune."[26] Shells were falling in the frigid city, the streets were covered with ice, and there were almost no vehicles in the street. Outside the railway station of the Chemin de Fer du Nord, homes were being destroyed and people were escaping from the ruins. The poor carried with them, through the deep snow, their children and their bedding. They crowded into the basement rooms of theatres, churches, and other public buildings. Nevertheless, Mme de Rothschild sold food on the 5th of January at fabulous prices to help needy women workers. A piece of sausage sold for twenty-five francs; a tiny terrine of foie gras raised 100 francs. Adam was thrilled that the boutique run by Betty de Rothschild realized thousands of francs for needy women workers. She concluded her thoughts about Betty with this observation: "Patriotism and charity efface rank, caste, prejudice, religion, political views, education, fortune and habits."[27]

Betty's continuing efforts to serve others is remarkable in the face of the disaster surrounding her. The noise of the bombardment and the poor diet took their toll on many, including Mme Morisot. She wrote to her daughter on January 8th:

We celebrated the birth of the New Year in sadness and tears. Berthe's health is visibly affected . . . The bombardment never stops. It is a sound that reverberates in your head night and day; it would make you feverish if you were not already in that state . . . Yet the bombs do not do much harm—all told there are not that many dead and but few wounded, and so far there is little destruction . . . Paris does not lose courage. I find it superb, and yet what suffering, what dire need. It is heart-rending.[28]

Eventually, even Betty began to despair. A letter to her English cousins from January noted that provisions were running out and that it would be almost criminal to expect the population to continue the struggle, which the whole nation had borne so courageously. She ended her letter with the hope that a brighter future awaited France.[29]

While the Parisians suffered hunger and cold, the Germans were stage-managing a dazzling ceremony at the Hall of Mirrors at Versailles to pay homage to Kaiser Wilhelm, invested as Emperor of Germany on January 18th. German dukes and princes assembled to glory in what was soon to be a German victory. An armistice was signed ten days later, and the siege of Paris was lifted on January 28th. It had continued for four months and twelve days, and the bombardment of the city lasted a full month. Since the 15th of January the ration of bread had been reduced to 300 grams a day and the ration of horse-meat since the 15th of December was only 30 grams a day. The mortality rate had more than tripled in the city. The French agreed to hold an election so that new leaders could negotiate the terms of surrender. During the next weeks, as election returns came in from the provinces, the mortality rate increased dramatically in Paris. Adolphe Thiers was elected President, and he went immediately to Versailles to meet with Bismarck.

The French Rothschilds shared some of the privations of their fellow Parisians, but when the siege lifted, their hunger was relieved with provisions sent by their English cousins. In January, Betty wrote to her cousin Charlotte thanking her for sending the most precious and delicious presents:

> Blessed by your loving hand that is offering us these gifts in such rich abundance and affording us the long-missed joy of feeding so many hungry friends and distributing to the hungry the last, long-stored rest of our provisions without exposing ourselves to starvation. Your sensitive heart thinks of all motherly concerns, of all needs of weakened stomachs and constitutions, and young and old find refreshment and nourishment in your hands . . . Mr. Bird, the gracious messenger of one of your shipments, will give you, dear friend, the best news about all of us. He personally occupied himself with the distribution of the food so magnanimously sent for our hungry population, and he can convey the deep impression he conceived looking a the suffering yet dignified poor.[30]

A few days later Betty again thanked Charlotte, confiding that her empathy for the French family and her baskets of food lifted Betty's spirits and brought solace to her heart. Alphonse added, "we fell like children on all the excellent things you sent us."[31] Betty thanked Charlotte for allowing the French Rothschilds to feed hungry friends and to distribute food to the needy.

On February 6th Betty wrote to Laurie, still in London:

> My beloved jewel,
>
> A few days ago I wrote you a long letter in response to the one so tender and so charming that you sent me on January 12: but I am told that the post

office is less reliable at this moment than the balloons because the Prussians want to let us experience the humiliation of our defeat, and therefore, even unsealed our letters are not sent from Versailles. I take advantage, in a hurry, of a messenger sent to Brussels, to entrust him with these tender thoughts for you, my beloved little Laurie, thanking you again for the so tender expressions of your heart. We are at this moment in the feverish period of elections in which our dear Alphonse found himself on almost all lists, even on those whose colors he does not like. But it is an irrefutable proof of his popularity and the appreciation of his character and mind, so we have to be flattered by such honorable and unanimous testimony. I regret that he could not accept the deputy mandate because our future Assembly will need good heads to counterbalance the bad ones. Bye, my dearest Angel, infinite tenderness to the little herd.[32]

As Betty's letter indicates Alphonse had been listed as a candidate for the National Assembly, but he did not accept the mandate. Alphonse, a Regent of the Bank of France and the head of Rothschild Frères, preferred to serve his country by negotiating with Bismarck for a lower indemnity. Betty's letter echoed the anger felt by many Parisians humiliated by the Germans. When the German Army took its victory march through Paris, Parisians stayed behind their shuttered windows and waited for the enemy to leave their city.

Shortly thereafter Betty wrote to Alphonse, who had joined his family in Boulogne. Betty inquired about the health of her grandson James, who had suffered a serious accident. She was happy that Alphonse was away from the horrible cannonading of Paris and hoped that he would be able to spend more time with his dear family, recently returned to France, and that the happiness he found with them will allow him to recuperate. Ever attentive to natural beauty, she added that she hopes that the change of air and scenery of Boulogne would calm Alphonse's nerves and fortify his soul.[33]

Alphonse went from Boulogne to Versailles where he successfully negotiated a reduction of the war indemnity from six to five billion francs. Betty was very proud of Alphonse's achievement. While the negotiations proceeded in Versailles, Paris continued to suffer from a shortage of food, continued cold weather, and growing armed conflict between those who supported the Commune and those who supported Thiers. The Morisot family left Paris for Versailles during these weeks.

On March 18th the Commune was declared. On the 26th Alphonse and Gustave again packed up their families for London and then left to assist the government in Versailles. Betty remained in Paris surrounded by her loyal staff. Outside the walls of rue Laffitte, violence was the order of the day. Led by Gustave Courbet, a band of rebels tore down the column on Place Vendôme. All symbols of wealth, of the monarchy, of the empire were subject to destruction. During the next two months many iconic structures were destroyed—the Tuileries was burned to the ground, the Palais-Royal, the Palais de Justice, the Légion d'honneur, the Ministry of Finance, and the Hôtel de Ville were all scorched. Remarkably, the Rothschild home on rue Laffitte was untouched.

Constance de Rothschild, Betty's cousin, was twenty-eight years old in 1871. In her memoirs she included a story about her Aunt Betty from this bloody period:

> When the Commune had brought mob-rule to dominate Paris, my aunt would not leave her house in the metropolis, the courtyard of which had been transformed into a hospital. One afternoon, returning from some charitable errand in her carriage and pair, she was stopped by an angry crowd in the Bois de Boulogne, and asked how she could dare to drive when people were starving and wanting horseflesh for food. The mob was about to unharness her horses when she, rising in her carriage, confronted the crowd and said: "Yes, take my horses if you will have them, but I am as good a patriot as any of you. Come and see my hospital in my own house; and do you not know that I have three sons all bearing arms and fighting for our country?" The mob cheered, and, forming themselves into a bodyguard, marched by the side of the carriage, accompanying my aunt triumphantly to the gates of her house.[34]

Finally, after much destruction of life and property, Bismarck agreed to release 80,000 French prisoners of war, led by General MacMahon, to suppress the rebellion. On May 22nd, Mme Morisot wrote to her daughter in Cherbourg with the good news: the fighting had ceased, and although their home in Passy lost all its windowpanes, it was otherwise unharmed. As for the rest of the city, Mme Morisot was fearful:

> We have not much hope that the place will soon be cleared. What is going to happen? I tremble to think. It is said that M. Thiers, once Paris is taken, will resign, and without him there will be nothing to restrain the reactionaries. We shall advance to a full-fledged monarchy, new struggles, open or hidden, with no respite. I am afraid that shall be our lot. I have read something about the financial terms, which if true will please me greatly; this arrangement will deliver us from these odious Prussians. They regale the terrace with their music every day. They are deployed and concentrated nearer to Paris. Their arrogance is extreme.[35]

On Monday, May 29, 1871, following a week known to historians as *la semaine sanglante* (the bloody week), William Gibson, an English minister living in Paris, received a letter from a member of his congregation living on rue de la Victoire, quite near Betty's home on rue Laffitte:

May 26: They fought all round our house from Monday morning until Tuesday evening. Our quarter was surrounded with barricades, one each at least in each of the following streets: rue de la Victoire . . . rue Joubert, rue Caumartin, rue de Provence, rue St Georges, rue Laffitte, rue Lafayette . . . You can not imagine what it is to hear the cannon, the *mitrailleuses*, and guns almost at one's door. The cannon of the troops were placed in the Square of the Trinity, near the church; those of the insurgents behind the barricade at the corner of the Boulevards . . . Numbers of insurgents who were taken were summarily shot in front on the church. I cannot tell you what joy we felt when we saw the real French flag (the tricolor as opposed to the red flag of the Commune). The army was greatly applauded throughout our quarter; cigars, wine and money were distributed to the soldiers; oranges and flowers were thrown out of windows.[36]

Mme Morisot wrote again on May 25th:

Paris on fire! This is beyond any description . . . Throughout the day the wind kept blowing in charred papers; some of them were still legible. A vast column of smoke covered Paris, and at night a luminous red cloud, horrible to behold, made it all look like a volcanic eruption. There were continual explosions and detonations; we were spared nothing . . . Latest official dispatch: the insurrection is now driven back to a very small part of Paris, the Tuileries is reduced to ashes, the Louvre survives, the part of the Finance Ministry building fronting on the Rue de Rivoli is on fire, the Cour des Comptes has been burned down . . . all the documents are being scattered to the winds.[37]

Finally, on May 28th fighting in Paris ended.
On June 5th Mme Morisot who had returned to the city noted:

I saw only the Hôtel de Ville the day after my arrival . . . What I saw was frightful. To think that this great massive building is ripped open from one end to the other! It was smoking in several places, and the firemen were still pouring water on it. It is a complete ruin. Your father would like all this debris to be preserved as a perpetual reminder of the horrors of popular revolution. It's unbelievable, a nation thus destroying itself! Going down by boat, I saw the remnants of the Cour des Comptes, of the Hôtel de la Légion d'Honneur, of the Orsay barracks, of a part of the Tuileries. The poor Louvre has been nicked by projectiles, and there are few streets that do not bear the traces of the struggle . . . one rubs one's eyes, wondering whether one is really awake.[38]

During the month of July, the city continued to heal its wounds. Betty, once again surrounded by her family, decided to provide *gratifications* (bonuses) to at least forty members of her staff who had stayed with her at rue Laffitte during the siege of the Commune or who had continued working at Ferrières during the German occupation.[39] The chief steward at Ferrières, Bergman, received 500 francs in recognition of his good work. The safety of Rothschild property was in question, and the physical hazards of those who served in the military as well as those who faced the difficulties of the siege were significant.

In August, cousin Ferdinand visited from London and reported that he was shocked at the "painfully green and yellow complexions of Alphonse and Gustave."[40] While the English family assisted in every way possible by providing shelter for French Rothschild women and children and by sending food and other support, the Frankfurt family remained loyal to the German government. As a result, when Alphonse and his brothers worked to help the French Government pay the indemnity, they specifically excluded the Frankfurt Rothschilds from participating in the loan. This rift in the family was not healed until 1877 when Edmond married Adelheid in Frankfurt.

Betty's patriotism grew during the months of the war. She was recognized by Juliette Adam for her philanthropic activities and for her personal bravery during the fighting; years later Paul Leroi, another journalist, concluded: "One does not recognize sufficiently Mme de Rothschild for her being an excellent Frenchwoman; never has a mother inspired her children more ardently with love of country."[41] Betty's desire to be officially recognized as French was a consequence of the war. During the Prussian siege of Paris, German residents were rounded up and evicted from the city. Suddenly, Betty's cosmopolitanism was no longer an asset. As the widow of James de Rothschild, Consul General of Austria in France, Betty maintained extraterritorial status. Following her involvement in the events of the Franco-Prussian War and in view of the fact that her children and grandchildren all held French citizenship, Betty applied for *admission à domicile,* or permanent resident status. The application, along with a thousand francs filing fee, was submitted on May 25, 1877. It was delayed for some time because it required a copy of Betty's marriage license that was filed in Frankfurt. The application read as follows:

Mme la Baronne Betty de Rothschild was born in Frankfurt-on-Main, on June 15, 1805. She was married in Frankfurt on July 11, 1824, to M. le Baron James or Jacques Meyer de Rothschild, already established for a few years in Paris as a banker. Since her marriage, she has not left France, where she always had her official residence. All her children were born in France and, at their majority they all claimed French citizenship, by virtue of article nine of the civil code. When she became a widow in 1868, Mme la Baronne de Rothschild continued to reside in France where all her real estate assets are and where her children and grandchildren, all French, occupy a high position due to their merit and high financial situation.

The feelings of Mme la Baronne de Rothschild towards France, her true adopted motherland, are so universally known and the testimony that she has not stopped giving is so evident that it is superfluous to demonstrate these facts.

Among the charitable works with which her name was so often associated we would like to point out the following:

She participated, with the Baron de Rothschild, her husband, in the founding of the Rothschild Hospital. She founded and endowed the orphanage on rue Lamblardie for one hundred orphans and the hospice for the incurable at rue Picpus with fifty beds. She presides over the Rothschild family foundation, the payment of the poor rent, registered at the charity office of each of the twenty Paris districts, without any religious distinction as well as the foundation to provide dowries for daughters of railway employees of the *Chemin de Fer du Nord*.

And concerning her private charity, it is so widespread, that the name of the Baronne de Rothschild is synonymous with benefactor to the sufferings of the poor. Madame la Baronne de Rothschild lives in Paris in her hotel at 19 rue Laffitte.[42]

On June 7, 1877, at the age of seventy-two, Betty was granted permanent residency in France and the right to profit from civil rights as long as she resided there.

Three years later, seeking a pleasant place to spend the frigid months, Betty spent her first winter in Cannes. Long frequented by the English and Russians, Cannes was first discovered by French high society in the 1870s. In 1881 Betty bought the villa Marie-Thérèse, razed it, and had a new one built to her specifications by a renowned local architect, Charles Baron. The villa, located in a residential neighborhood known as the Quartier des Anglais, was completed in one year. Her neighbors were Henry de Brougham, the Duchesse de Vallombrosa, Sir Charles Murray, and the Princesse de Sagan. Betty participated in the frequent formal receptions and less formal garden parties held by her neighbors. Soon every notable person traveling in Cannes was invited to the Villa Rothschild.

The house plan of the new Villa Rothschild was rectangular, rising five stories. The basement contained kitchens, laundry, and store rooms. The ground floor contained reception rooms. Bedrooms and private sitting rooms were on the next two levels. Servant quarters were in the attic. Graceful twin staircases led down to the gardens, which were planted with numerous exotic plant species. There were several fountains and displays of running water; classical references were present in both the exterior and interior of the villa. Betty brought to Cannes the famous wood panels that were removed from the Hotel Talleyrand, where Alphonse and Laurie lived in Paris.[43]

Betty returned to Cannes each winter until her death in 1886. Her son Alphonse and his family inherited the house, and in later years Edouard, Edmond, Maurice, and Philippe all spent time in the house and had several additional buildings constructed on the property. During the Second World War, the building was seized by the city. Today, the Municipal Library of Cannes is located in the house that Betty Rothschild built at the end of her life for herself and her children.

CHAPTER SEVEN

Legacy

On September 10, 1874, six years after the death of her beloved James, four years after her son-in-law Nathaniel's death, and two months after her brother Anselm died, Betty, following the family tradition, wrote a final message to her children. Written in her beautiful hand, on black-bordered notepaper, the letter runs to ten pages. It starts with sentiment, "When you read these pages, my very dear children, that bring you the last thoughts of my heart and the last gasp of my maternal tenderness, I will have ceased to exist."[1] Betty wished to comfort her "adored Charlotte and beloved sons" in death as she had during her lifetime. She assured them that she would rejoin loved ones who preceded her to the grave and that she would continue to watch over them from on high.

She blessed each of her children: "for the infinite joy which you have given me from the first days of your lives, for the respect which you have always shown me, for your excellent conduct and for your outstanding fulfillment of duty . . . for your generosity to all, for the tears you dry with charitable spirit, for your attachment to the religion of our fathers, which you practice with enlightenment and which you taught to your children from an early age." [2]

Betty's letter to her children was written twelve years before her demise. Her continuing efforts to guide them and her grandchildren were part of her daily life. After James's death, Edmond lived at rue Laffitte and at the chateau in Boulogne with his mother. All of the other children lived nearby. Charlotte lived in the Faubourg St. Honoré, with her bachelor son Arthur, a few doors away from Alphonse and Laurie who continued to live at the Hotel Talleyrand on the corner of rue St-Florentin and Place de la Concorde. Their home was a center of dinners and parties, reflecting the social standing of the couple and the social needs of their three maturing children: Bettina, Beatrice, and Edouard. Gustave and Cécile lived nearby on avenue Marigny, where they held frequent receptions. Their three daughters Zoé, Aline, and Bertha, and their son Robert enjoyed close relations with their cousins. Adèle, Salomon's widow, lived with Hélène on rue Berryer. Several years after his marriage, Edmond bought the Hotel Pontalba, whose garden on the Avenue Gabriel was one of the most beautiful in Paris. There, he and Adelheid raised three children: James, Maurice and Miriam. On holidays, the whole family gathered at Ferrières with grandchildren, servants, tutors and nannies.

Betty was privileged to live long enough to see her children develop into adulthood. She took pleasure in the fact that they continued to share the values she imparted to them in their youth. Betty remained attached to Jewish ritual, though she abandoned some customs over the years, deeming them unessential and incompatible with her aristocratic lifestyle. She was an unflagging proponent of secular education and of participation in the broader society, but she was also steadfast in her views on the importance of perpetuating Judaism by maintaining strongly identified Jewish families. All of her children married Jews; all but one married a Rothschild, following the family tradition started by Betty and James. Having watched the children of other Jewish families abandon their faith in youth or at marriage, she used her last letter to reiterate her views on the importance of filial respect and duty, generosity to all, and adherence to an enlightened Judaism.

The Rothschild family had only one experience with intermarriage during Betty's early years. In 1839, Hannah Mayer, Betty's niece, married Henry FitzRoy; the event was sharply criticized by James. Following this singular break in tradition, there were no more intermarriages in the Rothschild family for the next three decades. In 1873 Annie, daughter of Sir Anthony de Rothschild, married the Honorable Eliot Yorke. This time Betty was moved to write to Annie's mother, Louisa Montefiore, "The sentiments of sadness fill me more at this moment than I can express. They do not, however, stop me from assuring you of my greatest sympathy in your distress and in that of my dear nephew Sir Anthony." [3] Annie's sister Constance recalled that after the ceremony at the registry office: "Papa looked so sad. We all felt it dreadfully, Annie included."[4] A few years later, Constance married Cyril Flower, 1st Lord Battersea.

The next year, Constance's cousin Hannah, daughter of Mayer de Rothschild, married Philip Archibald Primrose, Earl of Rosebery. Rosebery's mother, the Duchess of Cleveland, was strongly opposed to her son's choice of "one who has not the faith and hope of Christ." She explained, "No two persons of different religions can marry without making a very great sacrifice, and, pardon me for adding, grieving and disappointing those who love them best . . . You must also expect to be judged unkindly by the world."[5] The Rothschild family shared these sentiments. Nevertheless, the daughters of the Naples branch of the family soon began to exhibit the same affinity for the aristocracy as had the English Rothschilds. Marguerite, daughter of Mayer Carl, married Agénor, Duc de Gramont in 1878. Four years later in 1882, her sister Bertha married Alexandre, Prince de Wagram.

Betty was determined that the French Rothschilds would not follow this path of marrying outside their faith. In 1874, Betty had one unmarried son and several unmarried grandchildren. The letter she addressed to her children was clear: "Continue, dear children, in the path of piety and charity and don't cease to watch over your children at the time when they escape from your direction so that none of them breaks off from our holy religion, this tree of holiness which is our guide against the uncertainties of life, our refuge and our consolation during days of testing."[6] Ten years later when she wrote her will, she returned to this subject. To equalize the funds available to her grandchildren, Betty left instructions to give extra sums to Gustave's children, the only grandchildren not to inherit from two Rothschild families; but Betty added that "should the children not marry in accord with their parents' wishes, the funds shall revert to their siblings."[7]

Betty was successful in passing her legacy of endogamous marriage to her children and grandchildren. Her children produced eighteen grandchildren, five of whom died in infancy or early childhood and one of whom remained a bachelor. Of the remaining twelve who married, two married Rothschilds, nine married into affluent Jewish families, and only one ignored her grandmother's wishes and married a Catholic of aristocratic lineage. A year after Betty's death, Hélène, Salomon's daughter, became the first French Rothschild to break the family code by marrying Baron Etienne van Zuylen de Nyevelt. Hélène's mother, the widow Adèle, followed Jewish tradition and went into mourning for her daughter;[8] she also disinherited her daughter, leaving her house on rue Berryer to the French government for the administration of fine arts.[9]

Constance Battersea, the daughter of Betty's cousin Sir Anthony de Rothschild, was among the more avid family chroniclers of her generation. She described Betty in the memoirs she published in 1923 as a remarkable woman. Betty's letters, written in French, were, according to Constance, marvels of epistolary power and grace. Constance also found Betty warm-hearted, generous, and deeply devoted to the Jewish people. She was, in her cousin's secular eyes, a woman devoted to religious observance who read Hebrew and continued to use the Judendeutsch of her childhood. Constance observed that James referred to his wife as "my good lady" when talking to his English relatives. Distancing himself from some of the religious practices followed by his wife, he would say: "My good lady never drives on the Sabbath," or "My good lady would not go out today, but I must do such and such things."[10]

For Betty, family togetherness and religious observance were always deeply connected. She urged her children to continue the family practice, so dear to her late husband, of gathering around the head of the family on religious holidays. Betty had lived surrounded by the rich and famous of the world; she knew the witty and talented, but for her the glittering social world could not rival the pleasures achieved in intimate family reunions. It was in these family events, imbued with religious sentiment and traditions that Betty had learned in childhood, that she felt completely secure. Betty believed, as had her husband before her, that these reunions were central to the moral strength of the Rothschild family. She asked her children to maintain these religious family observances and to regard their unity as a Jewish family as one of the key elements of their success.

Decades later when Alphonse wrote his final message to his children, he echoed Betty's thoughts:

> I urgently request that all my children, as well as other members of the family, continue as far as possible to gather together on the days of important religious holidays, in the rooms of our house at 19 rue Laffitte which were dedicated to this pious purpose by my late father and mother, in order to celebrate the event together, and to maintain the family solidarity in a united community of sentiments. This solidarity has always been our strength and our grandeur . . . [11]

The Jewish traditions practiced by the Rothschilds in Frankfurt were transported by Betty to rue Laffitte. In the midst of society balls, Betty's children celebrated Bar Mitzvah and Jewish festivals. Betty hired modern Jewish tutors for her children and she joined in their study sessions. She also enjoyed the friendship of leading Jewish artists of the day—Heine, Meyerbeer, Halévy, and Rachel, each one of whom juggled the duality of their identity in ways that informed Betty. This extended education gave her the ability to extract from modern French culture that which was compatible with Jewish values, and allowed her to form a strong identity as a French Israelite. Having attained a public role as a society lady in the 1830s, Betty moved into a public role in the

Jewish community in 1843 with the launching of the Société pour l'établisse-ment des jeunes filles israélites. Betty modeled a public role for Jewish women in maintaining the Jewish community; she extended this role to her daughter and daughters-in-law by her commitment to rotate the leadership of the lottery committee with them. She also encouraged hundreds of Jewish women to take part in the work of community building through philanthropy, mentoring, and leadership. After the devastations of the Franco-Prussian War and the Paris Commune, Betty was able to rebuild the organizations she nurtured in the pre-vious decades and see them regain a sound footing.

At the end of her life, Betty once again turned to thoughts of her family and of the role she had played to maintain family harmony. She knew from experience that misunderstandings and disagreements among family members occurred, and that they sometimes required mediation. Rothschild correspon-dence is replete with examples of interfamily squabbles, with the women of the family sometimes negotiating between brothers or fathers and sons. Betty had often served as the peacemaker between James and her sons, as well as between her own parents. Anticipating the need for someone to fill that role after her demise, Betty asked her sons to turn to their sister Charlotte, whom she appointed as her designate, capable of solving family problems. Of Charlotte, Betty wrote, "You will always find in her a wise counselor, fair and inspired by a developed reason." [12]

Charlotte also took over the role of mentor to the young English Roth-schilds. Just as Betty had provided interesting excursions for Leonora and Evelina in their youth, Charlotte entertained Constance Battersea and her sib-lings. Constance captured Charlotte's warm heart in her memoirs. She described frequent outings arranged by Aunt Charlotte to see the best plays in Paris followed by an ice at the fashionable Tortoni's. In this manner, Charlotte continued to foster Rothschild family ties, following her mother's footsteps.

Betty had also involved Charlotte in the Société pour l'établissement des jeunes filles israélites from its inception and in the annual lotteries that helped to fund the Société. Betty and Charlotte, as well as Laurie, Cécile, Adèle, and Adelheid were the catalysts for significant fundraising for the Jewish commu-nity in Paris until the end of the century. When Betty died, Charlotte took over the helm of the Société for several years. When Charlotte died, she followed her mother's example by leaving 10,000 francs as an endowment to produce an annual income of 1,500 francs for a dowry to be awarded to a deserving Jewish young woman. [13]

In addition to her philanthropic activities, Charlotte's principal interest was the arts. Several of her works hang in regional museums in France; additionally, she won many prizes for her watercolors in the 1880s and '90s. Having presented at the salons and participated in the Société des aquarellistes, she gained recog-nition as a talented amateur. [14] Charlotte was also a dedicated collector of art. While her mother bought only a small number of watercolors from her friend

Eugène Lami, Charlotte collected throughout her life and achieved recognition as a major arts philanthropist at the time of her death. She gave Greuze's *Milk-maid*, one of her father's first purchases, to the Louvre, along with fourteen Italian paintings, including selections by Fra Angelico and Tintoretto, and a series of Jacquemard watercolors. She donated a thirteenth century bust of a saint to the Cluny Museum along with several other Gothic objects, and several ancient instruments and manuscripts by Chopin and Rossini to the Music Conservatory. Charlotte gave the Museum of Decorative Arts ancient Moroccan leather boxes; she also gave a Chardin portrait and one by Boilly to the Hotel Carnavalet. In each instance Charlotte asked that her name be noted as donor; Betty would have approved of this act of visibility as it set a good example to others and demonstrated Rothschild family contributions to French institutions.[15]

Alphonse and Gustave, like their older sister, were socialized very early to philanthropy and the arts. Alphonse, who became head of the Rothschild Bank after his father's death, was already a member of the Central Consistory and later of the Alliance Israélite Universelle. Alphonse also served as president of the Rothschild Foundation until his death in 1905; he was followed by his brother Edmond who served until his death in 1934. The Foundation supported the continuous expansion and operating costs of the hospital, the hospice, and the orphanage founded by James in 1852 and expanded significantly by Betty in 1874. Gustave, Edmond, and later generations of French Rothschilds also made continuous contributions to these projects. In 1952, in recognition of the centenary of the Foundation, a booklet was published summing up the one hundred year history of the family commitment to helping others: 214,000 were treated at the Rothschild Hospital; 4,600 were cared for in the hospice; the orphanage educated 1,853 youngsters; the sanatorium opened in 1926 under the guidance of Baroness Adelheid at Hauteville in the Ain cared for 1,500 patients. In 1952, the annual budget of the four establishments run by the Foundation exceeded half a billion francs.[16]

In addition to their efforts to provide accessible healthcare, the Rothschilds devoted philanthropic effort to provide low-cost housing for the poor of Paris. In 1843, Betty had established a fund in memory of Nathalie de Rothschild, Charlotte and Nathaniel's first child who died at birth. This fund, administered by Betty for more than forty years, provided rent assistance for poor Parisians. In 1874, building on their mother's early initiative, Alphonse, Gustave and Edmond started donating 100,000 francs a year to the mayors of Paris to provide rent subsidies for those in need. Thirty years later the brothers created a new foundation with a donation of ten million francs. This Rothschild Foundation provided housing for workers on property owned by the family in Paris. In 1982, 1200 families lived in apartments subsidized by the Foundation.[17]

In addition to their work in finance and philanthropy, Alphonse and his brothers were also avid collectors. In 1885, Alphonse was elected to the Académie des Beaux-Arts. After his death twenty years later, the journal *L'Art* published an obituary describing Alphonse as legendary in the artistic world for his extraordinary ability to support artists in a tactful manner. Instead of distributing funds to artists directly, he bought engravings, sculptures, paintings, and other art objects every year at the Salon and other exhibits. Alphonse donated these works to provincial museums, to schools, and to municipalities. His most significant contribution was to the community where Betty built her last home; the Musée des Beaux-Arts de Cannes was known as Musée Alphonse de Rothschild from 1898–1939. Alphonse contributed 176 paintings, 92 watercolors and pastels, 203 lithographs, 40 ceramic sculptures, 100 engraved medals, and 419 photographs to this museum.[18]

Alphonse also left considerable sums to a variety of causes. He left 200,000 francs to the Académie des Beaux-Arts to establish a bi-annual award, leaving it to his colleagues to determine the conditions of the award. He left 250,000 francs to the Rothschild Hospital, continuing his family's efforts to provide for the sick. Following his mother's example, he provided 100,000 francs as an endowment to create dowries for the daughters of employees of the Chemin de Fer du Nord, started by James and chaired by Alphonse for many decades. In support of a project started by his tutor Albert Cohn and assisted by himself and his brothers, he left 200,000 francs to the Jewish Welfare Bureau. Smaller sums were left for the poor of Ferrières, Pontcarré, and Lagny.[19]

Gustave was a philanthropic supporter of the Paris Consistory, becoming its president in 1856 and holding the office until his death in 1911. Simultaneously, he participated with his brother in supporting the Rothschild Foundation and serving on its many committees. His philanthropy focused on care for the sick and needy, which he learned from his parents, and on education, which was of concern to his wife. When his son André died in 1877, he donated 12,000 francs to the Comité de Bienfaisance Israélite to be used in assisting convalescents leaving the hospital. In 1879, Gustave funded a consistorial school.[20]

Though Edmond had a desk at the bank, there was little need for him to work there. As a result, he had ample time to pursue his many interests. Edmond was a studious young man who passed his baccalaureate with distinction and was rewarded by the family with a trip to Egypt with his tutor Mayrarques. It was in Cairo in 1865 that twenty-year-old Edmond made his philanthropic entry to the world Jewish community. Edmond gave 3,500 francs to be used as follows: 500 francs for a boys' school; 500 francs for a girls' school; 500 francs for the poor; 1,000 to rededicate the synagogue. Back in Paris, Edmond worked to modernize the Rothschild Hospital. Later, he and Gustave each established a Jewish school: the Ecole Israélite Edmond de Rothschild opened on avenue Ségur in 1880 one year after the Ecole Consistoriale Israélite opened on rue des Feuillantines.[21]

Edmond had many other interests; from his youthful days at the Lycée Bonaparte, he was an avid collector of drawings. Ultimately, his collection included works by Michelangelo, Rembrandt, Fragonard, Boucher, and Watteau.

He donated 600,000 drawings to the Louvre, contributing to the creation of their collection. Edmond also acquired a magnificent home on Rue Faubourg St. Honoré, described by Edmond de Goncourt as "The most princely house I have ever seen in Paris."[22] An ancient mansion with a staircase worthy of the Louvre, attended by legions of liveried servants, today it houses the American embassy. While living in gilded surroundings and dining on Sèvres porcelain, Edmond continued to work with his brothers in the Alliance Israélite Universelle, where he came under the influence of Rabbi Zadok Kahn and Michael Erlanger, both of them Rothchild family friends.

In 1881, Russian Jews began to suffer direct physical assault due to the pogroms in the wake of the assassination of Tsar Alexander II. Leaders of the Alliance promulgated new solutions to the problems facing the five million Jews in Poland and Russia. In 1882, Rabbi Samuel Mohilever brought a proposal to Edmond to settle a group of Jewish farmers from Belorussia in Palestine. Another proposal came from Josef Feinberg who wanted money for an already existing colony named Rishon le Zion near present day Tel Aviv. The Rothschilds had supported a hospital, a school, and apprenticeship programs in Jerusalem since 1855. Gustave visited Palestine in 1853, Edmond went in 1855, and Alphonse visited in 1856; yet when Edmond gave Feinberg 25,000 francs to drill for water at Rishon le Zion, he was making a fateful commitment of another magnitude. Soon other settlers were encouraged to apply to him for aid. One of the first to apply was a group of Rumanian Jews at Samarin near Mount Carmel, later named Zikhron Ya'aqov in memory of James.

Edmond explained to Samuel Hirsch, head of the Mikveh Israel Agricultural College, that his aim was to create models of future settlements around which further groups of immigrants could subsequently settle. Edmond instructed Mohilever's settlers in Eqron, soon to be renamed Mazkeret Batya in memory of Betty, to attempt viniculture. He also pressed for experiments with silk manufacture at Rosh Pinna and perfume and glass production. By 1903, nineteen out of the twenty-eight Jewish settlements in Palestine were subsidized partially or wholly by Edmond.

In 1884 when Edmond and his wife Adelheid toured the country, he explained: "I am not a philanthropist . . . I have set out on this enterprise to see whether it is possible to establish Jews on Palestinian soil." Fifteen years later he said: "I did not come to your aid because of your poverty and suffering, for, to be sure, there were many other similar cases of distress in the world. I did it because I saw in you the realisers of the renaissance of Israel and of that ideal so dear to us all, the sacred goal of the return of Israel to its ancestral homeland."[23] Betty's youngest child, cognizant of the dire conditions of millions of Jews in Eastern Europe and Russia, believed that they could live better independent lives, at once Jewish and modern, in Palestine.

Although he was ambivalent about the politics of the Zionist movement, Edmond never wavered in fulfilling his duty as a Rothschild to be a leader in helping to regenerate his people. He visited the colonies he helped establish several times, but did not live to see the renaissance that he financed. He nevertheless hoped that with the passage of time and the arrival of additional settlers who were willing to devote themselves to the land, a new life for the Jewish people was possible.

Edmond strongly supported the efforts of Ben-Yehuda to modernize the Hebrew language and insisted that it be the primary language in the settlements he supported. In a gesture that would have delighted Betty, Ben-Yehuda dedicated his dictionary to Edmond. Toward the end of his life, Edmond made an unusual request to his son Jimmy, who had shared Edmond's Palestine vision. He asked Jimmy to move his coffin and that of Adelheid, his wife, to Palestine when it became a Jewish state. In 1954, 20 years after Edmond's death, his remains and those of his wife were disinterred from Père Lachaise in Paris and taken to Israel. The Rothchilds received a state funeral; the coffins were laid to rest on a hilltop overlooking the coastal plain near Caesarea.

In her last years, Betty was privileged to witness her children assume important philanthropic duties. Though she now spent several months a year in Cannes, Betty continued her philanthropic activities, working through her assistant Jodkowitz, who remained at rue Laffitte. She continued to receive voluminous requests for assistance until her death. A typical letter was dated November 29, 1882, from Ernestine Zadoc-Kahn, the wife of the chief rabbi, and a supporter of several of Betty's charitable projects:

Lady Baroness,

I am again asking for your kindness although I hesitated, as my husband thinks that I take advantage of your goodness. But I am so tormented, and you are so good, Lady Baroness. I am caring for numerous unfortunates at this time, which cause me serious worry. A very honorable mother wrote to me. Her husband has a shirt business and travels most of the year. He has been bedridden for several months with rheumatism. The wife works prodigiously doing the accounting for the business and raising six children, the oldest of whom is nine-years-old. They desperately need a few hundred francs to keep going. I am her only hope.

A thirty-year-old widow who lost her husband three months ago has three children, the youngest aged four months and the oldest five years. I have known this woman for a few years. She is the daughter of one of the best families of Metz. She received a very good education. If she weren't so distressed, she would try to take her exams, but she does not have the strength. Two younger children are with a wet nurse and I have been helping to pay the nurse's monthly fees for several months. She hopes to succeed by starting a small business, as she seems very business-minded. I would be very glad to be able to help her. I am a real solicitor, aren't I, Baroness, but it is so painful to see such great suffering that it emboldens me to ask you, and you have always encouraged me to do so, Lady Baroness!

Hoping your health is good, etc . . .
Ernestine Zadoc-Kahn[24]

Betty's reply to Ernestine was not saved, but her note to Jodkowitz about the matter remains. She instructed him to send a thousand francs with her enclosed card to Mme. Zadoc-Kahn.

Another letter found in Betty's papers came from the sisters of Saint-Vincent de Paul of Lagny, a religious community near Ferrières to which Betty had been a regular contributor. The letter, dated August 22, 1880, explained that the sisters were in mourning because "revolutionary fever is annihilating religious schools that taught religion and morality to the children of Lagny for over 40 years." They continued:

> Starting September first, that is, in a few days, the communal religious school shall be eliminated as well as the nursery room; in order to keep our religious instructors, we must find the necessary resources to purchase a building and pay the teachers. That latter part is taken care of by the priest of Lagny and with the help of a few charitable families. We have been offered a house large enough to accommodate the primary class of young girls and the nursery room for little children, at the capital of 30,000 francs, or for the yearly rent of this capital at 5%, that is 1500 francs.
>
> The members of the committee formed to support religious primary education and the nursery school of Lagny's sisters, present before you their plight and needs in the greatest confidence; help us, Mme Baroness, and may the members of your so good and loved family help us too![25]

Regrettably, Betty's reply to this request is unknown. Betty left money in her will for annual donations to a nursery school, but it is not clear whether this was the school administered by the Lagny sisters.

Some individuals even appealed to Betty by writing to her in the pages of *L'Univers Israélite*. L. Bloch wrote:

> Venerated Baroness,
>
> Deeply afflicted, I turn to you and appeal to your excessive kindness. The unfortunate deals I have made for the past few months led me to bankruptcy. There is absolutely nothing left to live on. The bankruptcy receiver told me I need to find a way to continue my business and obtain a settlement from my creditors that would enable me to partly pay them off. To that end I would need a sum of 4 to 5,000 francs to reopen my factory. The sum

would be guaranteed by the receiver, Mr. Normand and would therefore only be a loan, but it would save me and my family from ruin. Venerated Baroness, whose life has been full of generous deeds, you who were an angel of kindness for my father, who consoled him in his distress, please save me from sinking.

Without you, I am lost.[26]

In addition to reviewing and replying to individual philanthropic requests, Betty was actively involved in supervising the dispersal of funds to several accounts at the end of her life. She monitored the endowments for several organizations in which she had personal involvement: the fund for maternal and infant care, which she had started with her mother and daughter in 1843 and which now generated 4,300 francs per year; a fund for similar purposes based in Jerusalem, which she funded in 1855 and which produced 3,654 francs per year; the Nathalie de Rothschild rent relief program, which generated 7,500 francs per year; and the Société pour l'établissement des jeunes filles israélites, which Betty established in 1843 and which produced 3,600 francs per year. Betty, who was knowledgeable about the needs of these groups, frequently added to these sums.

In 1884, two years before her death, Betty wrote her final will. This massive document was designed to liquidate her estate which was valued at more than seventy-five million francs at the time of her death two years later. The property consisted of land, several homes, jewelry, a stock portfolio, and holdings in the Rothschild Bank. Betty's will follows family tradition: she provided roughly equal sums for her children and grandchildren, she left smaller sums to numerous charities and to a large number of individuals who were in her employ as well as to a list of people in need.[27]

The distribution of the estate showed Betty's continuing concern for her children's welfare. Betty noted the properties she had received from her father in article one: the Isle de Puteaux, the park of Suresnes, the house at 29 rue Laffitte, and the house at 13 rue Lafayette. Since Salomon had wished for these properties to pass from Betty to her sons or their descendants, she divided them among her three sons and Salomon's daughter Hélène. In subsequent articles, she explained how she had spent hundreds of thousands of francs on renovating some of these buildings as well as Ferrières. Following her improvements of the property, she gave some of her children additional sums of money to equalize the value of the inheritance. Betty wanted to bequeath the Villa at Cannes that she had built for herself in old age to Charlotte, who had spent so much time visiting her there. Nevertheless, she explained:

Earnestly desiring that the Villa at Cannes that I have had built and in which I reside in winter may remain in the family, I bequeath it to Alphonse, whose taste for beautiful nature most nearly approaches my own . . . I should have liked to leave my dear daughter Charlotte a souvenir of the happiness I have experienced in receiving her at my property at Cannes, but she has so manifestly made me understand that she only liked to reside in that pretty country for the pleasure of coming near me that I have been obliged to renounce this first idea and I beg her to accept the sum of one million francs by compensation as an extra share.

Betty's will also demonstrated her continuing affection for two women widowed in their youth: her daughter-in-law Adèle, the widow of Betty's son Salomon, and Laure-Thérèse, the widow of Betty's grandson Edouard. Both Adèle and Laure-Thérèse had assumed leadership roles in several philanthropic organizations that were dear to Betty. Betty left 600,000 francs to Adèle and 200,000 francs to Laure-Thérèse, supporting the continuation of their good works.

To equalize the inheritance for Gustave's children, Betty left 7,500,000 francs to be divided among the four siblings. She added:

Should, which may God forbid, any of my grandchildren contract a marriage opposed to the wish of his or her parents he or she shall be deprived of his or her legacy. I have perfect confidence that my well-beloved children will approve this provident disposition and that they will only see therein an act of justice.

Betty reaffirmed in her will the intent of her husband, who specified in his will that the estate at Ferrières go to Alphonse and that it continue to be used by all members of the family. The estate at Boulogne was divided among the children, but was ultimately bought by Edmond, who had spent many years there with his wife and mother during Betty's widowhood. Betty thoughtfully provided an annuity of 20,000 francs for the maintenance of Boulogne during the years it was not inhabited by any member of the family. She explained:

The object of this legacy is to offer even after my demise to my dear grandchildren and great grandchildren the pleasure that they have always had in meeting in this beautiful country—there to breathe good air and to enjoy all the amusements of their tender age.

Betty specified in her will that each of her children would receive approximately equal shares in her estate, calibrated after a review of the real property they received. Charlotte inherited 14, 272, 224 francs; Alphonse was left 13,765,870 francs; Gustave and Edmond each received 13,365,870 francs; Salomon's daughter Hélène received 11,275,276 francs.

The balance of her estate was left to charity, to individuals who had worked for Betty or had been employed by the organizations she supported, or to those who were simply needy. These gifts included capital donations for organizations supported by Betty and her family since the 1850s: the Rothschild Hospital received 10,000 francs to create a fund for convalescents; the Israelite Orphanage, funded by Betty in memory of her parents, received 50,000 francs for renovations and operations; the Berck Hospital, funded by James-Edouard, received 20,000 francs; the home for the elderly, part of the original Rothschild Hospital, received 6,000 francs; the hospice received 16,000 francs; the schools presided over by Cécile de Rothschild, Gustave's wife, received 10,000 francs and the Frankfurt Hospital, named for Mayer Amschel Rothschild by his sons, received 10,000 francs.

In addition to these sums, Betty provided for annual donations to be given to several of the above charities and to many others with which she was associated for many years. Betty indicated that each year, 1,000 francs was to be donated to the Israelite community of Paris; the Rothschild Hospital was to receive 2,000 francs; the hospice was due 1,000 francs; the orphanage would receive 3,000 francs for dowries; 200 francs was to be given to the home for the elderly; 600 francs was designated for the Nathalie de Rothschild Foundation dedicated to rent subsidies; 500 francs was to go to the Dames de Rothschild Foundation for maternity benefits; 1,000 francs was sent to the Jerusalem Hospital; an additional 300 francs was sent to Jerusalem to fund funeral candles and the recitation of the mourner's prayer; 200 francs was to be sent to Tetuan for medicine; 600 francs was spent for bread vouchers, and 300 francs were donated for the elderly in Boulogne; the community of Ferrières would receive 500 francs for clothing and funds for the poor; the nursery school of Ferrières would receive 150 francs; the community of Pont Carré was designated to receive 400 francs in clothing and general help for the poor; the poor of Cannes would receive 600 francs to be distributed by their priest, while the Petites Soeurs des Pauvres received 1,000 francs.

Betty's will also mentioned thirty-nine people who were to receive lifetime annuities, including Mme Cohn, the widow of Albert Cohn and her collaborator of many years; Mme Fabre, Betty's philanthropic assistant; and Dr. Neumann in Hambourg, the retired chief physician of the Jerusalem hospital. Several of these individuals and twenty others also received legacies, including Chief Rabbi Zadoc Kahn and Chief Rabbi Isidor. And in an additional category, Betty provided *gratifications* to her staff.

Finally, Betty addressed the needs of the major welfare institutions: the Assistance Publique received 50,000 francs; the mayoralities of Paris were given 41,000 francs; the mayorality of Boulogne received 2,000 francs; the mayoralities of Suresnes, Pont Carré, and Puteaux each received 500 francs; the mayoralities of Ferrières and Cannes received 1,000 francs each; the Israelite Welfare Committee was given 12,000 francs; and the Rothschild Hospital an additional 10,000 francs.

Betty added several personal notes to her will: she asked that her funeral be simple, with no flowers, no sermons, no pomp. During her long life, Betty was a tireless letter writer. She had also saved thousands of family letters. Now, she asked that the precious letters of her sainted mother, enclosed in an ebony box, be placed in her casket. Those of her dear husband, her dear father, and her dear brother, which probably contained financial information, she asked to be burned. The precious and charming letters of her deceased son Salomon from his trip to Spain and to America, as well as all of his photographs, kept in an ebony chest, she asked to be given to Hélène.

Betty asked that the portrait of James by Flandrin that she had kept by her side in Paris be returned to Ferrières where it was to be re-hung alongside Betty's portrait by Ingres. With the images of their parents looking down on them, Betty rejoiced in the idea that her children and grandchildren would spend time in Ferrières for decades to come. Betty asked that her apartments at rue Laffitte, in Boulogne, and in Ferrières be reopened at the end of one year's mourning period. She asked for mementos to be given to her personal maids. She also requested that her horses not be sold, but allowed to live out their lives with good care.

The will was signed and notarized in 1884. Two years later, in September 1886, Betty died in Boulogne. The room she occupied in her last weeks was on the first floor of the chateau. Facing north, she looked at the magnificent hill of St. Cloud. The baroness passed her days in an armchair and slept in a chaise longue at night; her children and grandchildren had stayed with her since the middle of June. When they left the room she said: "Adieu, my dear children; I am going far away, far from you . . ." Then she turned to the portrait of James and said, "Finally, I will be joining you . . ."[28] Charlotte and Adèle, her daughter and daughter-in-law, were her final companions and confidantes.

Obituaries appeared in all of the Parisian newspapers, many French newspapers, and the newspapers of capital cities where the Rothschild family lived. Crowds gathered at rue Laffitte to pay a condolence call on Betty's sons, grandsons, and great grandsons. Among the guests were the Marquis de Beauvoir and the Vicomte de Chevilly, devoted friends of the princes of Orleans, who represented them in all French ceremonies since the law of exile forbade their travel. Many other representatives of society were present, including Léon Say, Bischoffsheim, Cahen d'Anvers, and de Camondo. Major figures in the scientific world, the world of arts and letters, and the world of finances visited with the family. When the cortege left rue Laffitte bound for its final resting place in Père Lachaise, 5,000 people followed the simple coffin. Gaston Calmette wrote in Le Figaro:

> One could have spoken of her charity, which was immense and proverbial; of her patriotism during the difficulties of 1870; of the unequaled devotion that earned her the esteem of all the French; of that exquisite goodness

whose memory brought on so many tears for those who followed her coffin. On her express wish her friends did not state all of her virtues, nor her good deeds; they simply walked silently behind her.[29]

The cortege started at noon. Behind the simple hearse marched the Rothschild servants in mourning livery; at their head was Vidal, Betty's valet for the previous nineteen years. Among the delegations paying their final respects were children from both Catholic and Jewish orphanages and schools funded by Betty, and staff from the various hospitals, schools, and mansions associated with her. The *curé* of Notre Dame de Lorette followed the coffin until it reached the cemetery. Chief Rabbi Zadoc Kahn said a few words, summarizing that "She was an exceptional woman, who commanded, until her dying day, through her charity and her immense goodness, the respect and admiration of all."[30]

The obituary in *L'Evènement* recalled Betty's success as a salon hostess:

We remembered Prince Talleyrand, Alexandre de Humboldt, and Baron Louis were often at her salon; also, Dupuytren, Ingres, Halévy, Rossini, Meyerbeer, Balzac, Eugene Sue, Mignet, Thiers, Cousin, Claude Bernard, Paradol, etc. Baronne Rothschild defended Littré, whom she did not know, against the calumny of those who wished to close him out of the Académie Française.[31]

Others wrote about her tact and elegance; she was depicted as a charming conversationalist, knowledgeable about the smallest happenings, in the know about new books and new paintings. It was noted that although her portrait by Ingres, which appeared at the Universal Exposition des Beaux Arts in 1856, remained, "the traits of the *Baronne* are engraved on the heart of all those who had the honor of meeting her, all whom she helped, comforted."[32]

Finally, the *Moniteur universel* reprised her friendship with Queen Marie-Amélie:

Mme la baronne James de Rothschild was particularly close to Queen Marie-Amélie, whom she knew when she was the Duchess of Orleans. The respect for family and the feeling for charity were the ties that made them close . . . this admirable Christian admitted into her inner circle this Jewish woman who was worthy in her eyes. The baroness showed herself worthy of this august friendship. When the King died and when the Queen died as well she went into mourning and put her household into mourning too. During the Empire, despite all entreaties, she never appeared at Court.[33]

Betty de Rothschild died in 1886. Her memory was honored for decades by her family, and by the thousands whom she helped directly and the many more who never met her but benefited through her support. Her good works continued to thrive long after her demise; they were reflected in the daily activities of hospitals, schools, orphanages, hospices, and in the productive lives of those she helped to become useful citizens. Her personal struggle to adapt Jewish tradition to modern French life was a success, providing a model for her children and for the many French Jews who knew her or her work.

Today, more than a century after her death, there are few traces of her life in Paris, the city she loved. The famous Ingres portrait hangs privately in the home of one of her descendants. The magnificent Rothschild mansion on rue Laffitte, surrounded by streets bearing the names of many of her friends—Chopin, George Sand, Delacroix, and Balzac, was razed in 1987. The Rothschild Hospital, renovated many times, still stands on rue Picpus surrounded by a garden planted by Betty during the renovations of 1874. Today its walls carry plaques to the memory of hospital personnel and patients rounded up by the Nazis and sent to their death in 1944. Among those remembered is Dr. Zadoc Kahn, son of Betty's friends.

In the Père Lachaise cemetery, Betty lies next to James, surrounded by her extended family members. Her life story is a testament to the legacy she brought with her from Frankfurt and to her struggle to adapt the values of that legacy to modern life in Paris. As a result of her courage and perseverance, thousands beyond her immediate family were assisted to move into the modern world while retaining their identity as Jews.

Notes

☒ Chapter One

1. Hilde Spiel, *Fanny Von Arnstein: A Daughter of the Enlightenment, 1758–1818*, trans. Christine Shuttleworth (New York: St. Martin's Press, 1991) 320.

2. Egon Corti, *The Rise of the House of Rothschild* (New York: Cosmopolitan Book Corp., 1928) 210.

3. Alexander Dietz, *The Jewish Community of Frankfurt: A Genealogical Study 1349–1849*, trans. Frances Martin (Camelford, Cornwall, UK: Vanderher Publications, 1988) 290. Amos Elon, *Founder: A Portrait of the First Rothschild and His Time* (New York: Viking, 1996) 174.

4. It is possible that Salomon was not in Frankfurt in August 1819. See letter from Amschel to Nathan and Salomon, both in London, dated September 19, 1819, RAL.

5. Niall Ferguson, *The World's Banker: The History of the House of Rothschild* (London : Weidenfeld & Nicolson, 1998) 150.

6. Eleonore O. Sterling, "Anti-Jewish Riots in Germany in 1819: A Displacement of Social Protest," *Historia Judaica*, 12: 124.

7. Ferguson, 188–9.

8. See Jacob Katz, *Out of the Ghetto: The Social Background of Jewish Emancipation, 1770–1870* (Cambridge: Harvard University Press, 1973).

9. Herman Pollack, *Jewish Folkways in Germanic Lands (1648–1806): Studies in Aspects of Daily Life* (Cambridge, MIT Press, 1971) 87–88.

10. Elon, 50.

11. J.W. Goethe, *Dictung und Warheit*, (Frankfurt, no date), vol 1., bk. 4, 148.

12. Katz, 56.

13. RAL Marriage Contract of Salomon de Rothschild and Caroline Stern, 1800.

14. RAL letter from Caroline to Salomon 1820 cited in Ferguson, 221.

15. Ferguson, 174.

16. Dietz, 238.

17. Ferguson, 176.

18. Ferguson, 80.

19. About Carl's marriage to Adelheid, see Ferguson, 178.

20. Richard Bolster, *Marie D'Agoult : The Rebel Countess* (New Haven: Yale University Press, 2000) 29.

21. Ferguson, 205.

22. Freimann and Kracauer, 186.

23. Elon, 124. Arthur Galliner, <u>*The Philanthropin in Frankfurt*</u>: *Its Educational and Cultural Significance for Germany Jewry*. Leo Baeck Institute Year Book 1992, III (London: Secker & Warburg, 1958) 175.

24. Dietz, xiii.

25. Freimann and Kracauer, 206.

26. Ferguson, 176.

27. Freimann and Kracauer, 211.

28. RAL Caroline, Frankfurt, to Salomon, London, July 21, 1814.

29. Heidi Thomann Tewarson, *German-Jewish Identity in the Correspondence between Rahel Levin Varnhagen and Her Brother, Ludwig Robert: Hopes and Realities of Emancipation 1780–1830*, vol. 39, *Leo Baeck Institute Year Book 1994* (London: Secker & Warburg, 1994) 24.

30. Dietz, xviii.

31. RAL Caroline to Salomon, approximately 1813.

32. Herman Pollack, *Jewish Folkways in Germanic Lands: 1648–1806* (Cambridge, MA: M.I.T. Press, 1971) 155.

33. RAL Salomon, Paris, to Nathan, London, October 2, 1815 and December 16, 1815. See also, May 12, 1817.

34. Elon, 174.

35. RAL Caroline and Salomon, Rotterdam, to Hannah and Nathan, London, July 11, 1817.

36. RAL Betty, Schwalbach, to Charlotte, London, July 23, 1819.

37. RAL Caroline, Frankfurt, to Charlotte, London, September 22, 1820.

38. RAL Caroline to Salomon, September 26, 1820, cited in Ferguson, 197.

39. RAL Betty, Paris, to Charlotte, London, September 26, 1821.

40. Bolster, 42–3.

41. Georg Heuberger, ed., *The Rothschilds: Essays on the History of a European Family* (Frankfurt: Boydell & Brewer, 1994) 73.

42. Ferguson 168.

43. RAL Betty, Paris, to Charlotte, London, October 8, 1821.

44. RAL Betty, Frankfurt, to Charlotte, London, May 19, 1822.

45. Ibid.

46. RAL Betty, Vienna, to Charlotte, London, November 19, 1822.

47. RAL Betty, Vienna, to Charlotte, London, February 20, 1823.

48. RAL Hannah in Frankfurt to Nathan in London, July 7, 1824.

49. Freimann and Kracauer, 258–260.

50. Ibid.

⊠ CHAPTER TWO

1. Elon, 79–82.
2. Ibid, 102.
3. Ibid, 106. Selma Stern, *The Court Jew: A Contribution to the History of Absolutism in Europe*, trans. Ralph Weinman (New Brunswick, NJ: Transaction Books, 1950) introduction.
4. Anka Muhlstein, Baron James: *The Rise of the French Rothschilds* (New York: Vendome Press, 1982) 37–38.
5. Ferguson, 77–78. From 1812 until his death in 1836 Nathan was the head of the family.
6. Jules Bertaut, *La Bourse Anecdotique et Pittoresque* (Paris: Argenteuil: Impr. Coulouma, Editions du France, 1933) 99.
7. Prevost-Marcilhacy, "Un Hôtel de James de Rothschild," *Gazette des Beaux Arts*, (1994).
8. Ferguson, 204–205. Salomon also purchased property in Paris and in the countryside.
9. Corti, vol. 1, 257.
10. Ferguson, 215. Muhlstein, 69–72.
11. Philip Mansel, *Paris between Empires* (London: John Murray, 2001) 187.
12. Ferguson, 257.
13. Muhlstein, 74.
14. Prevost-Marcilhacy, "Un Hôtel de James de Rothschild," 37.
15. Anne Martin-Fugier, *La Vie Élégante ou la Formation du Tout-Paris: 1815–1848* (Paris: Fayard, 1990) 16.
16. Gary Tinterow and Philip Conisbee, ed., *Portraits by Ingres: Image of an Epoch* (New York: Metropolitan Museum of Art, 1999) 414.
17. See William Atwood, *The Parisian Worlds of Frederic Chopin* (New Haven: Yale University Press, 1999).
18. Lucien Capechot, "La Société sous le Règne de Louis-Philippe," *La Revue de Paris*, (1927) 65.
19. Harriet Countess Granville, *Letters of Harriet, Countess Granville, 1810–1845*, edited by the Hon. F Leveson-Gower, vol. 2 (London: Longmans, Green, 1894) 318.
20. Ibid, 358–9, 377.
21. Rodolphe (comte) Apponyi, *Vingt-Cinq Ans à Paris (1826–1850) Journal du Comte Rodolphe Apponyi, Attaché de l'ambassade d'Autriche-Hongrie à Paris*, (Paris: Plon-Nourrit, 1913) 7.
22. Boni Castellane, marquis de, *Journal du Maréchal de Castellane*, 3 vols. (Paris: E. Plon, Nourritt & Cie, 1896) v.2, 200. In 1827, James was 35, not 32.
23. Martin-Fugier, *La Vie Elégante ou la Formation du Tout-Paris: 1815–1848*, 8.
24. Ibid, 18.
25. Muhlstein, 93.
26. Tinterow, p.423, n.2.
27. Granville, 123.
28. Muhlstein, 110.
29. Atwood, 88.

30. Dorothée Dino, *Memoirs of the Duchesse de Dino* 1831–1835, (London: W. Heinemann, 1909) vol. 2, 224.

31. Apponyi, vol. 2, 297.

32. *Le Bon Ton,* vol. 4, 931.

33. Dino, vol. 3, 25–26.

34. *Le Bon Ton,* Feb. 8, 1842.

35. Apponyi, vol. 4, 11.

36. RAL étrennes list.

37. Granville, vol. 2, 150.

38. Prevost-Marcilhacy, "James de Rothschild à Ferrières: les projets de Paxton et de Lami," *Revue de l'Art,* 100, Sept. 1993, 58–73

39. Ary Scheffer, *Catalogue du Musée de la Vie Romantique,* 77.

40. Corti, 201.

41. Heinrich Heine, *Heinrich Heine; A Biographical Anthology,* Hugo Beiber, ed., (Philadelphia: Jewish Publication Society of America, 1956) 336.

42. RAL Heine to Betty, Paris July 20, 1855 and February 7, 1834.

43. RAL Heine to Betty, Paris May 1851.

44. Benita Eisler, *Chopin's Funeral* (New York: Alfred A. Knopf, 2003) 96.

45. Ibid, 164, 141, 171.

46. Atwood, 88.

47. Marguerite Louise Virginie Ancelot, *Les Salons de Paris* (Paris: Jules Tardieu, 1858) 99. Ferguson, 371. Muhlstein, 155.

48. RAL Betty's last letter.

49. Tinterow, 416–7, 422.

50. Cited in Tinterow, pp.418–9.

51. RAL, Diary of Louisa de Rothschild, 1844.

52. Ferguson, 347.

53. Ibid.

54. Apponyi, vol 3, 195–7.

55. *Le Bon Ton,* 20 March 1836, 396.

56. Delphine Gay [Vicomte de Launay] de Girardin, *Lettres Parisiennes* (Paris: Charpentier, 1843) vol 2, 29.

57. Ferguson, 454–5.

58. BHVP La Mésaventure Rothschild: Ferrières 1848 à Suresnes.

59. Muhlstein, 189.

60. RAL Betty's letter to Alphonse April 26, 1849.

61. Prevost-Marcilhacy, "Un Hotel De James De Rothschild" 50.

62. RAL Evelina to her parents Charlotte and Lionel, December 16, 1862.

⊠ CHAPTER THREE

1. Ferguson, 79.

2. Ibid, 316.

3. RAL James de Rothschild, Last Will and Testament, 1868.

4. RAL Hannah to Nathan, no date.

5. RAL Caroline (Frankfurt) to Salomon (Vienna) September 29, 1820.

6. Muhlstein, 153.

7. Ferguson, 338–344.

8. *Le Bon Ton*, vol.3, p.752.

9. Ferguson, 341.

10. RAL Betty to Alphone and Gustave, Oct. 8, 1838.

11. Ibid refers to Mathilde, daughter of Charlotte and Anselm.

12. Ibid.

13. RAL Betty to Alphonse and Gustave, Oct. 11, 1838.

14. RAL Betty to Alphonse and Gustave, Oct. 21, 1838.

15. RAL Betty to Alphonse and Gustave, Oct. 8, 1838.

16. RAL Betty to Alphonse and Gustave, Feb. 23, 1839.

17. Loeb, Isidore, *Biographie d'Albert Cohn*, (Paris: A. Durlacher, 1878), p.14.

18. RAL Letter from Salomon in Vienna to his brothers March 6, 1847.

19. Loeb, 18.

20. *Archive Israélite*, 1842 t.3, 191.

21. Marie-Amélie, Queen, *Journal de Marie-Amélie*, (Paris: Librairie Plon, 1838) 462.

22. G. Ben-Levi, *Moral and Religious Tales for the Young of the Hebrew Faith*, (London: Whittaker, 1846), 83–4, 115–117.

23. RAL Alphonse to Betty, Aug., 20, 1841.

24. RAL Thibault to Betty, August 21, 1841.

25. RAL Betty to Gustave, July 20, 1842.

26. RAL Betty to Gustave, July 21, 1842.

27. RAL Betty to Alphonse, Nov. 7, 1848.

28. RAL Betty to Alphonse, Nov. 23, 1848.

29. RAL Betty to Alphonse, Dec. 14, 1848.

30. RAL Betty to Alphonse, Dec. 27, 1848.

31. RAL Betty to Alphonse Dec. 30, 1848.

32. Ferguson, 574–577.

33. RAL Betty to Alphonse, December 30, 1848, (incorrectly noted as 1849).

34. RAL Betty to Alphonse, Feb. 7, 1849.

35. RAL Betty to Alphonse, March 7, 1849.

36. RAL Betty to Alphonse, May, 1848.

37. RAL Betty to Alphonse, Mar. 24, 1849.

38. RAL Betty to Alphonse, April 4, 1849.

39. RAL Betty to Alphonse, April 26, 1849

40. RAL Betty to Alphonse, May 10, 1849.

41. RAL Betty to Alphonse, May 16, 1949

42. RAL Betty to Alphonse, May 24, 1849.

43. RAL Betty to Gustave, April 10, 1851.

44. RAL Betty to Gustave, January 31, 1853.

45. Ibid.

46. RAL Betty to Gustave, March 1853.

47. RAL Betty to Gustave, March 10, 1853.

48. RAL Charlotte (Lionel), Diary, March 29, 1848.

49. Ibid.

50. *L'Univers Israélite*, Jan 1854, vol 9, 254. See also Graetz 100.

51. RAL Betty to Charlotte (Lionel), July 2, 1856.

52. See Pauline Metternich, *Souvenirs de la Princesse Pauline de Metternich*, (Paris: Plon Nourrit, 1922), 90, 112.

53. RAL Charlotte to Lionel, Natty, Alfred and Leopold, Feb. 2, Feb. 4, 1858,

54. RAL Betty to Charlotte, Boulogne, June 27, 1859.

55. RAL, Betty to Charlotte, Jan. 8, 1859.

56. *Le Monde Illustré*, February 19, 1858, III, 97.

57. Salomon de Rothschild, *A Casual View of America: The Home Letters of Salomon de Rothschild*, trans. Sigmund Diamond, (Stanford: Stanford University Press, 1967), introduction.

58. RAL Betty to Alphonse and Gustave, Oct. 7, 1839.

59. RAL Betty to Alphonse, 1848 undated.

60. *L'Universel Israélite*, 1861–62, Vol. 17, No. 8: 373.

61. Salomon de Rothschild, 4.

62. RAL Betty to Gustave, April 20, (1862).

63. Ibid.

64. Salomon de Rothschild, 5.

65. RAL Queen Marie-Amélie to Betty, 1864.

66. Margalith, I., *Le Baron Edmond de Rothschild et la Colonisation Juive en Palestine*, 1882–99 (Paris: Librairie Rivière, 1957), 66.

67. *L'Univers Israélite*, 1877–8, vol 33, 130–4.

⊠ CHAPTER FOUR

1. RAL Betty to Charlotte, Vienna, Nov. 19, 1822.

2. RAL Carl to brothers Salomon and James May 20, 1817.

3. RAL Salomon to Nathan Nov. 15, 1827.

4. RAL Betty to Alphonse, Nov. 1848.

5. RAL Betty to Alphonse, March 24,1849.

6. RAL Betty to Alphonse, April 4, 1849.

7. *L'Israélite français* (The French Israelite) was the title of the first Jewish journal in Paris, edited by Elie Halévy, father of noted composer Fromenthal Halévy and author Léon Halévy; this short-lived newspaper promulgated respect for Jewish tradition as well as participation in secular society.

8. RAL Charlotte (Nathan's daughter) to Hannah Nov 13, 1833.

9. RAL Betty to Alphonse April 26, 1849.

10. *Archives Israélites*,1864, vol.25, 567–9.

11. RAL Charlotte to Leopold, Oct 17, 1861

12. RAL Charlotte to Leopold, Oct 21, 1861.

13. RAL Charlotte to Nathaniel and Leopold, Sept 24, 1863.

14. *Conseiller des dames*, July 1848 details dinner party hosted by Caroline. The meal included lobster and other non-kosher delicacies.

15. RAL Salomon (Vienna) to brothers and Betty, March 6, 1847.

16. RAL Betty (Paris) to Alphonse (London), c. 1860.

17. Michaud, *Abrégé Chronologique de l'histoire de France*, 1836, in RAL.

18. Jonathan Frankel, *The Damascus Affair*, (Cambridge: Cambridge University Press, 1997), 367.

19. Comtesse de Gasparin, *Sabbat au Saint*-Sulpice, (Paris: Laffort, 1985), 672.

20. Albert Cohn, *Archives Israélites*, vol. 26, 1865, 34.

21. Ben-Levi, *Archives Israélites*, 1842.

22. See Laura Strumingher, "L'Ange de la Maison: Mothers and Daughters in Nineteenth Century France," *International Journal of Women's Studies*, vol. 2, no. 1: 51–61.

23. See Laure Adler, *A l'Aube du Feminisme*, (Paris: Payot, 1979), 75–115.

24. *Journal des femmes*, prospectus, 1832.

25. *Journal des femmes*, Sept. 1840, letter to readers.

26. Lisa Moses Leff, "Jewish Solidarity in Nineteenth Century France," *Journal of Modern History* 74 (2002), 75–115.

27. Diana Hallman, *Opera, Liberalism, and Antisemitism in Nineteenth Century France*, (Cambridge: Cambridge University Press, 2002), 3.

28. Halévy, La Juive, act V, scene iv in Hallman.

29. *Alliance Israélite*, 1849, vol.10, 236–44.

30. Forty women were helped in 1847, fifty in 1850, seventy-five in 1860, eighty-six in 1862 and 100 in 1882, *Annuaire parisien du culte Israélite*, 1882.

31. Evelyne Resnick, *Femmes et Associations, 1830–1880*, (Paris: Publisud, 1991), 182.

32. Ibid 184.

33. Resnick, 87.

34. Ibid 138.

35. Voix des femmes, April 3, 1848.

36. Ibid.

37. *L'Uinivers Israélite*, v. 9, 11: 48.

38. Kahn, Histoire des écoles, 486.

39. *L'Uinivers Israélite*, v.10, 1, 26.

40. Ibid, vol 10, 3, 124.

41. Ibid, vol. 10, 7: 374.

42. Ibid, vol. 11, 1: 37.

43. Ibid, vol. 11, 7: 324.

44. Grace Aguilar, *The Women of Israel*, (New York: Appleton and Co., 1871), vol. I: 11.

45. Ibid vol. I: 12.

46. Ibid vol. I: 15.

47. Ibid vol. II: 305.

☒ CHAPTER FIVE

1. *Archives Israélites*, May 1844, 341–7.

2. Ibid.

3. *Journal des femmes*, 1842, 141.

4. Phyllis Cohen Albert, *The Modernization of French Jewry*, (Hanover, NH: Brandeis University Press, 1977), 21–35.

5. Zosa Szajowski, *Poverty and Social Welfare Among French Jews*, (New York: Editions Historiques Franco-Juives, 1954), 62–5.

6. Leon Kahn, *Histoire des Ecoles*, (Paris: Durlacher, 1886), 29–35.

7. Jennifer Sartori, "Our Religious Future," (PhD Dissertation Emory University, 2004), 167–174.

8. Leon Kahn, *Société de secours mutuels*, (Paris: Durlacher, 1887), 137–9.

9. *Annuaire officiel du culte Israélite* records the beneficiaries.

10. Leon Kahn, *Professions manuelles*, (Paris: Durlacher, 1885), 43; L. Kahn, *Sociétés de secours mutuel*, 135–146.

11. AIU archives, letter from Mme Mund 1921.

12. RAL, Betty's account sheets are fragmentary; nonetheless, records from 1872–82 refer to Mme Fabre.

13. Kahn, *Professions manuelles*, 43.

14. *Archives Israélites*, May 1844, 341.

15. Ibid, 341.

16. J-N de Rothschild, "Bibliothèque de la Societé de patronage des apprentis et ouvriers israélites," *Bulletin de la Société de protection des apprentis et des enfants des manufactures*, 1869, 226–9.

17. *Archives Israélites*, May 1844, 337–41.

18. Kahn, *Comité de bienfaisance*, 159, and records in Consistoire archives.

19. Letters in the archives of the Consistoire de Paris attest to the role played by Betty de Rothschild.

20. *Annuaire parisien du culte israélite*, annual from 1850–1899.

21. *Archives Israélites*, July 1846.

22. *Archives Israélites*, January 1846.

23. *Archives Israélites*, July 1846.

24. *Archives Israélites*, April 1850, 237–41.

25. Ibid, 238.

26. *Archives Israélites*, April 1850.

27. Kahn, *Comité de bienfaisance*, 50.

28. *Inauguration de l'hôpital israélite*, Paris: 1852.

29. Ibid.

30. Graetz, 177.

31. *L'Illustration*, May 29, 1852.

32. *L'Univers Israélite*, July 1857.

33. Kahn, *Professions manuelles*, 50.

34. *L'Univers Israélite*, vol. 17, 1861–2, 462–5.

35. Nissim Levy, *The History of Medicine in the Holy Land*, 1998, 46.

36. Lipman, Sonia and V.D., *The Century of Moses Montefiore*, 280.

37. N.M Gelber, "Dr. Albert Cohn and His Visit to Jerusalem in 1854," *Jerusalem Quarterly History*, II, p.175–95. See also "The Saga of 1855" in *The Century of Moses Montefiore* Sonia and V. D. Lipman, eds., (Oxford: Oxford University Press, 1985).

38. RAL Betty's Account Books and letters to Jodkowitz.

39. Szajowski, *Poverty and Social Welfare*, 66.

40. RAL, Betty's Account Books.

41. RAL, Esther Schweitzer to Betty, Dec. 21, 1879.

42. RAL, Betty to Jodkowitz, Feb. 11, 1880.

43. RAL, E. Schweitzer to Jodkowitz, Sept. 23, 1880.

44. RAL, E. Schweitzer to Jodkowitz, Dec. 24, 1880.

45. RAL, E. Schweitzer to Jodkowitz, Dec. 30, 1880.

☒ CHAPTER SIX

1. "Les Rothschild," *Bulletin de la Société Historique de Gouvieux*, Oise 4, 1992.

2. Ibid.

3. Ibid.

4. Maurice Barres, *Le Voltaire*, September 7, 1886.

5. Centre des Archives du Monde de Travail, Collection Betty de Rothschild.

6. Ibid.

7. Ibid.

8. Stanley Weintraub, *Charlotte and Lionel*, (New York: Edwin Mellen Press, 1996), 233.

9. Robert Sibbet, *The Siege of Paris*, (Harrisburg, PA: Meyers, 1892), 31.

10. Sibbet, 86–92.

11. Sibbet, 86–92.

12. Pauline Metternich, *My Years in Paris*, (London: Nash and Grayson, 1922), 199.

13. Herbert Lottman, *The French Rothschilds*, (New York: Crown, 1995), 67 and Virginia Cowles, *The Rothschilds*, (New York: Knopf, 1973), 151.

14. Metternich, *My Years in Paris*, 209.

15. Sibbet, 113–133.

16. Berthe Morisot, *Berthe Morisot: The Correspondence*, (London: Moyer Bell Ltd., 1887), 53–4.

17. Cowles,152 and Weintraub, 237.

18. Adolphe Job, *Malades et blessés*, (Paris: Delahaye, 1871), 8–10.

19. Ibid, 50.

20. Maxime DuCamp, *Paris bienfaisant*, (Paris: Hachette, 1888), 335, 439.

21. Morisot, 55.

22. Morisot, 56.

23. Robert Baldrick, *The Seige of* Paris, (London: Batsford, 1964), 107,142. Sibbert, 250.

24. Morisot, 57.

25. Sibbert, 334.

26. Hollis Clayson, *Paris in* Despair, (Chicago: Chicago University Press, 2002), 128.

27. Ibid.

28. Morisot, 57.

29. Lucy Cohen, *Lady de Rothschild and Her Daughters*, (London: Heinemann, 1962), 146.

30. RAL Betty to Charlotte, c. Jan.-Feb. 1871.

31. Weintraub, 240.

32. RAL Betty, Paris to Laurie, London, Feb. 6, 1871.

33. RAL Betty, Paris to Alphonse, Bologne, c. Feb. 1871.

34. Constance Battersea, *Reminiscences*, (London: Macmillan, 1923), 75.

35. Morisot, 70–1.

36. William Fortescue, *The Third Republic in France, 1870–1940*, (London: Routledge, 2000), 19.

37. Ibid, 72.

38. Ibid, 73.

39. RAL Betty's Accounts.

40. RAL Ferdinand, Dieppe, to Lionel, Aug. 9, 1871.

41. Paul Leroi, *Le Courrier de l'Art*, September 10, 1886.

42. RAL Betty's application for Permanent Residency.

43. *Cannes Soleil*, 8, Avril 2002 and Cucurullo, José, *La Villa Rothschild*, (special collection Cannes Mediathèque).

⊠ CHAPTER SEVEN

1. RAL Betty to her children, Sept. 10, 1874.

2. Ibid.

3. Ferguson,765.

4. Ibid.

5. Ferguson, 766.

6. RAL Betty's letter to her children, Sept. 10, 1874.

7. RAL Betty Rothschild's Last Will and Testament October 26, 1884.

8. Guy de Rothschild, *The Whims of Fortune*, (New York: Random House, 1985), 253.

9. Ferguson,764.

10. Battersea, 73–4.

11. RAL Alphonse to his children, ©1900.

12. RAL Betty to her children, September 10, 1874.

13. Ibid.

14. E. Bénézit, *Dictionnaire des peintures, sculpteurs, dessinateurs et graveurs*, (Paris: Grand, 1924), vol.9, 119.

15. *Archives Nationales*, F19 11140, Charlotte de Rothschild, will.

16. *Fondation Rothschild: Hopital. Hospices. Orphelinat. Sanatorium. 1850–1937*, (Villeneuve-St.Georges: Union Typographiques, 1937). Christine Clerc, *Fondation Rothschild 130 ans de solidarité*, (Paris: BEBA, 1982).

17. Ibid.

18. Paul Leroi, "Le Baron Alphonse," *L'Art*, vol 64, 1905, pp.256–93.

19. G. Dargenty, "Les Derniers volontés de M. le baron Alphonse de Rothschild," *L'Art*, vol. 64, 1905, 366.

20. *L'Univers Israélite*, vol.33, 1877–78, 459–60.

21. *Archives Israélites*, vol.26, Feb. 26, 1865, 257.

22. Lottman, 97.

23. I. Margalith, *Baron Edmond de Rothschild et la colonisation juive en Palestine*, (Paris: Rivière, 1957). S. Schama, *Two Rothschilds and the Land of Israel*, (New York: Knopf, 1978), 17–19.

24. RAL letter to Betty de Rothschild from Ernestine Zadoc-Kahn, Dec. 9, 1882.

25. RAL letter from Sisters in Lagny, Aug 22, 1880.

26. *L'Univers Israélite*, July 10, 1880.

27. RAL Betty's will.
28. *Le Figaro*, September 5, 1886.
29. Ibid.
30. Ibid.
31. *L'Evènement*, September 4, 1886.
32. *La Patrie*, September 4, 1886.
33. *Moniteur Universel*, September 4, 1886.

Bibliography

PRIMARY SOURCES

A. ARCHIVAL SOURCES

Archives of the Alliance Israélite Universelle, Paris
Archives de Chaumet, Paris
Archives departementales des Hauts-de-Seine, Nanterre
Archives Nationales, Paris
Bibliotheque Nationale, Manuscript Collection
Centre des Archives Diplomatique, Nantes
Centre des Archives du Monde de Travail, Roubaix
Consistoire de Paris
The Rothschild Archives, London

B. NEWSPAPERS/PERIODICALS

Les Archives Israélites 1840–70
Annuaire Parisien du Culte Israélite 1871–1893
L'Univers Israélites 1844–70

C. PRINTED PRIMARY SOURCES

Abraham, A. *Moral and Religious Tales for the Young of the Hebrew Faith*. London: Whittaker and Co., 1846.
Adam, Juliette. *Mes Illusions et Nos Souffrances Pendant le Siège de Paris*. Paris: A. Lemerre, 1906.
Aguilar, Grace. *The Women of Israel*. New York: D. Appleton and Company, 1871.
Ancelot, Marguerite Louise Virginie. *Les Salons de Paris*. Paris: Jules Tardieu, 1858.

Apponyi, Rodolphe (comte). *Vingt-Cinq Ans à Paris (1826–1850) Journal du Comte Rodolphe Apponyi, Attaché de l'ambassade d'Autriche-Hongrie à Paris.* Paris: Plon-Nourrit, 1913.

● Battersea, Lady Constance. *Reminiscences.* London: Macmillan and Co., 1923.

Beaumont-Vassy, Edouard Ferdinand de la Bonninière, vicomte de, 1816–1875. *les Salons de Paris et la Société Parisienne sous Louis-Philippe.* Paris: Ferdinand Sartorius, 1866.

——. *les Salons de Paris, et la Société Parisienne sous Napoléon III.* Paris: Ferdinand Sartorius, 1868.

Ben-Levi, G. *Moral and Religious Tales for the Young of the Hebrew Faith.* London: Whittaker & Co., 1846.

Bertaut, Jules. *La Bourse Anecdotique et Pittoresque.* Paris: Argenteuil: Impr. Coulouma, Editions du France, 1933.

Boigne, Madame de. *Mémoires de Madame de Boigne.* Vol. 3. Paris: Emile-Paul Frères, 1922.

Capechot, Lucien. "La Société sous le Règne de Louis-Philippe." *La Revue de Paris* (1927): 58–90.

Castellane, Boni, marquis de. *Journal du Maréchal de Castellane.* 3 vols. Paris: E. Plon, Nourritt & Cie, 1896.

Chopin, Fréderic. *Selected Correspondence of Fryderyk Chopin: Abridged from Fryderyk Chopin's Correspondence.* Edited by Arthur Hedley. London: Heinemann, 1962.

● Cohen, Lucy. *Lady de Rothschild and Her Daughters, 1821–1931.* London: J. Murrary, 1935.

Compte-Rendu de la Société de Patronage des Apprentis et Ouvriers Israélites de Paris pour les Années 1872 à 1876, (1876).

Conseiller des Dames et Demoiselles (1848).

Dafau, P.A. "Lettres à une Dame sur la Charité." *Annales de la charité* (1847).

Delaborde, Henri, comte. *Ingres, Sa Vie, Ses Travaux, Sa Doctrine. d'après les Notes Manuscrites et les Lettres du Maître; Ouvrage Orné d'un Portrait Gravé Par Morse et du Fac-Simile d'un Autographe.* Paris: Plon, 1870.

Delacroix, Eugène. *The Journal of Eugène Delacroix,* trans. Lucy Norton, ed. Hubert Wellington. New York: Phaidon Publishers; distributed by Oxford University Press, 1951.

——. *Eugéne Delacroix: Selected Letters 1813–1863,* ed. Jean Stewart. Boston: MFA Publications, 1970.

Dino, Dorothée, duchesse de. *Memoirs of the Duchesse de Dino (Afterwards Duchesse de Talleyrand et de Sagan), 1831–1835,* ed. Princess Radziwill (née Castellane). 3 vols. London: W. Heinemann, 1909.

DuCamp, Maxime, *Paris bienfaisant.* Paris: Hachette, 1888.

"La Famille des Rothschild." *Revue Illustre* 14 (1892).

Finn, James. *A View from Jerusalem, 1849–1858: The Consular Diary of James and Elizabeth Anne Finn,* ed. Arnold Blumberg. Rutherford, NJ: Fairleigh Dickinson, 1980.

Galignani. *Galignani's New Paris Guide*. Paris: A. & W. Galignani, 1881.

Gasparin, Comtesse de . *Sabbat au Saint-Sulpice (1848)*, ed. Jean-Claude Berchet, *Anthologie des Voyageurs Français dans le Levant au XIXième Siècle*. Paris: Robert Laffort, 1985.

"La Gerbe: Etudes, Souvenirs, Lettres, Pensées Publiés à l'occasion du Cinquantenaire du Recueil Hebdomadaire." *les Archives Israélites-Politiques* (1890).

Girardin, Delphine Gay [Vicomte de Launay]. *Lettres Parisiennes*. Paris: Charpentier, 1843.

Granville, Harriet Countess. *Letters of Harriet, Countess Granville, 1810–1845; Edited by Her Son, the Hon. F. Leveson-Gower*. Vol. 2. London: Longmans, Green, 1894.

Guizot, M. (François). *Lettres de François Guizot et de la Princesse de Lieven*, ed. Jacques Naville. Vol. 1. Paris: Mercure de France, 1963.

Heine, Heinrich. *Lutéce: Lettres sur la Vie Politique, Artistique et Sociale de la France*. Paris: Michel Lévy Frères, 1855.

"Hospice Israélite de Paris." *l'Illustration: Journal Universel* (1852).

Kahn, Leon. *Histoire des Écoles Communales et Consistoriales Israelite de Paris (1809–84)*. Paris: A. Durlacher, 1884.

——. *Le Comité de Bienfaisance: l'Hôpital l'Orphelinat les Cimetiéres avec Gravures et Plans*. Paris: A. Durlacher, 1886.

——. *Les Sociétés de Secours Mutuels Philanthropiques et de Prévoyance*. Paris: A. Durlacher, 1887.

——. *Les Professions Manuelles*. Paris: A. Durlacher, 1885.

Kahn, Zadoc. *Sermons et Allocutions*. Paris: A. Durlacher, 1894.

Lemoisne, Paul-André. *l'Oeuvre d'Eugène Lami (1800–1890): Lithographies, Dessins, Aquarelles, Peintures: Essai d'un Catloque Raisonneé*. Paris: H. Champion, 1914.

Leroi, Paul. "Le Baron Alphonse." *l'Art* 64 (1905): 256–293.

Lewald, Fanny. *The Education of Fanny Lewald: An Autobiography*, trans. Hanna Ballin Lewis. Albany: State University of New York Press, 1992.

Loeb, Isidore. *Biographie d'Albert Cohn*. Paris: A. Durlacher, 1878.

Marie-Amélie, Queen, consort of Louis-Philippe. *Journal de Marie-Amélie de Bourbon des Deux-Siciles*. Paris: Librairie Plon, 1938.

La Mésaventure Rothschild: Février 1848 à Suresnes.

Metternich-Sándor, Pauline (Fürsten). *My Years in Paris*. London: E. Nash & Grayson, Ltd., 1922.

——. *Souvenirs de la Princess Pauline de Metternich (1859–1871)*, ed. Marcel Dunan. Paris: Plon Nourrit et cie, 1922.

Montefiore, Moses and Lady Montefiore. *Diaries of Sir Moses and Lady Montefiore*, ed. Louis Loewe. London: Jewish Historical Society of England, 1983.

Morisot, Berthe. *Berthe Morisot: The Correspondence with Her Family and Her Friends*, ed. Denis Rouart. London: Moyer Bell Limited, 1887.

Poëte, Marcel. *Comment s'est Formé Paris*. Paris: Hachete, 1925.

Poisson, Just, ed. *La Charité à Paris au XIXième Siécle*. Paris: Office Central des Oeuvres de Bienfaisance, 1900.

Ratisbonne, Théodore. *La Question Juive*. Paris: E. Dentu/Ch. Douniol, 1868.

Rothschild, Guy de. *The Whims of Fortune: The Memoirs of Guy de Rothschild*. New York: Random House, 1985.

Rothschild, James de. "Bibliothèques de la Société de Patronage des Apprentis et Ouvriers Israélites." *Bulletin de la Société de protection des apprentis et des enfants des manufacturers* (1869).

Rothschild, Salomon de. *A Casual View of America: The Home Letters of Salomon de Rothschild (1859–1861)*, ed. Sigmund Diamond. Stanford: Stanford University Press, 1961.

Sibbet, Robert Lowry. *The Siege of Paris by an American Eye-Witness, Robert Lowry Sibbet*. Harrisburg, PA: Meyers printing and publishing house, 1892.

Société d'Aquarellistes Français; Ouvrage d'art Pub. avec le Concours de Tous les Sociétaires; texte Par les Principaux Critiques d'art. Paris: H. Launette, 1883.

Status de l'école de Travail pour les Jeunes Filles Israélites. Paris: Eduard Blot et Fils.

Trognon, Auguste. *Vie de Marie-Amélie, Reine des Français*. Paris: Lévy, 1872.

Weill, Alexandre. *les Grandes Juives: A l'Usage des Jeunes Filles*. Paris: E. Dentu, undated.

D. PRINTED SECONDARY SOURCES

Adler, Laure. *A l'Aube du Féminisme: Les Premiéres Journalistes (1830–1850)*. Paris: Payot, 1979.

Adolphe, Job, *Malades et Blessés: Ambulance de l'hopital Rothschild pendant le siège de Paris 1870–1871*. Paris: Delahaye, 1871.

Albert, Phyllis Cohen. *The Modernization of French Jewry: Consistory and Community in the Nineteenth Century*. Hanover, NH: Brandeis Univ. Press, 1977.

Assouline, Pierre. *Le Dernier des Camondo*. Paris: Gallimard, 1997.

Atwood, William. *The Parisian Worlds of Frederic Chopin*. New Haven: Yale University Press, 1999.

Baader, Maria. "Inventing Bourgeois Judaism: Jewish Culture, Gender, and Religion in Germany, 1800–1870," PhD diss., Columbia University, 2000.

Baldick, Robert. *The Seige of Paris*. London: Batsford, 1964.

Balla, Ignatius. *The Romance of the Rothschilds*. New York: G. P. Putnam Sons, 1913.

Baskin, Judith R., ed. *Jewish Women in Historical Perspective*. Detroit: Wayne State University Press, 1991.

Beiber, Hugo, ed., *Heinrich Heine: A Biographical Anthology*, trans. Moses Hadas, Philadelphia: Jewish Publication Society of America, 1956.

Bembo, Bonifacio, et al. *The Rothschild Miscellany*. London: Facsimile Editions, 1989.

Ben-Arieh, Yehoshua. *Jerusalem in the Nineteenth Century*. Tel Aviv: MOD Books, 1989.

Benbassa, Esther. *The Jews of France: A History from Antiquity to the Present*. Translated by M.B. DeBevoise. Princeton, NJ: Princeton University Press, 1999.

Bénézit, E. *Dictionnaire des peintures, sculpteurs, dessinateurs et graveurs*. Paris: Grand, 1924.

Bergeron, Louis. *Les Rothschild et les Autres: la Gloire des Banquiers*. Paris: Perin, 1991.

Bergman-Carton, Janis. *The Woman of Ideas in French Art, 1830–1848*. New Haven: Yale University Press, 1995.

Birnbaum, Pierre. *Jewish Destinies: Citizenship, State, and Community in Modern Franc*, trans. Arthur Goldhammer. New York: Hill and Wang, 2000.

Birnbaum, Pierre and Ira Katznelson, ed. *Paths of Emancipation: Jews, States, and Citizenship*. Princeton, NJ: Princeton University Press, 1995.

Black, Gerry. *JFS: A History of the Jew's Free School, London since 1732*. London: Tymsder, 1998.

Bolster, Richard. *Marie d'Agoult: The Rebel Countess*. New Haven: Yale University Press, 2000.

Boursier-Mougenot, Ernest. "The Villa Ephrussi de Rothschild." *Beaux Arts (special issue)* 35, no. F. A catalogue of the Villa Ephrussi de Rothchild.

Brombert, Beth Archer. *Edouard Manet: Rebel in a Frock Coat*. Boston: Little, Brown, 1995.

Brownstein, Rachel M. *Tragic Muse: Rachel of the Comédie-Française*. New York: Alfred A. Knopf, 1993.

Charle, Christophe. *Social History of France in the Nineteenth Century*, trans. Miriam Kochan. Oxford: Berg, 1994.

Chouraqui, Andre. *l'Alliance Israélite Universelle et la Renaissance Juive Contemporaine, 1860–1960*. Paris: Presses universitaires de France, 1965.

Clark, T. J. *The Painting of Modern Life: Paris in the Art of Manet and His Followers*. Princeton, NJ: Princeton University Press, 1984.

Clayson, Hollis. *Paris in Despair: Art and Everyday Life under Siege (1870–71)*. Chicago: University of Chicago Press, 2002.

Clerc, Christine. *Fondations Rothschild: 130 Ans de Solidarité*. Paris: BEBA, 1982.

Conisbee, Philip and Gary Tinterow, eds. *Portraits by Ingres: Image of an Epoch*. New York: Metropolitan Museum of Art, 1999.

Corti, Egon. *The Rise of the House of Rothschild*. New York: Cosmopolitan Book Corp., 1928.

Cowles, Virginia. *The Rothschilds: A Family of Fortune*. New York: Alfred A. Knopf, 1973.

Cucurullo, José. *La Villa Rothschild*. Cannes. A pamphlet.

Dahan, Gilbert. *les Juifs au Regard de l'Histoire: Mélanges En l'Honneur de Bernhard Blumenkranz*, ed. Gilbert Dahan. Paris: Picard, 1985.

Davis, Richard. *The English Rothschilds*. London: Collins, 1983.

Dietz, Alexander. *The Jewish Community of Frankfurt: A Genealogical Study 1349–1849*, trans. Frances Martin. Cameford, Cornwall, UK: Vanderher Publications, 1988.

Duby, George and Michelle Perrot, eds. "Emerging Feminism from Revolution to World War." *A History of Women in the West*. Vol. 4. Cambridge, MA: Belknap Press of Harvard University Press, 1992.

Duprat, Catherine. *Usage et Pratiques de la Philanthropie: Pauvreté, Action Sociale et Lien Social, à Paris, au Cours du Premier XIXième Siècle*. Paris: Association pour l'étude de l'histoire de la sécurité sociale, 1997.

Eisler, Benita. *Chopin's Funeral*. New York: Alfred A. Knopf, 2003.

Elon, Amos. *Founder: A Portrait of the First Rothschild and His Time*. New York: Viking, 1996.

Ewals, Leo. *Ary Scheffer 1795–1858: Gevierd Romanticus*. Zwolle: Dordrecht Museum, 1995.

———. *Ary Scheffer, 1795–1858*. Museé de la Vie Romantique, 10 Avril–Juillet 1996, Paris: Paris–Musées, 1996.

Feliciano, Hector. *Le Musée Disparu: Enquête sur le Pillage des Oeuvres d'Art En France par les Nazis*. Paris: Austral, 1995.

Ferguson, Niall. *The World's Banker: the History of the House of Rothschild*. London: Weidenfeld & Nicolson, 1998.

Fondation de Rothschild: Hopital. Hospices. Orphelinat. Sanatorium. 1850–1937. Villeneuve-St-Georges: Union Typographique, 1937.

Fortescue, William. "The Role of Women and Charity in the French Revolution of 1848: The Case of Marianne de Lamartine." *French History* 11 (1997): 54–78.

———. *The Third Republic in France, 1870–1940*. London: Routledge, 2000.

Fout, John C., ed. *German Women in the Nineteenth Century: A Social History*. New York: Holmes & Meier, 1984.

Frankel, Jonathan. *The Damascus Affair: "Ritual Murder," Politics, and the Jews in 1840*. Cambridge: Cambridge University Press, 1997.

Freimann, A. and F. Kracauer. *Frankfort*. Translated by Bertha Szold Levin. Philadelphia: Jewish Publication Society of America, 1929.

Fuchs, Rachel Ginnis. *Poor and Pregnant in Paris: Strategies for Survival in the Nineteenth Century*. New Brunswick: Rutgers University Press, 1992.

Furet, François. *Revolutionary France, 1770–1880*, trans. Antonia Nevill. Oxford: Blackwell, 1992.

Galliner, Arthur. *The Philanthropin in Frankfurt: Its Educational and Cultural Significance for Germany Jewry*. Leo Baeck Institute Year Book 1992, III. London: Secker & Warburg, 1958.

Gelbart, Nina Rattner. *Feminine and Opposition Journalism in Old Regime France: Le Journal des Dames*. Berkeley: University of California Press, 1987.

Gelber, N.M. "Dr. Albert Cohen and His Visit to Jerusalem in the Year 5614 (1854)." *Jerusalem Quarterly History* II. 175–95.

Gilbert, Martin. *Jerusalem, Illustrated History Atlas*. Bnei Brak, Israel: Steimatzky, 1978.

Gille, Bertrand. *Histoire de la Maison Rothschild: Des Origines à 1848*. Vol. 1. Genève: Libraire Droz, 1965.

———. *Histoire de la Maison Rothschild: 1848–1970*. Geneva: Libraire Droz, 1967.

Goldstein, Robert Justin. *Censorship of Political Caricature in Nineteenth-Century France*. Kent, Ohio: Kent State University Press, 1989.

Graetz, Michael. *From Corporate Community to Ethnic-Religious Minority, 1750–1830*. Leo Baeck Institute Year Book 1992, XXXVII. London: Secker & Warburg, 1992.

———. *The Jews in Nineteenth Century France: From the French Revolution to the Alliance Israélite Universelle*, trans. Jean Marie Todd. Stanford: Stanford Univ. Press, 1996.

Gray, Francine du Plessix. *Rage and Fire: A Life of Louise Colet, Pioneer Feminist, Literary Star, Flaubert's Muse*. New York: Simon & Schuster, 1994.

Gray, Victor et al. *The Life and Times of N M Rothschild*. Edited by Victor Gray and Melanie Aspey. London: N M Rothschild & Sons, 1998.

Hachmey, Joseph et al. *Enduring Images: 19th Century Jerusalem through Lens and Brush*. Jerusalem: Bible Lands Museum, 2002.

Hallman, Diana R. *Opera, Liberalism, and Antisemitism in Nineteenth-Century France: The Politics of Halévy's la Juive*. Cambridge: Cambridge University Press, 2002.

Helfand, Jonathan I. "Passports and Piety: Apostasy in Nineteenth-Century France." *Jewish History* 3, no. 2 (1988): 59–84.

Hertz, Deborah. "Work, Love and Jewishness in the Life of Fanny Lewald." In *From East and West: Jews in a Changing Europe, 1750–1870*, edited by Frances Malino and David Sorkin, Cambridge: Basic Blackwell, 1990.

Hertz, Deborah Sadie. *Jewish High Society in Old Regime Berlin*. New Haven: Yale University Press, 1988.

Heuberger, Georg, ed. *The Rothschilds: Essays on the History of a European Family*. Frankfurt: Boydell & Brewer, 1994.

———. *Ludwig Börne: A Frankfurt Jew Who Fought for Freedom*. Frankfurt: Jewish Museum, Frankfurt on Main, 1996.

Heuberger, Rachel and Salomon Korn. *The Synagogue at Frankfurt's Börneplatz*. Frankfurt: Jewish Museum, Frankfurt on Main, 1996.

Hurel, Roselyne and Diana Scarisbrick. *Chaumet: Two Centuries of Fine Jewelry*. Paris: Musée Carnavalet, 1998.

Hyman, Paula E. *The Emancipation of the Jews of Alsace: Acculturation and Tradition in the Nineteenth Century*. New Haven: Yale University Press, 1991.

———. *The Jews of Modern France*. Berkeley: Univ. of California Press, 1998.

Isser, Natalie. *Antisemitism During the French Second Empire, American University Studies*. New York: Peter Lang, 1991.

Jurgrau, Thelma, ed. *Story of My Life: The Autobiography of George Sand*. Albany: State University Press of New York, 1991.

Kale, Steven D. "Women, the Public Sphere, and the Persistence of Salons." *French Historical Studies* 25, no. 1 (2002).

Kaplan, Marion A., ed., *The Marriage Bargain: Women and Dowries in European History*. New York: Harrington Park Press, 1985.

———. *The Life of Marie d'Agoult, Alias Daniel Stern*. Baltimore: Johns Hopkins University Press, 2000.

Katz, Jacob. *Out of the Ghetto: The Social Background of Jewish Emancipation, 1770–1870*. Cambridge: Harvard University Press, 1973.

Kenney, Elise K. *The Pear: French Graphic Arts in the Golden Age of Caricature*. South Hadley, Mass. : Mount Holyoke College Art Museum, 1991.

Kertzer, David I. *The Kidnapping of Edgardo Mortara*. New York: Alfred A. Knopf, 1997.

La Berge, Ann F. "Medicalization and Moralization: The Creches of Nineteenth-Century Paris." *Journal of Social History* 25, no. 1 (fall 1991).

Leff, Lisa Moses. "Jewish Solidarity in Nineteenth-Century France: The Evolution of a Concept." *The Journal of Modern History* 74 (2002).

——. *The Making of Modern Solidarity: French Jews and World Jewry, 1789–1889.* PhD diss., University of Chicago, 2000.

Lejeune-Resnick, Evelyne. *Femmes et Associations (1830–1880).* Paris: Publisud, 1991.

Lenarz, Michael. *The Old Jewish Cemetery in Frankfurt on Main.* Frankfurt: Jewish Museum, Frankfurt on Main, 1996.

Levy, Nissim. *The History of Medicine in the Holy Land: 1799–1948.* Haifa, Israel: Hakibbutz Hameuchad: 1998.

Liberles, Robert S. *A Tale of Two Cities: Jewish Life in Fankfurt and Istanbul, 1750–1870,* ed. Vivian B. Mann. New York: Jewish Museum, 1982.

Lipman, Sonia and V. D. Lipman, eds., *The Century of Moses Montefiore.* Oxford: Oxford University Press, 1985.

Lottman, Herbert R. *The French Rothschilds: The Great Banking Dynasty through Two Turbulent Centuries.* New York: Crown, 1995.

Lowenstein, Steven M. "Jewish Upper Crust and Berlin Jewish Enlightenment: The Family of Daniel Itzig." *From East and West: Jews in a Changing Europe, 1750–1870,* ed. Frances Sorkin and David Malino, Cambridge: Basic Blackwell, 1990.

Maille, duchesse de. *Souvenirs des Deux Restaurations, Journal Inédit Présenté Par X. de la Fournière.* Paris: Perrin, 1984.

Mainardi, Patricia. *Art and Politics of the Second Empire: The Universal Expositions of 1855 and 1867.* New Haven: Yale University Press, 1987.

Malino F. and Phyllis Cohen Albert, eds., *Essays in Modern Jewish History: A Tribute to Ben Halpern.* Rutherford, NJ: Fairleigh Dickinson University Press, 1982.

Mann, Vivian B. and Richard I. Cohen, eds., *From Court Jews to the Rothschilds: Art, Patronage, and Power: 1600–1800.* New York: Prestel-Verlag, 1996.

Mansel, Philip. *Paris between Empires.* London: John Murray, 2001.

Margalith, Israel. *Le Baron Edmond de Rothschild et la Colonisation Juive en Palestine, 1882–1899.* Paris: Librairie M. Rivière, 1957.

Martin-Fugier, Anne. *La Vie Élégante ou la Formation du Tout-Paris: 1815–1848.* Paris: Fayard, 1990.

McCarthy, Kathleen D., ed. *Women, Philanthropy, and Civil Society.* Bloomington, IN: Indiana University Press, 2001.

Merk, Georg Heuberger and Anton, eds., *Moritz Daniel Oppenheim: Die Entdeckung des Jüdischen Selbstbewusstsseins in Der Kunst.* Cologne: Wienand, 1999.

Meyer, Michael A. *The Origins of the Modern Jew: Jewish Identity and European Culture in Germany 1749–1824.* Detroit: Wayne State University Press, 1967.

Mollier, Jean-Yves. "de Rachel aux Rothschild, la Place des Juifs dans la Bourgeoisie Parisienne Entre 1850 et 1914." *Quarante-huit/quatorze* 4 (1990–91): 37–43.

Mondonico-Torri, Cécile. "les Réfugiés en France sous la Monarchie de Juillet: l'Impossible Statut." *Revue d'Histoire Moderne et Contemporaine* 47, no. 4 (2000).

Morton, Frederic. *The Rothschilds; a Family Portrait*. New York: Antheneum, 1962.

Muhlstein, Anka. *Baron James: The Rise of the French Rothschilds*. New York: Vendome Press, 1982.

Mülsch, Elisabeth-Christine. "Creativity, Childhood, and Children's Literature, or How to Become a Woman Writer: The Case of Eugénie Foa." *Romance Languages Annual VIII* (1997).

———. "Eugénie Foa and the Institut des Femmes." *Women Seeking Expression: France 1789–1914*, eds. Rosemary Lloyd and Brian Nelson. Victoria: Monash University, 2000.

Neumann, Bernhard. *Die Heilige Stadt und Deren Bewohner in Inhren Naturhistorischen, Culturgeschichtlichen, Socialen und Medicinischen Verhältnissen*. Hamburg: Der Verfasser, 1877.

Perrot, Philippe. *Fashioning the Bourgeoisie: A History of Clothing in the Nineteenth Century*, trans. Richard Bienvenu. Princeton, NJ: Princeton University Press.

Piette, Christine. *Les Juifs de Paris (1808–1840): La Marche vers l'Assimilation*. Québec: Les Presses de l'Université Laval, 1983.

Pollack, Herman. *Jewish Folkways in Germanic Lands (1648–1806)*. Cambridge, MA: M.I.T. Press, 1971.

Prawer, Siegbert Salomon. *Heine's Jewish Comedy: A Study of His Portraits of Jews and Judaism*. Oxford; New York: Clarendon Press, 1983.

Prévost-Marcilhacy, Pauline. "James de Rothschild à Ferriéres: les Projets de Paxton et de Lami," *Revue de l'Art* 100, no. 9 (1993).

———. *Les Rothschilds: Bâtisseurs et Mècénes*. Paris: Flammarion, 1995.

———. "Un Hotel de James de Rothschild." *Gazette des Beaux Arts* (1994).

Resnick, Evelyne. *Femmes et Associations, 1830–1880: Vraies Démocrates ou Dames Patronesses?* Paris: Publisud, 1991.

Ribeiro, Aileen. *Ingres in Fashion: Representations of Dress and Appearance in Ingre's Images of Women*. New Haven: Yale University Press, 1999.

Richard I. Cohen, et al. *The Emergence of Jewish Artists in Nineteenth-Century Europe*, ed. Susan Tumarkin Goodman. New York: Merrell in association with the Jewish Museum under the auspices of the Jewish Theological Seminary of America, 2001.

Riot-Sarcey, Michèle. *De la Liberté des Femmes: "Lettres de Dames" au Globe, 1831-1832*. Paris: Côté femmes, 1992.

———. *La Démocratie à l'Épreuve des Femmes: Trois Figures Critiques du Pouvoir, 1830–1848*. Paris: A. Michel, 1994.

Robb, Graham. *Balzac: A Biography*. London: Picador, 1994.

Robert Forster, and Joseph N. Moody. *Enterprise and Entrepreneurs in Nineteenth- and Twentieth-Century France*. Edited by Edward C. Carter II. Baltimore: Johns Hopkins University Press, 1976.

Rodrigue, Aron. "Abraham de Camondo of Istanbul: The Transformation of Jewish Philanthropy." *From East and West: Jews in a Changing Europe*,

1750–1870, eds. Frances Malino and David Sorkin. Cambridge: Basic Blackwell, 1990.

The Rothschild Archive: Review of the Year April 1999-March 2000, London: Rothchild Archive, 2000.

Sartori, Jennifer. "'Our Religious Future': Girls' Education and Jewish Identity in Nineteenth-Century France." PhD diss. Emory University, 2004.

Schama, Simon. *Two Rothschilds and the Land of Israel*. New York: Knopf, 1978.

Shelton, Andrew Carrington. "Ingres Versus Delacroix." *Art History*. 23, no. 5 (2000).

Smith, Bonnie G. *Ladies of the Leisure Class: The Bourgeoises of Northern France in the Nineteenth Century*. Princeton, NJ: Princeton University Press, 1981.

Sorkin, David Jan. *The Transformation of German Jewry, 1780–1840*. New York: Oxford University Press, 1987.

Soubiran, Jean-Roger. *Renaissance du Musée des Beaux-Arts de Cannes*. Cannes: Musée de la Castre, 1983.

Spiel, Hilde. *Fanny Von Arnstein: A Daughter of the Enlightenment, 1758–181*, trans. Christine Shuttleworth. New York: St. Martin's Press, 1991.

Sterling, Eleonore O. "Anti-Jewish Riots in Germany in 1819: A Displacement of Social Protest." *Historia Judaica* 12 (October 1950).

Stern, Selma. *The Court Jew: A Contribution to the History of Absolutism in Europe*, trans. Ralph Weiman. New Brunswick, NJ: Transaction Books, 1950.

Stock-Morton, Phyllis. *The Life of Marie d'Agoult, Alias Daniel Stern*. Baltimore: Johns Hopkins University Press, 2000.

Szajkowski, Zosa. *Poverty and Social Welfare among French Jews (1800–1880)*. New York: Editions Historiques Franco-Juives, 1954.

——. *Jews and the French Revolution of 1789, 1830 and 1848*. New York: Ktav Publishing House, 1970.

——. *Jewish Education in France, 1789–1939*, ed. Tobey B. Gitelle. New York: Columbia University Press, 1980.

Thomann Tewarson, Heidi."German-Jewish Identity in the Correspondence between Rahel Levin Varnhagen and Her Brother, Ludwig Robert: Hopes and Realities of Emancipation 1780–1830." *Leo Baeck Institute Year Book*, vol. 39. London: Secker & Warburg, 1994.

Walton, Whitney. *France at the Crystal Palace: Bourgeois Taste and Artisan Manufacture in the Nineteenth Century*. Berkeley, CA: University of California Press, 1992.

——. *Eve's Proud Descendants: Four Women Writers and Republican Politics in Nineteenth-Century France*. Stanford, CA: Stanford University Press, 2000.

Waserman, Manfred and Samuel S. Kottek, eds., *Health and Disease in the Holy Land: Studies in the History and Sociology of Medicine from Ancient Times to the Present*. Lewiston, New York: Edwin Mellen Press, 1996.

Weintraub, Stanley. *Charlotte and Lionel: A Rothschild Love Story*. New York: Free Press, 2003.

Weissbach, Lee Shai. "The Jewish Elite and the Children of the Poor: Jewish Apprenticeship Programs in Nineteenth-Century France." *AJS Review* 12, no. 1 (Spring 1987): 123–142.

Wolff, Alexander. *Die treue Anhänglichkeit zu Jerusalem und die liebe zu Zion, Salomon Lewynsohn*. Wollstein, 1855.

Wynne, George G. *Frankfurt through the Centuries*. Frankfurt-am-Main: Kramer, 1957.

Index

Network Rings inc family